D1101455

THE CHASE

THE GREATEST CHASES

THE CHASE

THE GREATEST CHASES

HAVE YOU GOT WHAT IT TAKES?

Foreword by Bradley Walsh

An Hachette UK Company
www.hachette.co.uk

First published in Great Britain in 2016 by Hamlyn,
a division of Octopus Publishing Group Ltd
Carmelite House
50 Victoria Embankment
London EC4Y 0DZ
www.octopusbooks.co.uk

The Chase The Greatest Chases © 2016 ITV Studios Limited

All rights reserved. No part of this work may be reproduced or utilized
in any form or by any means, electronic or mechanical, including
photocopying, recording or by any information storage and retrieval
system, without the prior written permission of the publisher.

ISBN 978-0-600-63281-8

A CIP catalogue record for this book is available from the British Library.

Printed and bound in the UK.

10 9 8 7 6 5 4 3 2 1

The Chase is a trade mark of ITV Studios Limited. All rights reserved.

Jacket images ITV Studios Limited.

Contents

FOREWORD

Hello and welcome to the second *Chase Quizbook*.

This book is all about the Final Chase, where the contestants who have made it through to the final have one more chance to outrun the chaser and take an equal share of the money home.

We have a lot of fun making *The Chase*. My job is not just to ask the questions, but also to watch the back of the contestants and wind up the Chasers as much as I can. That's the only way I can help the contestants because, unless the question is about *Carry On* films, Monopoly or custard creams, I just don't know the answers. That's why I ask the questions. I play along with the contestants, sharing their joy if they get back or their pain if they get caught.

But, when it comes to the Final Chase, there is always an air of great anticipation in the studio. The fun is over; it's time for business. The contestants want to win that pot of money but, for the Chaser, it's not about the money, it's the chase, the catch, the pride.

We have now reached Series 10 of *The Chase* and we have recorded over 1,000 shows. I have met more than 4,000 contestants. Of those 4,000, more than 2,500 have made it through to the Final Chase, playing for nearly £20 million – of which more than £6 million has been won. This money has been spent on many things from holidays, cars and house improvements to 'a new back door' and 'a blind kitten for my mum'.

In every show I ask around 115 questions, so that's over 130,000 asked since we began all those years ago, and – if you really want to feel sorry for me – that's approximately 1.5 million words.

But, I still love it. So, enjoy the book, set a target as high as you can in order to beat the Chaser, whether it be The Barrister, The Beast, The Vixen, The Sinnerman or old Frosty Knickers herself, The Governess, and remember, it's the thrill of *The Chase*.

Bradley Walsh, 2016

HOW TO USE THIS BOOK

The hugely successful television quiz show, *The Chase,* with its host Bradley Walsh, was launched in 2009. Over the years scores of players – and many celebrities – have confronted the intellectual might of the show's resident Chasers: the Governess, the Beast, the Sinnerman, the Barrister and the Vixen.

In this book you can either take on the challenge alone or join with friends and family to outrun the Chaser of your choice. Each of the 5 chapters, which feature a particular Chaser, has 10 quiz segments. So there are 50 exciting quizzes in which you can have fun pitting your wits against best quiz brains in the country.

Each quiz segment mirrors the format of the show, with four sets of Head-to-Head questions – one for each contestant – followed by a Final Chase. The questions included in the Final Chase are those asked in a show in which the Chaser was outrun by the contestants. The target number of correct answers and the prize money quoted are what the contestants actually achieved and won on the show.

There are lots of possibilities for using this book as a source of fun quiz games for family parties or personal amusement. The guidelines below are simply suggested scenarios, but quiz enthusiasts will undoubtedly devise their own variations.

Lone players:

Round 1

For those brave enough to take on the Chase on their own, you can tackle all four sets of Head-to-Head questions. You'll need 5 correct answers out of 7 in each set to qualify for Round 2 – the Final Chase.

Round 2

If you achieve the target score, you can then go on to face the Chaser in the Final Chase and attempt to match the winning total stated at the beginning of that round, which was achieved by actual contestants.

HOW TO USE THIS BOOK

Playing as a team:

Round 1

Teams of players can each take on a set of Head-to-Head questions labelled for contestants 1 to 4. And if you have enough players you may wish to appoint a non-playing member of the party to ask the questions and check the answers. Those members of the team who fail to answer 5 questions correctly cannot qualify for the Final Chase and, just as in the show, are eliminated.

Round 2

Team members who achieved the total of 5 correct answers in the first Head-to-Head round go on to participate in the Final Chase. Working as a team, players can pool their knowledge to achieve the winning total specified for that quiz – and outrun the Chaser. You may want to impose the rule, as used in the show, that whichever team member first indicates they can answer the question has to answer correctly or the point is lost.

Checking your answers:

At the end of each round you can check whether you have answered correctly using the Answers section at the back of the book (see pages 332–83). Cover the answers on the facing page (or better still, have a non-player to check for you), so as not to spoil your fun when you try the next quiz.

GOOD LUCK AND ENJOY THE CHASE!

QUESTIONS

The
GOVERNESS

The Governess

Dubbed Miss Frosty Knickers by Bradley Walsh, Anne Hegerty, aka The Governess, is a formidable opponent. Her on-screen persona of an authoritarian headmistress from times gone by (likened by one contestant to Miss Trunchbull from Roald Dahl's *Matilda*) has the potential to freeze the boldest of contestants.

But this Chaser is not just an intimidating presence, she is also a highly knowledgeable and experienced player of *The Chase*. Able to confidently and quickly answer questions on subjects from ancient history to contemporary TV soap operas, she is always a danger to any player she chases.

Anne also holds the distinction of having successfully 'caught' a contestant in the Final Chase who had jointly achieved the highest score of 26 but failed to outrun the Chaser. She was also involved in a Final Chase for the lowest prize (£500) on record – a contest to which, characteristically, she nevertheless gave her all.

Yet The Governess also has a softer side and, just like all good teachers, is always encouraging contestants at the end of each round.

The Governess Quiz 1: Contestant 1

Answer at least 5 questions correctly to progress on to the Final Chase.

1/1 ▶ Human blood is mainly composed of what?

> **A** RED BLOOD CELLS **B** PLATELETS **C** PLASMA

1/2 ▶ A red and white embroidery pattern appears down the hoist side of which national flag?

> **A** BELARUS **B** ARMENIA **C** UKRAINE

1/3 ▶ Who once said 'grass grows, birds fly, waves pound the sand. I beat people up'?

> **A** BIG DADDY **B** MUHAMMED ALI **C** JOHN PRESCOTT

1/4 ▶ At which course of a meal would you normally serve the Italian dish *semifreddo*?

> **A** STARTER **B** MAIN **C** DESSERT

1/5 ▶ What was the title of the first UK Top 5 hit single for Destiny's Child?

> **A** 'BILLS BILLS BILLS' **B** 'JUMPIN' JUMPIN'' **C** 'NO NO NO'

1/6 ▶ Which of these was a car made by Nissan?

> **A** CHERRY **B** PLUM **C** LEMON

1/7 ▶ Which of these rival middle-distance runners was the oldest?

> **A** SEBASTIAN COE **B** STEVE OVETT **C** STEVE CRAM

The Governess Quiz 1: Contestant 2

Answer at least 5 questions correctly to progress on to the Final Chase.

1/1 ▶ In Scrabble, which three consecutive letters have the same value?

> **A** ABC **B** LMN **C** RST

1/2 ▶ Which of these characters does NOT appear in the *1,001 Arabian Nights*?

> **A** ALADDIN **B** ALI BABA **C** ALAN-A-DALE

1/3 ▶ Which acting brothers appeared in the film *Good Will Hunting*?

> **A** CASEY AND BEN AFFLECK **B** LUKE AND OWEN WILSON
> **C** JOE AND PAUL MCGANN

1/4 ▶ Having shot down 40 Japanese planes, who was the greatest American fighter pilot of World War Two?

> **A** PERCY BING **B** WILLIE BANG **C** DICK BONG

1/5 ▶ The name of which shipping area is also that of a sailing race?

> **A** FASTNET **B** FORTIES **C** FISHER

1/6 ▶ What is the largest US state by population?

> **A** CALIFORNIA **B** ILLINOIS **C** NEW YORK

1/7 ▶ Which of these French phrases was the name of a 1998 Number One hit?

> **A** *BON VOYAGE* **B** *C'EST LA VIE* **C** *DÉJÀ VU*

The Governess Quiz 1: Contestant 3

Answer at least 5 questions correctly to progress on to the Final Chase.

1/1 ▶ Safety matches ignite as a result of the heat produced by what force?

> **A** TENSION **B** AIR RESISTANCE **C** FRICTION

1/2 ▶ Which of these Shakespeare plays begins closest to Stratford-upon-Avon?

> **A** *HAMLET* **B** *A MIDSUMMER NIGHT'S DREAM* **C** *TROILUS AND CRESSIDA*

1/3 ▶ Which of these was NOT the title of an *Only Fools and Horses* Christmas special?

> **A** 'TO HULL AND BACK' **B** 'MIAMI TWICE' **C** 'BEND IT LIKE PECKHAM'

1/4 ▶ What style of skirt is traditionally worn by a cheerleader?

> **A** RA-RA **B** A-LINE **C** PENCIL

1/5 ▶ *Be Careful What You Wish For* by Simon Jordan is about his time as owner of what football club?

> **A** CRYSTAL PALACE **B** MIDDLEBOROUGH **C** WALSALL

1/6 ▶ Each of the Emirates that form the UAE can also be described as what?

> **A** SHEIKDOMS **B** KINGDOMS **C** SULTANATES

1/7 ▶ What blocked tubes can cause popping noises in your ears?

> **A** BRONCHIAL **B** EUSTACHIAN **C** FALLOPIAN

The Governess Quiz 1: Contestant 4

Answer at least 5 questions correctly to progress on to the Final Chase.

1/1 ▶ Who said 'Socialist governments traditionally do make a financial mess. They always run out of other people's money'?

> **A** MARGARET THATCHER **B** EDWARD HEATH **C** JOHN MAJOR

1/2 ▶ Which couple, who had a 1970s hit with 'Love Will Keep Us Together', announced their divorce in 2014?

> **A** CAPTAIN & TENNILLE **B** ASHFORD & SIMPSON **C** WOMACK & WOMACK

1/3 ▶ The mythical Egyptian phoenix resembled which bird?

> **A** OWL **B** EAGLE **C** VULTURE

1/4 ▶ In 1995, which TV cook is said to have caused a nationwide shortage of cranberries after featuring them in recipes?

> **A** JAMIE OLIVER **B** DELIA SMITH **C** NIGELLA LAWSON

1/5 ▶ Which golfer lost his chance of winning the 1999 Open after he hit his ball into the water on the last hole?

> **A** SERGIO GARCÍA **B** BERNHARD LANGER **C** JEAN VAN DE VELDE

1/6 ▶ Which of these letters is worth the most in Scrabble?

> **A** X **B** Y **C** Z

1/7 ▶ What boy band had their debut Number One in 2014 with 'Me and My Broken Heart'?

> **A** RADFORD **B** RIGHTON **C** RIXTON

The Governess Quiz 1: Final Chase

★ Prize fund in the Final Chase was £21,000

★ Your target is 20 correct

Four contestants reached the final in this programme, and provided 16 correct answers to set a 20-step target for the Chaser. The team cemented their solid initial performance by executing all 9 of the push back opportunities offered by The Governess, outrunning her by an amazing 10 steps.

1/1 ▷ What currency replaced the lira in Italy?

1/2 ▷ On what TV singing contest do coaches sit in red swivel chairs?

1/3 ▷ Who became Timothy Laurence's mother-in-law in 1992?

1/4 ▷ What country is the setting for the play *Hedda Gabler*?

1/5 ▷ What's three-quarters of 120?

1/6 ▷ Which member of Blue was in *Celebrity Big Brother* 2014?

1/7 ▷ What's the earliest month that Mother's Day can fall?

1/8 ▷ What's the capital of Ecuador?

1/9 ▷ Serbian Ana Ivanovic is a star of what sport?

1/10 ▷ Which former Girls Aloud singer had a baby in February 2014?

THE GOVERNESS

1/11 ▶ Who was the first US President to serve two consecutive terms?

1/12 ▶ 'No More Tears' is the slogan for what brand of baby shampoo?

1/13 ▶ Which poet wrote the 'The Lady of Shallot'?

1/14 ▶ Clare of Assisi was a follower of which Italian saint?

1/15 ▶ Who played Dr Ellen Sanders in the US TV series *Hostages*?

1/16 ▶ What was the city of Bombay renamed in 1995?

1/17 ▶ Hamsters belong to what order of mammals?

1/18 ▶ In 2011, who became Liverpool Football Club's record signing?

1/19 ▶ Ivan the Fourth of Russia is known by what nickname?

1/20 ▶ 'I'm Not a Girl, Not Yet a Woman' was a hit for which pop star?

1/21 ▶ What vegetables is a clever person said to know?

1/22 ▶ Which TV cook wrote the book *Gino's Italian Escape*?

1/23 ▶ Nick Frost stars as Bruce in what 2014 dance film?

1/24 ▶ The liver turns what simple sugar into glycogen?

1/25 ▶ Oahu is the third-largest island in what US state?

The Governess Quiz 2: Contestant 1

Answer at least 5 questions correctly to progress on to the Final Chase.

2/1 ▶ Which writer said '...such is the human race. Often it does seem such a pity that Noah didn't miss the boat'?

> **A** LOUISA MAY ALCOTT **B** HENRY JAMES **C** MARK TWAIN

2/2 ▶ Which of these fruits has hairy drupelets?

> **A** COCONUT **B** GOOSEBERRY **C** RASPBERRY

2/3 ▶ In which Charles Dickens novel is Master Bates a young member of a gang of pickpockets?

> **A** *GREAT EXPECTATIONS* **B** *OUR MUTUAL FRIEND* **C** *OLIVER TWIST*

2/4 ▶ Facebook was originally limited to students at which American university?

> **A** HARVARD **B** PRINCETON **C** YALE

2/5 ▶ In 1929, the Newport Pottery was given over entirely to the decoration of which ceramic designer's work?

> **A** CLARICE CLIFF **B** BERNARD LEACH **C** LUCIE RIE

2/6 ▶ Which of these monarchs reigned the longest?

> **A** QUEEN ANNE **B** QUEEN MARY II **C** QUEEN VICTORIA

2/7 ▶ What shape is the line on a graph representing normal distribution?

> **A** DIAGONAL LINE **B** BELL-SHAPED CURVE **C** PARABOLA

The Governess Quiz 2: Contestant 2

Answer at least 5 questions correctly to progress on to the Final Chase.

2/1 ▶ Which of these songs topped the UK charts before the others?

> **A** 'ALBATROSS' **B** 'PRETTY FLAMINGO' **C** 'LITTLE RED ROOSTER'

2/2 ▶ Which novel by William Golding is about schoolboys stranded on an uninhabited island?

> **A** *THE INHERITORS* **B** *LORD OF THE FLIES* **C** *RITES OF PASSAGE*

2/3 ▶ Which stately home has the postcode DE45 1PP?

> **A** BLENHEIM PALACE **B** CASTLE HOWARD **C** CHATSWORTH HOUSE

2/4 ▶ Which US President said, 'if you want to test a man's character, give him power'?

> **A** GEORGE WASHINGTON **B** ABRAHAM LINCOLN **C** BILL CLINTON

2/5 ▶ In 1981, which classic sitcom debuted with an episode called 'Big Brother'?

> **A** *ONLY FOOLS AND HORSES* **B** *FAWLTY TOWERS* **C** *THE GOOD LIFE*

2/6 ▶ Founded in 1797, Hatchards of Piccadilly claims to be London's oldest surviving what?

> **A** RESTAURANT **B** BOOKSHOP **C** TAILOR

2/7 ▶ How many strings does a cello have?

> **A** FOUR **B** FIVE **C** SIX

The Governess Quiz 2: Contestant 3

Answer at least 5 questions correctly to progress on to the Final Chase.

2/1 ▶ What type of coarse flour is the main ingredient in the dark brown bread 'pumpernickel'?

> **A** BUCKWHEAT **B** SPELT **C** RYE

2/2 ▶ Who is the first person to have won both an Oscar and a Turner Prize?

> **A** DAMIEN HIRST **B** SAM TAYLOR-WOOD **C** STEVE MCQUEEN

2/3 ▶ To what order of architecture does Nelson's Column belong?

> **A** CORINTHIAN **B** DORIC **C** TUSCAN

2/4 ▶ Which of the actors who played the Doctor in *Doctor Who* famously wore a long scarf?

> **A** TOM BAKER **B** WILLIAM HARTNELL **C** PETER DAVISON

2/5 ▶ 'Look to her, Moor, if thou hast eyes to see' is a line from which Shakespeare play?

> **A** *HAMLET* **B** *MACBETH* **C** *OTHELLO*

2/6 ▶ Which of these is the name of the explorer who claimed Canada for France in the 16th century?

> **A** CARTIER **B** LONGINES **C** TISSOT

2/7 ▶ Which organ of the human body is made up of four chambers?

> **A** HEART **B** KIDNEY **C** LIVER

The Governess Quiz 2: Contestant 4

Answer at least 5 questions correctly to progress on to the Final Chase.

2/1 ▶ What is the only US state to border just one other state?

> A MAINE B NORTH DAKOTA C OHIO

2/2 ▶ According to legend, the shape of tortellini pasta was reputedly inspired by what part of Venus's body?

> A LIPS B EAR C NAVEL

2/3 ▶ To gain the gift of 'eloquent speech' when kissing the Blarney Stone, you have to be what?

> A LAUGHING B HANGING UPSIDE DOWN C NAKED

2/4 ▶ In the song 'I Know an Old Lady Who Swallowed a Fly', what animal did she swallow to catch the spider?

> A CAT B DOG C BIRD

2/5 ▶ The leader of which South American country is often called 'the world's poorest president'?

> A URUGUAY B BRAZIL C BOLIVIA

2/6 ▶ Which of these is a traditional gift for the sixth wedding anniversary?

> A SALT B SUGAR C SAUSAGES

2/7 ▶ Which of these countries is an absolute monarchy?

> A IRAQ B QATAR C YEMEN

The Governess Quiz 2: Final Chase

⭐ Prize fund in the Final Chase was £45,000

⭐ Your target is 20 correct

The final featured 3 contestants. Their impressive score of 20 was largely thanks to top scorer Dave, a 60-year-old primary school teacher from Rugby, who contributed an amazing 13 correct answers. The Governess motored through her questions, only stumbling towards the end, losing 6 push backs, 4 of which were executed to clinch victory for the team.

2/1 ▶ Original Ribena contains what fruit?

2/2 ▶ The tree *Salix babylonica* is known as the 'weeping...' what?

2/3 ▶ Which actor plays Danny Dyer's father in *EastEnders*?

2/4 ▶ In the *Twilight* series what is Bella's married surname?

2/5 ▶ 'Vista' was a version of what Microsoft operating system?

2/6 ▶ 'Myriad' originally referred to how many thousands?

2/7 ▶ What country is the opera *Porgy and Bess* set in?

2/8 ▶ A Mai Tai cocktail contains the juice of what citrus fruit?

2/9 ▶ Which Bond actor won an Oscar for *The Untouchables*?

2/10 ▶ What colour does albumen become when cooked?

2/11 ▶ What nationality was Arctic explorer Willem Barents?

THE GOVERNESS QUIZ 2: Final Chase

THE GOVERNESS

2/12 ▶ The Chair of St Augustine is in which English cathedral?

2/13 ▶ The Gulf of Tunis is an inlet of what sea?

2/14 ▶ Winnie the Pooh is a 'Bear of Very Little...' what?

2/15 ▶ In dressage, how many errors lead to disqualification?

2/16 ▶ Complete the proverbial saying 'Like father, like...' what?

2/17 ▶ Paul McCartney was born in what decade?

2/18 ▶ Who played Mick Travis in the 1960s film *If...*?

2/19 ▶ The word 'abattoir' comes from what language?

2/20 ▶ What organs are covered by the visceral pleura?

2/21 ▶ What Welsh football club's nicknamed 'The Swans'?

2/22 ▶ How many centigrams make a gram?

2/23 ▶ What's the opposite of a neap tide?

2/24 ▶ A cobnut's a variety of what nut?

2/25 ▶ What's the only US state with a 'J' in its name?

2/26 ▶ Aby is a short name for what cat breed?

2/27 ▶ How many wings does a bee have?

The Governess Quiz 3: Contestant 1

Answer at least 5 questions correctly to progress on to the Final Chase.

3/1 ▶ Which of these Canadian cities is closest to Niagara Falls?

> **A** TORONTO **B** MONTRÉAL **C** QUEBEC

3/2 ▶ François Mitterrand was a member of what French political party?

> **A** ECOLOGY **B** REPUBLICAN **C** SOCIALIST

3/3 ▶ Which of these songs was a hit before the others?

> **A** 'AGADOO' **B** 'VINDALOO' **C** 'WATERLOO'

3/4 ▶ London and what other British city has a Charing Cross Railway Station?

> **A** SHEFFIELD **B** BRISTOL **C** GLASGOW

3/5 ▶ What completes the full title of an 1871 book by Lewis Carroll *Through the Looking-Glass, and What Alice...*?

> **A** DID THERE **B** SAW THERE **C** FOUND THERE

3/6 ▶ The puma is also called the 'mountain...' what?

> **A** COYOTE **B** LION **C** RACCOON

3/7 ▶ To achieve a Duke of Edinburgh's Award, all activities must be completed by which birthday?

> **A** 16TH **B** 20TH **C** 25TH

The Governess Quiz 3: Contestant 2

Answer at least 5 questions correctly to progress on to the Final Chase.

3/1 ▶ The American soprano, famed for her inability to sing, was 'Florence Foster...' who?

> **A EVANS B WILLIAMS C JENKINS**

3/2 ▶ The location of origin of which of these cheeses is furthest north?

> **A DOUBLE GLOUCESTER B RED LEICESTER C CORNISH YARG**

3/3 ▶ What musical is set around the production of a musical called *Pretty Lady*?

> **A** *42ND STREET* **B** *FIVE GUYS NAMED MOE* **C** *HALF A SIXPENCE*

3/4 ▶ Italian majolica is a type of what?

> **A POTTERY B GLASS C LACE**

3/5 ▶ What species is General Sherman, the world's largest living tree?

> **A GIANT SEQUOIA B EASTERN COTTONWOOD C SUGAR MAPLE**

3/6 ▶ What sporting event from *The Pickwick Papers* was formerly depicted on a 10-pound note?

> **A CRICKET MATCH B FOOTBALL MATCH C RUGBY MATCH**

3/7 ▶ During the early 18th century, a 'commode' was a fashionable piece of women's clothing worn where?

> **A ABOVE THE ANKLE B AROUND THE WAIST C ON THE HEAD**

The Governess Quiz 3: Contestant 3

Answer at least 5 questions correctly to progress on to the Final Chase.

3/1 ▶ What is the full name of the chart-topping Australian boy band 5SOS?

> **A** 5 SECONDS OF SUMMER **B** 5 SIX OR SEVEN **C** 5 STARS OF SYDNEY

3/2 ▶ In Roman numerals, an X with a dash above it indicates what number?

> **A** 100 **B** 10,000 **C** 1,000,000

3/3 ▶ James Moriarty, the arch-enemy of Sherlock Holmes, is a professor in which academic subject?

> **A** CHEMISTRY **B** LATIN **C** MATHEMATICS

3/4 ▶ Lochnagar, mentioned in the title of a children's book by Prince Charles, is on what royal estate?

> **A** SANDRINGHAM **B** WINDSOR **C** BALMORAL

3/5 ▶ In 1983, Dame Mary Donaldson became the first woman to hold what post in the City of London?

> **A** YEOMAN CAPTAIN **B** LORD MAYOR **C** MASTER OF THE MINT

3/6 ▶ Which of these countries does NOT have a border with Afghanistan?

> **A** KAZAKHSTAN **B** PAKISTAN **C** UZBEKISTAN

3/7 ▶ Which of these French numbers is even?

> **A** *SOIXANTE* **B** *NEUF* **C** *QUINZE*

The Governess Quiz 3: Contestant 4

Answer at least 5 questions correctly to progress on to the Final Chase.

3/1 ▶ Which religious figure lays claim to 'the Power of the Keys'?

> **A** DALAI LAMA **B** CHIEF RABBI **C** THE POPE

3/2 ▶ Which of these brand names is the oldest?

> **A** DADDIES SAUCE **B** PAPA JOHN'S **C** UNCLE BEN'S

3/3 ▶ What is the name of the wheeled platform used on film sets to move cameras?

> **A** DOLLY **B** MOLLY **C** POLLY

3/4 ▶ Which of these letters is NOT the symbol of a chemical element?

> **A** A **B** B **C** C

3/5 ▶ In 2014, what was the surname of the first father and son to play at the same US Masters golf championship?

> **A** COUPLES **B** ZOELLER **C** STADLER

3/6 ▶ Corned beef mixed and fried with potatoes and seasoning is known as 'corned beef...' what?

> **A** HASH **B** MESS **C** SHAMBLES

3/7 ▶ The 1981 novel *The Dead of Jericho* was adapted into the first episode of which ITV crime drama?

> **A** *INSPECTOR MORSE* **B** *MAIGRET* **C** *MIDSOMER MURDERS*

The Governess Quiz 3: Final Chase

★ Prize fund in the Final Chase was £17,000

★ Your target is 19 correct

The 3 contestants in this final produced a target of 19 for The Governess to aim at. Katy, a 22-year-old receptionist from London, was their most prolific scorer, but all team members made contributions. In the Final Chase The Governess failed to answer 6 questions and the team executed 3 push backs. This was sufficient to secure a win.

3/1 ▶ What word means both a sauce for salad and putting clothes on?

3/2 ▶ The Baltic Sea is part of what ocean?

3/3 ▶ Scottish outlaw Robert MacGregor was known by what nickname?

3/4 ▶ Which Swedish author created the character Mikael Blomkvist?

3/5 ▶ Barnyard Dawg featured in cartoons starring which rooster?

3/6 ▶ Patrick Moore was famous for wearing what optical aid?

3/7 ▶ The Unseen University is in what Terry Pratchett book series?

3/8 ▶ In what country is the Soelden ski resort?

3/9 ▶ Which explorer landed in Honduras in 1502?

3/10 ▶ What's the last of Sergio Leone's *Dollars* film trilogy?

THE GOVERNESS

3/11 ▶ How is the 'Hundred Guinea Cup' more commonly known?

3/12 ▶ The sensory cortex is in what organ of the body?

3/13 ▶ Which playwright wrote *The History Boys*?

3/14 ▶ Operation Torch was a military campaign in what war?

3/15 ▶ Dunstable Downs is the highest point in what county?

3/16 ▶ 'Door-step' is slang for a thick slice of what food product?

3/17 ▶ Meryl Streep plays Donna Sheridan in what film musical?

3/18 ▶ Who was the first Labour MP to be Justice Secretary?

3/19 ▶ Which Lord Mayor of London is the subject of a pantomime?

3/20 ▶ Which future 'King of Scots' was excommunicated in 1306?

3/21 ▶ Maui is an island in what US state?

3/22 ▶ In what city was the Irish Stock Exchange founded in 1793?

3/23 ▶ Dinah Morris is a female preacher in what George Eliot novel?

3/24 ▶ What's the Italian word for vengeance?

3/25 ▶ In what Vera Lynn hit did she sing 'Keep smiling through'?

The Governess Quiz 4: Contestant 1

Answer at least 5 questions correctly to progress on to the Final Chase.

4/1 ▶ Which of these was a hit single for Flo Rida in 2012?

A 'WHISTLE' B 'HUM' C 'TOOT'

4/2 ▶ How were England's two 17th-century Lord Protectors related?

A BROTHERS B FATHER AND SON C UNCLE AND NEPHEW

4/3 ▶ What mathematical symbol was introduced by John Wallis in 1655?

A SQUARE ROOT B PI C INFINITY

4/4 ▶ Which TV character lived above the garage at 565 North Clinton Drive, Milwaukee?

A WALNUT B MAGNUM C FRASIER

4/5 ▶ The peach is closely related to what culinary nut?

A WALNUT B HAZELNUT C ALMOND

4/6 ▶ A horse with a height of 15 hands is how tall?

A 5 FEET B 6 FEET C 7 FEET

4/7 ▶ Which trio of Greek goddesses was believed to control human life?

A FATES B DESTINIES C SOOTHSAYERS

The Governess Quiz 4: Contestant 2

Answer at least 5 questions correctly to progress on to the Final Chase.

4/1 ▶ Which of these joints in the human body is NOT a ball-and-socket joint?

> **A** ANKLE **B** HIP **C** SHOULDER

4/2 ▶ Who wrote the 'Dam Busters March'?

> **A** MALCOLM ARNOLD **B** PERCY GRAINGER **C** ERIC COATES

4/3 ▶ The Bay City Rollers had a Number One single with a cover version of what song?

> **A** 'HELLO GOODBYE' **B** 'BYE, BYE, BABY' **C** 'TIME TO SAY GOODBYE'

4/4 ▶ In which of these decades did a British coronation take place?

> **A** 1920S **B** 1930S **C** 1940S

4/5 ▶ The full title of the novel by Robert Louis Stevenson describes the story of *Dr Jekyll and Mr Hyde* as a what?

> **A** AMAZING ADVENTURE **B** TALE OF TERROR **C** STRANGE CASE

4/6 ▶ In what book of the Bible does God help Moses to part the Red Sea?

> **A** ECCLESIASTES **B** ESTHER **C** EXODUS

4/7 ▶ The team from which of these places had to travel furthest to the 2014 Commonwealth Games?

> **A** ST HELENA **B** ST KITTS AND NEVIS **C** ST LUCIA

The Governess Quiz 4: Contestant 3

Answer at least 5 questions correctly to progress on to the Final Chase.

4/1 ▶ Hammurabi was King of what ancient city?

A BABYLON B HALICARNASSUS C TROY

4/2 ▶ Ant and Dec returned to the UK charts in 2013 with the song 'Let's Get Ready To...' what?

A MHUMBLE B RHUMBLE C FHUMBLE

4/3 ▶ Father Lankester Merrin is a major character in what 1971 novel?

A *THE EXORCIST* B *THE GODFATHER* C *THE HERETIC*

4/4 ▶ What is the longest division of geologic time?

A EON B EPOCH C ERA

4/5 ▶ What bear has a scientific name that means 'decorated bear'?

A BROWN BEAR B POLAR BEAR C SPECTACLED BEAR

4/6 ▶ In the final episode of *Friends* which character says 'I got off the plane'?

A PHOEBE B RACHEL C MONICA

4/7 ▶ Which of these was a middle name of the World Cup-winning captain Bobby Moore?

A ARSENAL B FULHAM C CHELSEA

The Governess Quiz 4: Contestant 4

Answer at least 5 questions correctly to progress on to the Final Chase.

4/1 ▶ In the human body, the neocortex is part of what organ?

> **A** BRAIN **B** HEART **C** STOMACH

4/2 ▶ Named after the man who predicted its position, the Le Verrier Ring surrounds what planet?

> **A** JUPITER **B** NEPTUNE **C** SATURN

4/3 ▶ According to the 1920s film *The Crowd*, 'marriage isn't a word, it's a...' what?

> **A** CHAPTER **B** PARAGRAPH **C** SENTENCE

4/4 ▶ In 2014, Manchester United broke the British record in spending around £60m on which footballer?

> **A** ANDER HERRERA **B** ANGEL DI MARIA **C** MARIO BALOTELLI

4/5 ▶ In 2014, David Cameron claimed the Queen made what noise on hearing the Scottish independence result?

> **A** MIAOW **B** HISS **C** PURR

4/6 ▶ In Mary Shelley's novel, in what country does Victor Frankenstein create his monster?

> **A** GERMANY **B** HUNGARY **C** ROMANIA

4/7 ▶ The spotted skunk commonly uses which of these feats to ward off potential attackers?

> **A** HANDSTAND **B** SKIPPING **C** JUGGLING

The Governess Quiz 4: Final Chase

★ Prize fund in the Final Chase was £16,000

★ Your target is 21 correct

Four contestants reached the final. They set an excellent total of 21 for the Chaser to pursue, with Dom, a 31-year-old website content writer from Hitchin, contributing an amazing 14 correct answers. The team did equally well in the Final Chase against The Governess, with 4 executed push backs from 7 opportunities allowing them to romp home.

4/1 ▷ 'iamwill' is the Twitter username of which rapper and producer?

4/2 ▷ Altogether, how many sides do a dozen triangles have?

4/3 ▷ In what film does Simon Pegg play policeman Nicholas Angel?

4/4 ▷ Which Lake Poet wrote 'The World Is Too Much With Us'?

4/5 ▷ What American landmark has broken shackles at its base?

4/6 ▷ Who sang lead vocals on the Jam's 'A Town Called Malice'?

4/7 ▷ What colour tail and mane does a Palomino horse usually have?

4/8 ▷ Which Liberal Prime Minister was nicknamed 'Old Squiffy'?

4/9 ▷ Petunia Pig is which cartoon character's girlfriend?

4/10 ▷ Which King Richard was the nephew of John of Gaunt?

THE GOVERNESS

4/11 ▷ 'Down Under' was a Number One hit for which Australian group?

4/12 ▷ 'Crazy' and 'Mini' are leisure forms of what sport?

4/13 ▷ In what decade was the boxer Muhammad Ali born?

4/14 ▷ What colour is the cross on the flag of Finland?

4/15 ▷ Which musical actress narrated the Disney film *Enchanted*?

4/16 ▷ Ivories is slang for what part of the human body?

4/17 ▷ Bletchley Park was known as Station X during what war?

4/18 ▷ Columbia is the capital of what American state?

4/19 ▷ What's the closest planet to the Sun named after a goddess?

4/20 ▷ *True Grit* is a book by which TV adventurer?

4/21 ▷ Which noble gas is often used to fill party balloons?

4/22 ▷ Alcatraz prison's in what American bay?

4/23 ▷ Nick Nack was a villain in what James Bond film?

4/24 ▷ The Punta Balena strip is part of what Mallorcan resort?

4/25 ▷ In a rising musical scale, what note follows 'lah'?

4/26 ▷ What US boundary line was named after two English surveyors?

The Governess Quiz 5: Contestant 1

Answer at least 5 questions correctly to progress on to the Final Chase.

5/1 ▶ Psy's hit song 'Gangnam Style' takes its name from a district in which Asian capital city?

> A HANOI B MANILA C SEOUL

5/2 ▶ At the 2014 Golden Globes, Andy Samberg won Best Leading Comedy Actor for which comedy?

> A *GIRLS* B *MODERN FAMILY* C *BROOKLYN NINE-NINE*

5/3 ▶ In what year was the voting age for women reduced to 21?

> A 1918 B 1928 C 1938

5/4 ▶ What is a male zebra called?

> A BUCK B RAM C STALLION

5/5 ▶ In the lyrics to the 1960s hit 'Aquarius', Jupiter aligns with which other planet?

> A MARS B VENUS C EARTH

5/6 ▶ The film *Candyman* is based on a short story by which author?

> A CLIVE BARKER B STEPHEN KING C MARY SHELLEY

5/7 ▶ In *The Office*, David Brent claimed that his infamous dance 'fused Flashdance with...' which rapper?

> A LL COOL J B EMINEM C MC HAMMER

The Governess Quiz 5: Contestant 2

Answer at least 5 questions correctly to progress on to the Final Chase.

5/1 ▶ What is the only Belgian city to have hosted the Olympic Games?

> **A** ANTWERP **B** BRUGES **C** BRUSSELS

5/2 ▶ What name links a popular Fendi handbag and a children's game?

> **A** PEEKABOO **B** TAG **C** HOPSCOTCH

5/3 ▶ Electricity is the flow of what?

> **A** PROTONS **B** NEUTRONS **C** ELECTRONS

5/4 ▶ What was the most-watched TV programme on Christmas Day 2013?

> **A** *DOCTOR WHO* **B** *MRS BROWN'S BOYS* **C** *DOWNTON ABBEY*

5/5 ▶ Whose right to the throne was challenged by Lady Jane Grey?

> **A** EDWARD VI **B** ELIZABETH I **C** MARY I

5/6 ▶ What's an alternative name for the dots on dominoes?

> **A** SEEDS **B** PIPS **C** NUTS

5/7 ▶ A straw boater appears on the badge of what football club?

> **A** NORTHAMPTON TOWN **B** IPSWICH TOWN **C** LUTON TOWN

The Governess Quiz 5: Contestant 3

Answer at least 5 questions correctly to progress on to the Final Chase.

5/1 ▶ Which British actor was born Michael Dumble-Smith?

A MICHAEL GAMBON **B** MICHAEL CRAWFORD **C** MICHAEL YORK

5/2 ▶ The ilium is the largest of the three bones in what part of the body?

A ANKLE **B** EAR **C** PELVIS

5/3 ▶ The 1908 Olympics are the longest ever, lasting how many days?

A 37 **B** 97 **C** 187

5/4 ▶ Which of these hands beats the others in a game of poker?

A STRAIGHT **B** TWO PAIR **C** FOUR OF A KIND

5/5 ▶ What birds appear in the lyrics of the song 'My Favourite Things'?

A DOVES **B** GEESE **C** LARKS

5/6 ▶ Which of these is NOT a book by Roger Hargreaves?

A *LITTLE MISS SOMERSAULT* **B** *LITTLE MISS DOTTY* **C** *LITTLE MISS ANGRY*

5/7 ▶ An audiologist would treat which of these medical problems?

A ANOSMIA **B** MYOPIA **C** TINNITUS

THE GOVERNESS QUIZ 5: Contestant 3

The Governess Quiz 5: Contestant 4

Answer at least 5 questions correctly to progress on to the Final Chase.

5/1 ▶ Formed in Victorian times, what did members of the 'Band of Hope' pledge to avoid?

> **A** ALCOHOL **B** GAMBLING **C** SMOKING

5/2 ▶ Which king was made a saint by the Church of England?

> **A** WILLIAM II **B** EDWARD V **C** CHARLES I

5/3 ▶ *The Splash* and *A Little Splash* are works by which British artist?

> **A** LUCIAN FREUD **B** DAVID HOCKNEY **C** L S LOWRY

5/4 ▶ The cartoon character Danger Mouse had his secret base in what feature on London's Baker Street?

> **A** POLICE BOX **B** PILLAR BOX **C** TELEPHONE BOX

5/5 ▶ Which former world champion boxer retired in 1982, 1984, 1987, 1991 and 1997?

> **A** MARVIN HAGLER **B** ROBERTO DURÁN **C** SUGAR RAY LEONARD

5/6 ▶ What name is given to a ruler who uses their power to steal their country's resources?

> **A** OMNICRAT **B** KLEPTOCRAT **C** BUREAUCRAT

5/7 ▶ Which of these is a character in Shakespeare's *The Tempest*?

> **A** ELLEN **B** MIRANDA **C** ROSEANNE

The Governess Quiz 5: Final Chase

★ Prize fund in the Final Chase was £9,000

★ Your target is 15 correct

Just 2 contestants confronted The Governess in this final. They achieved a creditable 15, but would need to execute as many push back opportunities as possible to outrun the Chaser. They were able to take advantage of 5 out of 6 stumbles by The Governess to win by the narrow margin of 1 step.

5/1 ▷ Plaque and tartar build up on what parts of the body?

5/2 ▷ In what country was the sitcom *Kath and Kim* made?

5/3 ▷ What kind of insect is a Speckled Wood?

5/4 ▷ What Old Testament book features Deborah, Gideon and Samson?

5/5 ▷ The poet Dylan Thomas was born in what Welsh city?

5/6 ▷ What film company acquired Marvel Entertainment in 2009?

5/7 ▷ In cricket, it's said that 'catches win...' what?

5/8 ▷ The fabric hessian is named after a place in what country?

5/9 ▷ What's half of 360?

5/10 ▷ Before 1981, UK telecoms were controlled by what body?

THE GOVERNESS

5/11 ▶ Which American crime novelist wrote *City Primeval*?

5/12 ▶ What place name is both 'upon Thames' and 'upon Hull'?

5/13 ▶ Which of the Teletubbies carries a red handbag?

5/14 ▶ What does the 'N' stand for in the American TV network NBC?

5/15 ▶ The writer of *Being John Malkovich* was 'Charlie...' who?

5/16 ▶ A Cockney is from the east side of what city?

5/17 ▶ The egg in the dish kedgeree is cooked by what method?

5/18 ▶ Which *Glee* actress released the book *Brunette Ambition*?

5/19 ▶ Which former Prime Minister died aged 90 in 1965?

5/20 ▶ Methane is formed by carbon and what gaseous element?

5/21 ▶ What group had seven consecutive Number Ones in the 1960s?

5/22 ▶ *The Code of the Woosters* is a novel by who?

5/23 ▶ In figure skating, a single axel jump turns how many degrees?

5/24 ▶ What UK capital city is on the River Lagan?

5/25 ▶ What surname links singers Norah, Tom and Grace?

The Governess Quiz 6: Contestant 1

Answer at least 5 questions correctly to progress on to the Final Chase.

6/1 ▶ Which musical brothers played the lead roles in the 1990 film *The Krays*?

> **A** GARY AND MARTIN KEMP **B** MATT AND LUKE GOSS **C** MAURICE AND ROBIN GIBB

6/2 ▶ What European country has a capital with a three-word name?

> **A** ANDORRA **B** MOLDOVA **C** SAN MARINO

6/3 ▶ Dr Gordon Freeman is the protagonist of what video-game series?

> **A** 'QUAKE' **B** 'CALL OF DUTY' **C** 'HALF-LIFE'

6/4 ▶ What farm animal goes before 'parsley' to give the name of a plant with white flowers?

> **A** COW **B** PIG **C** HEN

6/5 ▶ Macaulay Culkin featured in the music video for which Michael Jackson song?

> **A** 'BLACK OR WHITE' **B** 'BILLIE JEAN' **C** 'THRILLER'

6/6 ▶ Which author described Winston Churchill as 'simply a radio personality who outlived his prime'?

> **A** EVELYN WAUGH **B** ALDOUS HUXLEY **C** AGATHA CHRISTIE

6/7 ▶ In the Bible, the newborn Christ was visited by wise men who came from which direction?

> **A** THE EAST **B** THE NORTH **C** THE WEST

The Governess Quiz 6: Contestant 2

Answer at least 5 questions correctly to progress on to the Final Chase.

6/1 ▶ What is the only English club football team to have a Number One single?

> **A** CHELSEA **B** TOTTENHAM HOTSPUR **C** MANCHESTER UNITED

6/2 ▶ Which of these Channel Islands does NOT allow cars?

> **A** ALDERNEY **B** GUERNSEY **C** SARK

6/3 ▶ In Jane Austen's *Emma* what are described as 'the best fruit in England'?

> **A** STRAWBERRIES **B** PINEAPPLES **C** MANGOES

6/4 ▶ Which of these men would be most likely to use crampons?

> **A** CHRIS BROAD **B** CHRIS BOARDMAN **C** CHRIS BONINGTON

6/5 ▶ In *Are You Being Served?*, what was Mrs Slocombe's first name?

> **A** BETTY **B** KITTY **C** FANNY

6/6 ▶ Which of these colours does NOT appear on the flag of Argentina?

> **A** BLUE **B** RED **C** WHITE

6/7 ▶ How many full-length novels did Arthur Conan Doyle write about Sherlock Holmes?

> **A** 4 **B** 14 **C** 24

The Governess Quiz 6: Contestant 3

Answer at least 5 questions correctly to progress on to the Final Chase.

6/1 ▶ Which of these sports fields the largest team?

> **A** RUGBY UNION **B** GAELIC FOOTBALL **C** AUSSIE RULES

6/2 ▶ Which of these is NOT a bone in the ear?

> **A** ANVIL **B** HAMMER **C** BELLOW

6/3 ▶ Which reality TV star released the 'Hollywood' gaming app, where the object of the game is to become a 'celebrity'?

> **A** PARIS HILTON **B** KIM KARDASHIAN **C** HEIDI PRATT

6/4 ▶ The full title of what Dickens novel includes the phrase 'Which He Never Meant to Publish on Any Account'?

> **A** *DAVID COPPERFIELD* **B** *MARTIN CHUZZLEWIT* **C** *NICHOLAS NICKLEBY*

6/5 ▶ What row of letters on a standard keyboard has no vowels?

> **A** TOP **B** MIDDLE **C** BOTTOM

6/6 ▶ Which of these beaches is closest to the United Kingdom?

> **A** BONDI **B** COPACABANA **C** WAIKIKI

6/7 ▶ Tocology is the science of what?

> **A** METABOLISM **B** CHILDBIRTH **C** SPEECH

THE GOVERNESS

The Governess Quiz 6: Contestant 4

Answer at least 5 questions correctly to progress on to the Final Chase.

6/1 ▶ Which former politician presents the TV series *Great Continental Railway Journeys*?

> **A** MICHAEL PORTILLO **B** KENNETH CLARKE **C** NIGEL LAWSON

6/2 ▶ In law, a legatee will in due course find themselves what?

> **A** UNDER ARREST **B** BANNED **C** RICHER

6/3 ▶ Whose 28-year-old 1,500-metres British record did Mo Farah break in 2013?

> **A** SEB COE **B** STEVE OVETT **C** STEVE CRAM

6/4 ▶ Which of these is NOT a classification for clouds?

> **A** CIRRUS **B** CUMULUS **C** CONIC

6/5 ▶ The Mediterranean flatbread socca is made with what legume?

> **A** CHICKPEAS **B** BLACK-EYED PEAS **C** MANGETOUT

6/6 ▶ In 2013, which celebrity received the 2,500th star on the Hollywood Walk of Fame?

> **A** QUEEN LATIFAH **B** CHER **C** JENNIFER LOPEZ

6/7 ▶ Which of these sports requires the team in possession to attempt to score within 24 seconds of getting the ball?

> **A** BASKETBALL **B** HURLING **C** POLO

The Governess Quiz 6: Final Chase

★ Prize fund in the Final Chase was £13,000

★ Your target is 14 correct

Two contestants made it through to the final in this programme. Top scorer Nathan, a 32-year-old civil servant from London, provided 10 of the modest 14-step target. But an impressive performance on push backs – executing 6 of the 9 opportunities offered – enabled them to convincingly outrun The Governess.

6/1 ▶ What two months start with the letter 'A'?

6/2 ▶ Which member of the X-Men has retractable metal claws?

6/3 ▶ Five and 10-pence coins were first introduced in what decade?

6/4 ▶ The Dhammapada is a set of teachings in what religion?

6/5 ▶ What type of dairy product is Hereford Hop?

6/6 ▶ 'At sixes and sevens with you' is a line from what musical song?

6/7 ▶ On what island could you visit Parkhurst Forest?

6/8 ▶ The Chequers ring belonged to which Tudor monarch?

6/9 ▶ *L.A. 7* was a kids' TV show featuring what pop band?

6/10 ▶ 'Leg theory' is a term from which sport?

THE GOVERNESS

6/11 ▷ What Japanese motor company was founded by Jujiro Matsuda?

6/12 ▷ Fez and Marrakesh are former capitals of what country?

6/13 ▷ The nightingale belongs to what family of birds?

6/14 ▷ What type of vehicle was the British Army's Challenger One?

6/15 ▷ Which pop star sang on the John Mayer song 'Who You Love'?

6/16 ▷ World War Two lasted just under how many years?

6/17 ▷ Exeter and what other English city have an 'X' in their name?

6/18 ▷ What card game has a variant called Kansas Lowball?

6/19 ▷ Which mythical gorgon is depicted on the flag of Sicily?

6/20 ▷ 'A Pirate's Life' is a song from what Disney film?

6/21 ▷ The word 'vodka' comes from what language?

6/22 ▷ If you cause your own downfall, you 'dig your own...' what?

6/23 ▷ Which saint founded the order of 'Black Friars' in 1216?

6/24 ▷ The novel *Little Women* was first published in what century?

The Governess Quiz 7: Contestant 1

Answer at least 5 questions correctly to progress on to the Final Chase.

7/1 ▶ In the nursery rhyme, when Jack broke his crown, how was it fixed?

> **A** MILK AND A TEA CLOTH **B** VINEGAR AND BROWN PAPER
> **C** STICKY TAPE AND LOO ROLL

7/2 ▶ Who declared that the marriage between Henry VIII and Catherine of Aragon was void?

> **A** THOMAS CRANMER **B** THOMAS MORE **C** THOMAS WOLSEY

7/3 ▶ Which city was the first to host both the Olympic Games and the FIFA World Cup final?

> **A** PARIS **B** ROME **C** MUNICH

7/4 ▶ In musical notation, what term indicates that all the instruments should be played together?

> **A** TUTTI **B** FRUTTI **C** AU RUTTI

7/5 ▶ The 'Hawaiian Missionaries' are a famous and highly collectable set of what?

> **A** COINS **B** BUTTERFLIES **C** POSTAGE STAMPS

7/6 ▶ In what year was a waxwork of Winston Churchill first displayed at Madame Tussauds?

> **A** 1908 **B** 1938 **C** 1968

7/7 ▶ In what way were the royals played by Colin Firth and Helen Mirren in their Oscar-winning roles related?

> **A** HUSBAND AND WIFE **B** BROTHER AND SISTER **C** FATHER AND DAUGHTER

The Governess Quiz 7: Contestant 2

Answer at least 5 questions correctly to progress on to the Final Chase.

7/1 ▶ What is an alternative name for 1662's 'Great Ejection', when 2,000 ministers were expelled from the Church of England?

> **A** BLACK BARTHOLOMEW'S DAY **B** PINK PERCY'S DAY
>
> **C** SCARLET SEBASTIAN'S DAY

7/2 ▶ The name of which African country means 'Land of Incorruptible People'?

> **A** BURKINA FASO **B** ERITREA **C** MOZAMBIQUE

7/3 ▶ What type of birds can be described as 'raptors'?

> **A** BIRDS OF PREY **B** FLIGHTLESS BIRDS **C** SONGBIRDS

7/4 ▶ In the binary system, 1-0-0-0 represents what number?

> **A** TWO **B** FOUR **C** EIGHT

7/5 ▶ Which Founding Father of the United States wrote under the pseudonyms 'Polly Baker' and 'Alice Addertongue'?

> **A** BENJAMIN FRANKLIN **B** THOMAS JEFFERSON **C** GEORGE WASHINGTON

7/6 ▶ What name is given to a golf course built on sandy ground by the seaside?

> **A** KNOTS **B** SHACKLES **C** LINKS

7/7 ▶ With what country does France share its longest border?

> **A** GERMANY **B** SWITZERLAND **C** SPAIN

The Governess Quiz 7: Contestant 3

Answer at least 5 questions correctly to progress on to the Final Chase.

7/1 ▶ What piece of furniture does NOT appear in the title of one of the *Chronicles of Narnia*?

> **A** BED **B** CHAIR **C** WARDROBE

7/2 ▶ Who sang the title theme song for the James Bond film *Diamonds Are Forever*?

> **A** SHEENA EASTON **B** CARLY SIMON **C** SHIRLEY BASSEY

7/3 ▶ Which of these short words is also a symbol for a chemical element?

> **A** IS **B** IT **C** IN

7/4 ▶ How many bones are there in the human skull?

> **A** 11 **B** 22 **C** 33

7/5 ▶ Which of these Soviet leaders died after less than 15 months in office?

> **A** ANDROPOV **B** BREZHNEV **C** GORBACHEV

7/6 ▶ What is the occupation of Ichabod Crane in Washington Irving's story 'The Legend of Sleepy Hollow'?

> **A** BLACKSMITH **B** FARMER **C** SCHOOLTEACHER

7/7 ▶ According to Guinness World Records, which country has the greatest number of official languages?

> **A** CHINA **B** INDONESIA **C** ZIMBABWE

The Governess Quiz 7: Contestant 4

Answer at least 5 questions correctly to progress on to the Final Chase.

7/1 ▶ In Hitchcock's film *The Lady Vanishes,* how is Miss Froy travelling when she disappears?

> **A** TRAIN **B** BOAT **C** PLANE

7/2 ▶ The Jewish festival of Rosh Hashanah begins at what time of day?

> **A** SUNRISE **B** MIDDAY **C** SUNSET

7/3 ▶ Which of these performers used the name of their pet and the street they grew up on to devise their stage name?

> **A** BRUNO MARS **B** IGGY AZALEA **C** PALOMA FAITH

7/4 ▶ Loud upper-class toffs are commonly called what?

> **A** HOORAY HENRYS **B** JOLLY JONNIES **C** WHOOPEE WALTERS

7/5 ▶ What country has borders with both the Czech Republic and Belarus?

> **A** POLAND **B** ROMANIA **C** SLOVAKIA

7/6 ▶ Orogenesis is the natural formation of what geographical features?

> **A** DESERTS **B** MOUNTAINS **C** RIVERS

7/7 ▶ Which song in *Mary Poppins* was inspired by the child of lyricist Robert Sherman getting a polio vaccine at school?

> **A** 'CHIM CHIM CHER-EE' **B** 'STAY AWAKE' **C** 'A SPOONFUL OF SUGAR'

The Governess Quiz 7: Final Chase

★ Prize fund in the Final Chase was £18,000

★ Your target is 21 correct

Featuring 3 contestants, the team amassed a challenging score of 21 for the chaser to pursue. Pete, a 46-year-old shop owner from Anglesey, supplied a healthy 15 of the correct answers. In spite of an uninterrupted final sprint, The Governess was ultimately thwarted by 3 executed push backs from 6 of her missed questions.

7/1 ▶ The French seaport of Nice is on the coast of what sea?

7/2 ▶ In texting, 'msg' is short for what word?

7/3 ▶ Which king did the Queen call Grandpa England?

7/4 ▶ A standard netball court is how many feet wide?

7/5 ▶ What first name links the composers Mahler and Holst?

7/6 ▶ Shakespeare's Juliet marries into what family?

7/7 ▶ Which author created the half-elven character Elrond?

7/8 ▶ Who was Prime Minister between Rosebery and Balfour?

7/9 ▶ What animal usually appears on a malted milk biscuit?

7/10 ▶ In 1513, James the Fifth became king of what country?

THE GOVERNESS

7/11 ▶ What Puccini opera features a 'Flower Duet'?

7/12 ▶ What's the opposite of the nautical term 'windward'?

7/13 ▶ What type of creature is an oldwife?

7/14 ▶ The postal abbreviation 'CT' refers to what American state?

7/15 ▶ What primary colour is carminic acid?

7/16 ▶ Who did Lucy Griffiths play in the BBC drama *Robin Hood*?

7/17 ▶ In 1498, which Italian explorer discovered Trinidad?

7/18 ▶ What Rudyard Kipling novel has the shortest title?

7/19 ▶ What's the last month of the year to begin with a vowel?

7/20 ▶ Queen Victoria erected a statue at Balmoral to which ghillie?

7/21 ▶ The film *Ferry Cross the Mersey* is set in what city?

7/22 ▶ On an automatic gearbox, what does 'P' stand for?

7/23 ▶ What name is given to Welsh Rarebit with a poached egg on top?

7/24 ▶ What does a necrologist write for newspapers?

7/25 ▶ Felicity Jones played Emma Grundy in what radio series?

The Governess Quiz 8: Contestant 1

Answer at least 5 questions correctly to progress on to the Final Chase.

8/1 ▶ When you have one final opportunity to do something right, you are said to be 'drinking in the last chance...' what?

> **A** BAR **B** CAFÉ **C** SALOON

8/2 ▶ 'Marching as to war' is the second line of what famous hymn?

> **A** 'ABIDE WITH ME' **B** 'MORNING HAS BROKEN' **C** 'ONWARD CHRISTIAN SOLDIERS'

8/3 ▶ Which of these novels was published first?

> **A** *LITTLE DORRIT* **B** *LITTLE LORD FAUNTLEROY* **C** *LITTLE WOMEN*

8/4 ▶ Nintendo character Mario originally had what occupation?

> **A** CARPENTER **B** CHOREOGRAPHER **C** COMPOSER

8/5 ▶ What is the name of the setting for the cult 1960s TV drama *The Prisoner*?

> **A** THE PARISH **B** THE TOWN **C** THE VILLAGE

8/6 ▶ Which of these is the name of a variety of cabbage?

> **A** JANUARY KING **B** MARCH MADNESS **C** MAY BALLS

8/7 ▶ What film title is used as an alternative name for Ronald Reagan's 'Strategic Defense Initiative'?

> **A** STAR WARS **B** STAR TREK **C** STAR STRUCK

The Governess Quiz 8: Contestant 2

Answer at least 5 questions correctly to progress on to the Final Chase.

8/1 ▶ Which European capital fell to the Germans in September 1939?

> **A** BRUSSELS **B** WARSAW **C** LISBON

8/2 ▶ Jackie Harris was the sister of the title character in what sitcom?

> **A** *ELLEN* **B** *MIRANDA* **C** *ROSEANNE*

8/3 ▶ The motto of which of the UK armed forces is usually translated from Latin as 'through adversity to the stars'?

> **A** ARMY **B** NAVY **C** AIRFORCE

8/4 ▶ Former England manager Graham Taylor had two spells as boss of which Midlands club?

> **A** ASTON VILLA **B** NOTTS COUNTY **C** WEST BROMWICH ALBION

8/5 ▶ In the name of the Government department DEFRA, what does the A stand for?

> **A** ADMINISTRATION **B** AFFAIRS **C** AUTHORITY

8/6 ▶ Which of these kings ruled England first?

> **A** WILLIAM II **B** HENRY II **C** GEORGE II

8/7 ▶ Reed Richards is the original name of which fictional character?

> **A** MR SINISTER **B** MR FANTASTIC **C** MR TICKLE

The Governess Quiz 8: Contestant 3

Answer at least 5 questions correctly to progress on to the Final Chase.

8/1 ▶ Due to its shape, the ANZAC Bridge in Sydney was given what nickname?

> **A** GAGA'S STILETTO **B** MADONNA'S BRA **C** KYLIE'S HOTPANTS

8/2 ▶ Which of these snooker players was born in Scotland?

> **A** JOHN HIGGINS **B** RONNIE O'SULLIVAN **C** MARK WILLIAMS

8/3 ▶ Prior to becoming an MP, who was sacked from *The Times* newspaper for falsifying a quote?

> **A** BORIS JOHNSON **B** ED BALLS **C** VINCE CABLE

8/4 ▶ German composer Johann Sebastian Bach was closely associated with which period of music?

> **A** RENAISSANCE **B** BAROQUE **C** ROMANTIC

8/5 ▶ Which of these is NOT the name of a major UK celebrity gossip magazine?

> **A** *CLOSER* **B** *SPOTTED!* **C** *REVEAL*

8/6 ▶ Tommy Lee Jones won an Oscar for his role as a US Marshal in which film?

> **A** *JFK* **B** *NO COUNTRY FOR OLD MEN* **C** *THE FUGITIVE*

8/7 ▶ A jack-rabbit is actually a type of what?

> **A** GOPHER **B** SQUIRREL **C** HARE

The Governess Quiz 8: Contestant 4

Answer at least 5 questions correctly to progress on to the Final Chase.

8/1 ▶ Which of these songs was NOT a Pet Shop Boys hit?

> **A** 'WEST END GIRLS' **B** 'WILD WEST HERO' **C** 'GO WEST'

8/2 ▶ Which year's US Presidential campaign saw the first televised debate between candidates?

> **A** 1960 **B** 1964 **C** 1968

8/3 ▶ Which of these Shakespeare plays does NOT open in a street in Italy?

> **A** *THE MERCHANT OF VENICE* **B** *OTHELLO* **C** *TWELFTH NIGHT*

8/4 ▶ What name is shared by an English philosopher and a Dublin-born painter?

> **A** FRANCIS BACON **B** FRANCIS LAMB **C** FRANCIS VEAL

8/5 ▶ In *EastEnders*, what did Michelle Fowler call the baby girl she had with Dennis Watts?

> **A** DENISE **B** ALBERTA **C** VICKI

8/6 ▶ Which of these is a large mandolin?

> **A** MANDOCELLO **B** MANDOFLUTE **C** MANDOBELL

8/7 ▶ What name is given to the young of a hamster?

> **A** PUP **B** KITTEN **C** CUB

The Governess Quiz 8: Final Chase

★ Prize fund in the Final Chase was £45,000

★ Your target is 19 correct

This 3-contestant final produced a target score of 19. All 3 team members contributed to the total. The Governess embarked on a spirited chase. She conceded only 5 push back opportunities, including a disconcerting 'brain-freeze' on a cricket question, but the team executed 4 of these, which enabled them to outrun her by 2 steps.

8/1 ▶ The Phillies are a baseball team from what American city?

8/2 ▶ What daytime game show involved a series of trolley dashes?

8/3 ▶ Marian Robinson is the mother-in-law of which world leader?

8/4 ▶ The order of Knights Templar was founded in what century?

8/5 ▶ Which tennis star was born in Mallorca in 1986?

8/6 ▶ What constellation is named after the wife of Perseus?

8/7 ▶ In a 1977 hit, what hotel did the Eagles sing about?

8/8 ▶ Which French novelist wrote *Toilers of the Sea*?

8/9 ▶ Twelve minutes is what fraction of an hour?

THE GOVERNESS

8/10 ▷ What is boxer Manny Pacquiao's full first name?

8/11 ▷ The city of Pisco is in what South American country?

8/12 ▷ The Everly Brothers had their first hit song in what decade?

8/13 ▷ In *The Flintstones*, who is Bamm Bamm's mother?

8/14 ▷ On a cricket scorecard, what form of dismissal is 's.t.'?

8/15 ▷ What Martin Amis novel shares its name with a Hackney park?

8/16 ▷ Who's the second oldest child of the Queen?

8/17 ▷ Louisville, Kentucky is named after a king of what country?

8/18 ▷ *Get Lifted* was a 2004 album by which soul singer?

8/19 ▷ What part of a shoe can be 'block'?

8/20 ▷ What's the common alternative name for the harebell flower?

8/21 ▷ Wheat is ground to make what ingredient in bread?

8/22 ▷ A selfish person is said to look out for what number?

8/23 ▷ In America, a silencer on a car exhaust is known as what?

The Governess Quiz 9: Contestant 1

Answer at least 5 questions correctly to progress on to the Final Chase.

9/1 ▶ Which term describes a people with no fixed residence who roam from place to place?

> **A** SPORADIC **B** NOMADIC **C** PERIODIC

9/2 ▶ At the Broadcast Awards in 2015, which Ricky Gervais series was named 'Best programme of the last 20 years'?

> **A** *THE OFFICE* **B** *EXTRAS* **C** *LIFE'S TOO SHORT*

9/3 ▶ Who became US President 16 years after first becoming Vice President?

> **A** JIMMY CARTER **B** RICHARD NIXON **C** GERALD FORD

9/4 ▶ In which of these years was there NOT a female monarch on the English throne?

> **A** 1300 **B** 1600 **C** 1900

9/5 ▶ In electric circuit diagrams, two parallel lines of different lengths represent what?

> **A** BATTERY **B** SWITCH **C** MOTOR

9/6 ▶ In 2012, who created 'Diamond Jubilee Chicken' for thousands of hampers given away by the Queen at a picnic?

> **A** JAMIE OLIVER **B** MICHEL ROUX JR **C** HESTON BLUMENTHAL

9/7 ▶ What is the name of the musical based on the life of Susan Boyle?

> **A** *DAYDREAM BELIEVER* **B** *DON'T DREAM IT'S OVER* **C** *I DREAMED A DREAM*

The Governess Quiz 9: Contestant 2

Answer at least 5 questions correctly to progress on to the Final Chase.

9/1 ▶ Marble is a form of what type of rock?

> A IGNEOUS B METAMORPHIC C SEDIMENTARY

9/2 ▶ In 2014, how many places in Scotland had official city status?

> A TWO B FIVE C SEVEN

9/3 ▶ Which of these joints is furthest up the arm?

> A CARPUS B ELBOW C KNUCKLE

9/4 ▶ Which Shakespeare play features the quote 'My father's spirit in arms! All is not well. I doubt some foul play'?

> A *HAMLET* B *MACBETH* C *OTHELLO*

9/5 ▶ Which of these film stars was married the most times?

> A TONY CURTIS B REX HARRISON C MICKEY ROONEY

9/6 ▶ Which international crisis began in October 1973?

> A SUEZ CRISIS B OIL CRISIS C CUBAN MISSILE CRISIS

9/7 ▶ Nicknamed the 'Invincibles', which football team was undefeated during the entire 2003–04 Premier League season?

> A ARSENAL B CHELSEA C MANCHESTER UNITED

The Governess Quiz 9: Contestant 3

Answer at least 5 questions correctly to progress on to the Final Chase.

9/1 ▶ Which former James Bond actor plays Sir Malcolm Murray in the TV drama *Penny Dreadful?*

> **A** PIERCE BROSNAN **B** TIMOTHY DALTON **C** ROGER MOORE

9/2 ▶ In 2015, women were reportedly turned away from the red carpet at the Cannes Film Festival for not wearing what?

> **A** HATS **B** GLOVES **C** HIGH HEELS

9/3 ▶ Which of these American states does NOT have a coastline on the Atlantic Ocean?

> **A** NEW JERSEY **B** NEBRASKA **C** NORTH CAROLINA

9/4 ▶ Which star of *Friends* played Michael J Fox's girlfriend in the sitcom *Family Ties?*

> **A** JENNIFER ANISTON **B** COURTENEY COX **C** LISA KUDROW

9/5 ▶ Voters who switch allegiance from one party to another between elections are called what?

> **A** SWING VOTERS **B** ROUNDABOUT VOTERS **C** SLIDE VOTERS

9/6 ▶ The Kandinsky Prize is a prestigious Russian award in which field?

> **A** LITERATURE **B** ART **C** CINEMA

9/7 ▶ In the King James Version of the Bible, which Gospel consists of the most chapters?

> **A** MATTHEW **B** MARK **C** LUKE

The Governess Quiz 9: Contestant 4

Answer at least 5 questions correctly to progress on to the Final Chase.

9/1 ▶ According to the saying 'virtue is its own...' what?

> **A** CONSOLATION **B** REWARD **C** VICTORY

9/2 ▶ What kind of children's toy is a dreidel?

> **A** SPINNING TOP **B** RAG DOLL **C** HOOP

9/3 ▶ Which island issued a 'Man of Steel' stamp collection to mark local boy Henry Cavill playing Superman in the 2013 film?

> **A** GUERNSEY **B** ISLE OF MAN **C** JERSEY

9/4 ▶ When buying property, a sequence of interlinked purchases is known as a what?

> **A** STRING **B** CHAIN **C** NECKLACE

9/5 ▶ Which of these is a nickname for a South Australian?

> **A** CROW EATER **B** EMU CHASER **C** PIGEON KISSER

9/6 ▶ Which of these tennis players was never beaten in a Wimbledon Singles final?

> **A** JIMMY CONNORS **B** PETE SAMPRAS **C** ROD LAVER

9/7 ▶ Which of these novels has NOT been adapted as a feature film?

> **A** *THE DAY OF THE TRIFFIDS* **B** *THE DAY OF THE JACKAL* **C** *THE DAY OF THE SCORPION*

The Governess Quiz 9: Final Chase

★ Prize fund in the Final Chase was £11,000

★ Your target is 19 correct

Three contestants qualified for the final in this programme. Pam, a 61-year-old visitor assistant from Newquay, was the team's top scorer with 9 correct answers contributing to the total of 19. The Governess failed to answer 9 questions and the team executed 4 push backs, which was sufficient to outrun the Chaser by 5 steps.

9/1 ▶ Egg-white omelettes are made by removing what from the eggs?

9/2 ▶ Websters' Auto Centre is a garage in what TV soap?

9/3 ▶ Which planet is named after Jupiter's father?

9/4 ▶ Bertrand Russell was awarded the Nobel Prize in what field?

9/5 ▶ Who played the title character in the film *Ghost*?

9/6 ▶ What racecourse is 13 miles east of Cambridge?

9/7 ▶ Who became the head of state of Canada in February 1952?

9/8 ▶ Adam Driver stars in what Lena Dunham sitcom?

9/9 ▶ Who succeeded F W de Klerk as South African President?

THE GOVERNESS QUIZ 9: Final Chase

THE GOVERNESS

9/10 ▷ In economics, what does the 'D' in GDP stand for?

9/11 ▷ What motorway connects Liverpool and Hull?

9/12 ▷ In the *Harry Potter* books, what animal is Fang?

9/13 ▷ The Mount of Olives is in what Middle East city?

9/14 ▷ In what decade did the Kinks have three UK Number One hits?

9/15 ▷ What Puccini opera features near-destitute artist Marcello?

9/16 ▷ What's half of 34?

9/17 ▷ 'The Judgement of Paris' is a story from which mythology?

9/18 ▷ In what English county is the Furness peninsula?

9/19 ▷ Who composed the musical song 'The Naming of Cats'?

9/20 ▷ What city is home to the Utah Jazz basketball team?

9/21 ▷ The month of July has how many days?

9/22 ▷ Arbroath has a coastline on what sea?

9/23 ▷ Who became Rod Stewart's first wife in 1979?

The Governess Quiz 10: Contestant 1

Answer at least 5 questions correctly to progress on to the Final Chase.

10/1 ▶ Salvatore and Cherilyn were the real first names of what singing duo?

A PEACHES AND HERB B RENÉE AND RENATO C SONNY AND CHER

10/2 ▶ What makes up most of the diet of a gannet bird?

A BERRIES B INSECTS C FISH

10/3 ▶ French courtesan Marie Duplessis inspired which opera?

A *TOSCA* B *LA TRAVIATA* C *THE BARBER OF SEVILLE*

10/4 ▶ What did J Paul Getty install at his Sutton Place mansion so guests did not need to think they were imposing on the host?

A PAYPHONE B DRINKS VENDING MACHINE C LAUNDERETTE

10/5 ▶ According to the latest available figures, which organisation is the largest UK landowner?

A THE FORESTRY COMMISSION B THE NATIONAL TRUST C THE RSPB

10/6 ▶ In Norse myth, the Aesir and the Vanir are races of what?

A GODS B GOBLINS C GIANTS

10/7 ▶ Which industry is associated with the names Chatto & Windus and Jonathan Cape?

A BOOKS B FASHION C MUSIC

The Governess Quiz 10: Contestant 2

Answer at least 5 questions correctly to progress on to the Final Chase.

10/1 ▶ Which of these is NOT the name of the wife of a 20th-century British king?

> **A** ELIZABETH **B** MARY **C** VICTORIA

10/2 ▶ To the on-screen compliment 'Goodness, what beautiful diamonds', who replied 'Goodness had nothing to do with it'?

> **A** MARLENE DIETRICH **B** MARILYN MONROE **C** MAE WEST

10/3 ▶ Samuel Taylor Coleridge's poem 'Kubla Khan' ends 'For he on honey-dew hath fed, And drunk the...' what?

> **A** MILK OF PARADISE **B** MILK OF ROSES **C** MILK OF MAGNESIA

10/4 ▶ On what type of medieval building would you be most likely to see crenellations?

> **A** CASTLE **B** WINDMILL **C** CHURCH

10/5 ▶ Who took the unusual step of contesting Commons Speaker John Bercow's constituency in the 2010 General Election?

> **A** NIGEL FARAGE **B** MARTIN BELL **C** GEORGE GALLOWAY

10/6 ▶ The sitcom *Green Wing* was set in what type of establishment?

> **A** BIRD SANCTUARY **B** HOSPITAL **C** PRISON

10/7 ▶ Brought back to the US by servicemen after World War Two, the word 'honcho' means 'group leader' in which language?

> **A** CANTONESE **B** JAPANESE **C** TAGALOG

The Governess Quiz 10: Contestant 3

Answer at least 5 questions correctly to progress on to the Final Chase.

10/1 ▶ Lord's Cricket Ground also has facilities for the playing of which of these sports?

> **A** BOWLS **B** POLO **C** REAL TENNIS

10/2 ▶ What size of poodle is less than 11 inches tall?

> **A** ELFIN **B** PETITE **C** TOY

10/3 ▶ Which of these is the name of an Oscar Wilde play?

> **A** *LADY WINDERMERE'S FAN* **B** *LORD CONISTON'S GLOVES*
> **C** *MAJOR BUTTERMERE'S WALLET*

10/4 ▶ Which singer featured on Calvin Harris's 2012 Number One single 'Sweet Nothing'?

> **A** ELLIE GOULDING **B** RITA ORA **C** FLORENCE WELCH

10/5 ▶ Which of these items originated in the Americas?

> **A** TEA **B** COFFEE **C** TOBACCO

10/6 ▶ Which James Bond actor played Inspector Clouseau in *Curse of the Pink Panther*?

> **A** PIERCE BROSNAN **B** SEAN CONNERY **C** ROGER MOORE

10/7 ▶ What percentage of the London Underground network is actually underground?

> **A** 45% **B** 65% **C** 85%

The Governess Quiz 10: Contestant 4

Answer at least 5 questions correctly to progress on to the Final Chase.

10/1 ▶ Which of these is a process of curing fish by smoking them for a short time?

> **A** BALLOONING **B** BILLOWING **C** BLOATING

10/2 ▶ What phrase usually appeared in the opening titles of *The X-Files*?

> **A** I WANT TO BELIEVE **B** THE TRUTH IS OUT THERE **C** TRUST NO-ONE

10/3 ▶ Which metal has the highest thermal conductivity?

> **A** GOLD **B** SILVER **C** PLATINUM

10/4 ▶ A person described as having a 'fit of pique' is experiencing a temporary feeling of what?

> **A** CONFUSION **B** HAPPINESS **C** RESENTMENT

10/5 ▶ A famous literary festival was founded in the 1980s in which of these towns?

> **A** HAY-ON-WYE **B** STRATFORD-UPON-AVON **C** NEWARK-ON-TRENT

10/6 ▶ Which of these is the full name of an Oscar-winning actress?

> **A** KATHARINE HOWARD HEPBURN **B** ANNE BOLEYN BANCROFT
>
> **C** JANE SEYMOUR FONDA

10/7 ▶ Echography is used to investigate the body's internal structures by means of what?

> **A** ULTRASOUND **B** CONTRAST X-RAYS **C** FIBRE OPTICS

The Governess Quiz 10: Final Chase

★ Prize fund in the Final Chase was £40,000

★ Your target is 23 correct

In this programme 3 contestants reached the final. All contributed to the magnificent final score of 23. However, their execution of push backs failed to match up – with only 1 out of 5 opportunities being executed. The Governess's impressive final sprint was halted by the clock and the team were victorious.

10/1 ▷ On what part of the body would you wear a balaclava?

10/2 ▷ 'New Orleans' is a style of what music genre?

10/3 ▷ A hexaploid organism has how many sets of chromosomes?

10/4 ▷ In what decade did the Fascists come to power in Italy?

10/5 ▷ Tamwar Masood is a character in what TV soap?

10/6 ▷ What is the name of the UK's nuclear weapons programme?

10/7 ▷ In what type of race did Ben-Hur compete against Messala?

10/8 ▷ In reptiles, ectothermic is another name for being what?

10/9 ▷ 'Oh, please yourself' was a catchphrase of which comedian?

10/10 ▷ What's the national currency for the territory of Guam?

THE GOVERNESS

10/11 ▷ Which rap mogul released the 2015 album *Compton*?

10/12 ▷ Armament factory workers started what London football club?

10/13 ▷ What's the first name of Hollywood director Van Sant?

10/14 ▷ 'Bracelets' is a slang term for what piece of police equipment?

10/15 ▷ Voltaire and Victor Hugo are buried in what Paris building?

10/16 ▷ What's half of 82?

10/17 ▷ The character Horatio Hornblower is a member of what service?

10/18 ▷ Sam Burgess is a famous name in what sport?

10/19 ▷ How many people are playing a 'four-handed' piece on a piano?

10/20 ▷ What berry is dried to make a craisin?

10/21 ▷ What type of creature is the salmon-crested cockatoo?

10/22 ▷ Which singer-turned-actress was born Leian Piper?

10/23 ▷ The painter Edward Burne-Jones lived in what century?

10/24 ▷ Shudra is the fourth caste in what major Asian religion?

10/25 ▷ The holder of what cabinet post is also 'Master of the Mint'?

The
SINNERMAN

The Sinnerman

Paul Sinha, The Sinnerman, is *The Chase*'s 'iron fist in a velvet glove'. Also dubbed The Smiling Assasin and Sarcasm in a Suit by Bradley Walsh, Paul's friendly demeanour seems to offer an easy ride to contestants – that is, until the famous sarcastic humour kicks in. A typical quip was telling a competitor in a colourful shirt that he didn't think it was possible [for him] to be as bright as his shirt. Deceptively relaxed, in fact, he can be as competitive as any of his fellow Chasers. And he likes to show off his in-depth knowledge, often providing extra information to show that his correct answers are no fluke.

Paul holds the record for the lowest negative offer made and accepted by a contestant – minus £15,000. This offer was taken through to the Final Chase successfully by the player. The highest score he has caught in the Final Chase is 24. The Sinnerman's lowest winning score in the Final Chase was 14.

Always guaranteed to get players and audience alike giggling, The Sinnerman is nevertheless a tough opponent for any contestant.

The Sinnerman Quiz 1: Contestant 1

Answer at least 5 questions correctly to progress on to the Final Chase.

1/1 ▶ A Long Island Iced Tea cocktail should be served in what type of glass?

> **A** FLUTE **B** SNIFTER **C** HIGHBALL

1/2 ▶ *The Man Who Made Murray* is the subtitle of a 2014 biography of which retired tennis star?

> **A** BORIS BECKER **B** TIM HENMAN **C** IVAN LENDL

1/3 ▶ Attar is an essential oil most commonly obtained from the petals of which flower?

> **A** JASMINE **B** LILY **C** ROSE

1/4 ▶ Edward J Smith was the captain of which sunken passenger liner?

> **A** *LUSITANIA* **B** *COSTA CONCORDIA* **C** *TITANIC*

1/5 ▶ ABBA made an unsuccessful attempt to represent Sweden in the 1973 Eurovision Song Contest with which song?

> **A** 'RING RING' **B** 'I DO, I DO, I DO, I DO, I DO' **C** 'HONEY HONEY'

1/6 ▶ The triathlon was introduced as a sport at which Olympics?

> **A** BARCELONA 1992 **B** ATLANTA 1996 **C** SYDNEY 2000

1/7 ▶ Which character in *EastEnders* was originally played by Jo Warne?

> **A** ANGIE WATTS **B** ZOË SLATER **C** PEGGY MITCHELL

The Sinnerman Quiz 1: **Contestant 2**

Answer at least 5 questions correctly to progress on to the Final Chase.

1/1 ▶ If you ordered '*gambas*' on a Spanish menu, what would you get?

> **A** CRAB **B** LOBSTER **C** PRAWNS

1/2 ▶ Which of these historical events took place first?

> **A** MUTINY ON THE BOUNTY **B** BOSTON TEA PARTY **C** STORMING OF THE BASTILLE

1/3 ▶ Where is a Philip Treacy creation most likely to be worn?

> **A** ON THE FEET **B** AROUND THE WAIST **C** ON THE HEAD

1/4 ▶ Which of these films is categorised as a comedy?

> **A** *28 DAYS LATER* **B** *THE NUMBER 23* **C** *22 JUMP STREET*

1/5 ▶ Which of these is NOT a place in Dorset?

> **A** SCRATCHY BOTTOM **B** HAPPY BOTTOM **C** SLACK BOTTOM

1/6 ▶ After the retreat from Moscow in 1812, Napoleon reputedly said 'There is only one step from the sublime to...' what?

> **A** THE OUTRAGEOUS **B** THE RIDICULOUS **C** THE ADULTEROUS

1/7 ▶ Members of the chart-topping group Liberty X were rejects from which TV talent show?

> **A** *POP IDOL* **B** *THE X FACTOR* **C** *POPSTARS*

The Sinnerman Quiz 1: Contestant 3

Answer at least 5 questions correctly to progress on to the Final Chase.

1/1 ▶ In the Bible, who led the Israelite invasion of Canaan and brought his people to the Promised Land?

> **A ABRAHAM B MOSES C JOSHUA**

1/2 ▶ What vegetable is a traditional ingredient of a Glamorgan sausage?

> **A CARROT B POTATO C LEEK**

1/3 ▶ In 1988, which player ended Martina Navratilova's run of six consecutive Wimbledon Ladies' Singles titles?

> **A STEFFI GRAF B MONICA SELES C GABRIELA SABATINI**

1/4 ▶ Lisfranc injuries affect what part of the body?

> **A HAND B RIBCAGE C FOOT**

1/5 ▶ Which of these birds is NOT flightless?

> **A CASSOWARY B KIWI C PTARMIGAN**

1/6 ▶ Which Stephen Sondheim composition won the 1975 Grammy Award for 'Song of the Year'?

> **A 'I FEEL PRETTY' B 'LOSING MY MIND' C 'SEND IN THE CLOWNS'**

1/7 ▶ Which painter was described by Cézanne as 'only an eye, but my God what an eye!'?

> **A GAUGUIN B VAN GOGH C MONET**

The Sinnerman Quiz 1: Contestant 4

Answer at least 5 questions correctly to progress on to the Final Chase.

1/1 ▶ What did Katie Price name her second daughter, born in 2014?

> **A** BUNNY **B** KITTY **C** HORSEY

1/2 ▶ In 2014, the European Space Agency successfully landed the space probe *Philae* on what type of body?

> **A** ASTEROID **B** COMET **C** DWARF PLANET

1/3 ▶ Which of these cities does NOT stand on the River Rhine?

> **A** AMSTERDAM **B** BASEL **C** COLOGNE

1/4 ▶ The Paisley Gateway is an entrance at what football ground?

> **A** ANFIELD **B** ELLAND ROAD **C** VILLA PARK

1/5 ▶ The signature of which Bank of England official appears on English banknotes?

> **A** CHIEF CASHIER **B** GOVERNOR **C** DIRECTOR

1/6 ▶ What snake derives its name from a monstrous serpent in Greek mythology?

> **A** COBRA **B** MAMBA **C** PYTHON

1/7 ▶ Which fictional castaway found 'the print of a man's naked foot on the shore'?

> **A** BEN GUNN **B** LEMUEL GULLIVER **C** ROBINSON CRUSOE

The Sinnerman Quiz 1: Final Chase

★ Prize fund in the Final Chase was £35,000

★ Your target is 19 correct

Four contestants reached the final in this programme. Sandy, a 52-year-old logistics controller from Edinburgh, was the top scorer for the team, providing 12 of their 15 correct answers. Working as a team, the contestants managed to execute 7 out of 8 push back opportunities to frustrate The Sinnerman in the Final Chase.

1/1 ▶ Margaret Thatcher was an MP for what party?

1/2 ▶ Ricky Tomlinson played Bobby Grant in what TV soap?

1/3 ▶ Iron sulphide is often mistaken for what metal?

1/4 ▶ The mountain Scafell Pike is in what county?

1/5 ▶ How many slices of bread make a double-decker sandwich?

1/6 ▶ Which French DJ had a 2014 Number One with 'Lovers On The Sun'?

1/7 ▶ Longboarding and shortboarding are styles of what water activity?

1/8 ▶ Traditionally, a pally-ass mattress is filled with what?

1/9 ▶ The human heart has how many valves?

1/10 ▶ In the *Spider-Man* films, which character is referred to as MJ?

THE SINNERMAN QUIZ 1: Final Chase

THE SINNERMAN

1/11 ▶ Achilles is the hero of what epic poem by Homer?

1/12 ▶ What name links actresses with the surnames Davis and Midler?

1/13 ▶ The city of Albacete is in what European country?

1/14 ▶ In what sport did Harry Vardon win the Open six times?

1/15 ▶ William Beech is a war evacuee in what children's novel?

1/16 ▶ What colour's associated with environmental awareness?

1/17 ▶ The original Speakers' Corner is in what London park?

1/18 ▶ 'Heartless' was a 2008 hit for which hip-hop artist?

1/19 ▶ Traditionally, on what type of map does X mark the spot?

1/20 ▶ How many Tudor kings were named Henry?

1/21 ▶ Traditionally, what animals are said to 'moo'?

1/22 ▶ What sport is played in Japan's 'J League'?

1/23 ▶ Mayim Bialik plays Amy Farrah Fowler in what US sitcom?

1/24 ▶ In the name of the exam, what did CSE stand for?

The Sinnerman Quiz 2: Contestant 1

Answer at least 5 questions correctly to progress on to the Final Chase.

2/1 ▶ Little Jimmy Osmond's 'Long Haired Lover' of his 1970s hit came from what part of the country?

> **A** HUMBERSIDE **B** TYNESIDE **C** MERSEYSIDE

2/2 ▶ Which variety of apple was originally called Mullin's Yellow Seedling?

> **A** GOLDEN DELICIOUS **B** GALA **C** GRANNY SMITH

2/3 ▶ 'Gnu' is another name for which mammal?

> **A** WILDEBEEST **B** WARTHOG **C** WILD OX

2/4 ▶ What type of vessel was the world's first nuclear-powered warship?

> **A** AIRCRAFT CARRIER **B** BATTLESHIP **C** SUBMARINE

2/5 ▶ Which Englishman played in a ninth consecutive Ryder Cup in 2014?

> **A** JUSTIN ROSE **B** IAN POULTER **C** LEE WESTWOOD

2/6 ▶ Which Roman god was said to be lame?

> **A** MERCURY **B** VULCAN **C** MARS

2/7 ▶ In text messages, what does 'XOXO' mean?

> **A** TOO MUCH SWEARING **B** NOT SURPRISED **C** HUGS AND KISSES

The Sinnerman Quiz 2: Contestant 2

Answer at least 5 questions correctly to progress on to the Final Chase.

2/1 ▶ Which was the last English queen whose sister had also been monarch?

> A ELIZABETH I B ANNE C VICTORIA

2/2 ▶ The 'bat-eared' is a species of what mammal?

> A FOX B RABBIT C SQUIRREL

2/3 ▶ The tales in the *Arabian Nights* were told to whom?

> A THE EMIR B THE IMAM C THE SULTAN

2/4 ▶ Which of these policing duos appeared on TV first?

> A CAGNEY & LACEY B DEMPSEY & MAKEPEACE C STARSKY & HUTCH

2/5 ▶ What is the national currency of Fiji?

> A DOLLAR B POUND C FRANC

2/6 ▶ Which boxer claimed 'I should be a postage stamp. That's the only way I'll ever get licked!'?

> A MUHAMMAD ALI B SONNY LISTON C GEORGE FOREMAN

2/7 ▶ In which Monty Python film is the deadly Rabbit of Caerbannog killed with the Holy Hand Grenade of Antioch?

> A *LIFE OF BRIAN* B *THE MEANING OF LIFE* C *THE HOLY GRAIL*

The Sinnerman Quiz 2: Contestant 3

Answer at least 5 questions correctly to progress on to the Final Chase.

2/1 ▶ Which of these states was NOT one of the original 13 colonies of the USA?

> **A** RHODE ISLAND **B** SOUTH CAROLINA **C** TENNESSEE

2/2 ▶ Which girl's name means 'little bear'?

> **A** VERONICA **B** URSULA **C** WANDA

2/3 ▶ Which of these elements has a single letter for its chemical symbol?

> **A** SILVER **B** SODIUM **C** SULPHUR

2/4 ▶ The Icelandic delicacy of *Hákarl* is made from what?

> **A** ROTTEN SHARK **B** SMOKED PUFFIN **C** FERMENTED POLAR BEAR

2/5 ▶ Red mercuric sulphide is another name for what pigment?

> **A** ULTRAMARINE **B** OCHRE **C** VERMILION

2/6 ▶ Which of these bands did NOT originate in Wales?

> **A** CATATONIA **B** STEREOPHONICS **C** TEARS FOR FEARS

2/7 ▶ Which dog breed does The Kennel Club describe as 'the canine equivalent of the Laughing Cavalier'?

> **A** BLOODHOUND **B** GERMAN PINSCHER **C** SAMOYED

The Sinnerman Quiz 2: Contestant 4

Answer at least 5 questions correctly to progress on to the Final Chase.

2/1 ▶ In 2010, who or what did *Rolling Stone* magazine call a 'great vampire squid wrapped around the face of humanity'?

> **A** STARBUCKS **B** GOLDMAN SACHS **C** SIMON COWELL

2/2 ▶ Which of these is a city in Alberta, Canada?

> **A** MEDICINE HAT **B** DENTIST CHAIR **C** SURGICAL GLOVE

2/3 ▶ Which chocolate assortment shares its name with a 2004 hit for the group OutKast?

> **A** QUALITY STREET **B** CELEBRATIONS **C** ROSES

2/4 ▶ Which of these actresses did NOT win a Best Actress Oscar for a role in a musical film?

> **A** JULIE ANDREWS **B** BARBRA STREISAND **C** JUDY GARLAND

2/5 ▶ Which politician said 'My chances of being PM are about as good as the chances of finding Elvis on Mars'?

> **A** BORIS JOHNSON **B** NIGEL FARAGE **C** NICK CLEGG

2/6 ▶ According to the saying, 'Caesar's wife must be above...' what?

> **A** BOARD **B** SUSPICION **C** SEA LEVEL

2/7 ▶ The brainchild of John Spilsbury, the first jigsaw puzzle was created in what century?

> **A** 16TH CENTURY **B** 17TH CENTURY **C** 18TH CENTURY

The Sinnerman Quiz 2: Final Chase

⭐ Prize fund in the Final Chase was £35,000

⭐ Your target is 19 correct

Three players made it to the final, where they amassed an impressive total of 19. The top scorer was Adam, a 41-year-old mental health nurse from Bristol, who provided 11 of the correct answers. Conceding 6 push back opportunities, of which the team were able to execute 5, The Sinnerman was beaten, in spite of an excellent final run.

2/1 ▶ What day of the week is three days after Sunday?

2/2 ▶ The posterior cruciate ligament is in what part of the leg?

2/3 ▶ Brad Pitt forms a pugilist group in what 1999 film?

2/4 ▶ Which British Prime Minister signed the Good Friday Accord?

2/5 ▶ How many minutes in one-sixth of an hour?

2/6 ▶ Redback spiders are native to what country?

2/7 ▶ What surname links father and daughter singers Marty and Kim?

2/8 ▶ What Cornwall pub gave its name to a Daphne du Maurier novel?

2/9 ▶ What relation by marriage is Tim Laurence to Prince William?

THE SINNERMAN

2/10 ▷ What letter represents the lowest Council Tax band?

2/11 ▷ Which retired boxer became Mayor of Kiev in 2014?

2/12 ▷ Which queen did Angel Coulby play in the TV series *Merlin*?

2/13 ▷ The dish *Wiener Schnitzel* originated in what country?

2/14 ▷ The V-1 flying bomb was used by the Germans in what war?

2/15 ▷ Hallowmass is another name for what November feast day?

2/16 ▷ What 1978 film begins on the planet Krypton?

2/17 ▷ Cohiba cigars were created for which Cuban president?

2/18 ▷ Which Italian composed the opera *The Girl of the Golden West*?

2/19 ▷ RI is the postal abbreviation for what American state?

2/20 ▷ 'Watch the Throne' was a tour by Jay-Z and which other rapper?

2/21 ▷ In fashion, what are flats and lace-ups?

2/22 ▷ What semi-precious stone is a type of lignite or coal?

2/23 ▷ In Roman numerals, what two letters represent the number 60?

THE SINNERMAN QUIZ 2: Final Chase

The Sinnerman Quiz 3: Contestant 1

Answer at least 5 questions correctly to progress on to the Final Chase.

3/1 ▶ Which of these is a sandwich biscuit?

> **A** NICE **B** MALTED MILK **C** BOURBON

3/2 ▶ The Pope sacked the head of the Swiss Guard in 2014 because he was what?

> **A** TOO LAZY **B** TOO HIGHLY PAID **C** TOO STRICT

3/3 ▶ In the TV series, which of the Tracy brothers was the pilot of *Thunderbird Two*?

> **A** ALAN **B** GORDON **C** VIRGIL

3/4 ▶ The Frans Hals painting *Young Man Holding a Skull* has been thought to be of which Shakespeare character?

> **A** HAMLET **B** OTHELLO **C** MACBETH

3/5 ▶ Which of these sports stars won Olympic gold at the longest distance?

> **A** KATHERINE GRAINGER **B** REBECCA ADLINGTON **C** SALLY GUNNELL

3/6 ▶ Which of these former US Presidents did NOT die on 4 July 1826?

> **A** THOMAS JEFFERSON **B** JOHN ADAMS **C** JAMES MONROE

3/7 ▶ The sleep disorder 'Pavor Nocturnus' is commonly known as what?

> **A** NIGHT TERROR **B** NIGHT HORROR **C** NIGHT PANIC

The Sinnerman Quiz 3: Contestant 2

Answer at least 5 questions correctly to progress on to the Final Chase.

3/1 ▶ Which literary character said courage is 'when you know you're licked before you begin, but you begin anyway'?

> **A** ALBUS DUMBLEDORE **B** ATTICUS FINCH **C** WINSTON SMITH

3/2 ▶ Famous for its tonic wine, Buckfast Abbey is in what county?

> **A** DEVON **B** DORSET **C** CORNWALL

3/3 ▶ Which film gave Walt Disney his only Best Picture Oscar nomination?

> **A** *BEDKNOBS AND BROOMSTICKS* **B** *SONG OF THE SOUTH* **C** *MARY POPPINS*

3/4 ▶ The shipping forecast area FitzRoy is named after the captain of what famous ship?

> **A** *BEAGLE* **B** *MARY ROSE* **C** *VICTORY*

3/5 ▶ Albert Einstein was an accomplished amateur player of which instrument?

> **A** FLUTE **B** ORGAN **C** VIOLIN

3/6 ▶ Which of these is NOT a part of the Penguin publishing group?

> **A** PARTRIDGE **B** PELICAN **C** PUFFIN

3/7 ▶ How many states does Florida have land borders with?

> **A** ONE **B** TWO **C** THREE

The Sinnerman Quiz 3: Contestant 3

Answer at least 5 questions correctly to progress on to the Final Chase.

3/1 ▶ In Formula 1, a half white, half black flag with a car's number on it is a warning for what?

> **A** A MECHANICAL PROBLEM **B** REFUELLING IMMINENT **C** UNSPORTING BEHAVIOUR

3/2 ▶ 'Empty belly life! Rotten smelly life!' is a lyric from what musical theatre song?

> **A** 'FOOD GLORIOUS FOOD' **B** 'IT'S THE HARD-KNOCK LIFE' **C** 'MANCHESTER ENGLAND'

3/3 ▶ Where is Paul Van Hoeydonck's artwork *Fallen Astronaut*?

> **A** KENNEDY SPACE CENTER **B** THE MOON **C** INTERNATIONAL SPACE STATION

3/4 ▶ The triquetral and trapezium bones are in what joint of the human body?

> **A** ANKLE **B** KNEE **C** WRIST

3/5 ▶ In which city was escapologist Harry Houdini born?

> **A** BERLIN **B** BORDEAUX **C** BUDAPEST

3/6 ▶ Which scientist gives his name to an SI unit of pressure and a computer programming language?

> **A** NEWTON **B** TESLA **C** PASCAL

3/7 ▶ Which of these queens was the mother of two English monarchs?

> **A** ELEANOR OF AQUITAINE **B** CATHERINE OF ARAGON **C** MARY OF MODENA

The Sinnerman Quiz 3: Contestant 4

Answer at least 5 questions correctly to progress on to the Final Chase.

3/1 ▶ The literary character Pippi Longstocking wears her hair in what style?

> **A** PIGTAILS **B** BUN **C** DREADLOCKS

3/2 ▶ What is a 'funambulist' most likely to walk on?

> **A** HOT COALS **B** TIPTOES **C** TIGHTROPE

3/3 ▶ Planet Mondas was the original home of which foes in TV's *Doctor Who*?

> **A** CYBERMEN **B** DALEKS **C** SLITHEEN

3/4 ▶ As the crow flies, which UK capital city is closest to Edinburgh?

> **A** BELFAST **B** CARDIFF **C** LONDON

3/5 ▶ Which of these German numbers has the highest value?

> **A** ELF **B** SIEBEN **C** ZWÖLF

3/6 ▶ Billionaire Boys Club and Ice Cream are clothing lines by which musician?

> **A** KANYE WEST **B** WILL.I.AM **C** PHARRELL WILLIAMS

3/7 ▶ What is the motto of Alexandre Dumas' Three Musketeers?

> **A** UNITED IN DIVERSITY **B** ALL FOR ONE, ONE FOR ALL **C** THREE'S COMPANY

The Sinnerman Quiz 3: Final Chase

★ Prize fund in the Final Chase was £35,000

★ Your target is 19 correct

The final involved 3 contestants, who racked up a total of 19 steps for The Sinnerman to chase. Forty-five-year-old B & B owner Darren was the top scorer, contributing 13 correct answers. The team stalled The Sinnerman's pursuit by executing 4 out of 6 push back chances and were able to outrun him with 5 steps to spare.

3/1 ▷ *Le Chat Noir* was a 19th-century cabaret club in what city?

3/2 ▷ Heinz Spaghetti Hoops are covered with what flavour sauce?

3/3 ▷ Which Poet Laureate became a Dame in 2015?

3/4 ▷ At 84, which Victorian was Britain's oldest Prime Minister?

3/5 ▷ What is Catalonia's most populous city?

3/6 ▷ How many contestants take part in the TV quiz *Tipping Point*?

3/7 ▷ *Miss E... So Addictive* is an album by which female rapper?

3/8 ▷ 'Hello, Gorgeous' is a line from what Barbra Streisand film?

3/9 ▷ Osiris is the ladies' reserve rowing team at what university?

THE SINNERMAN QUIZ 3: Final Chase

THE SINNERMAN

3/10 ▷ Which mutineer got married in Tahiti in June 1789?

3/11 ▷ Adam Brody starred as Seth Cohen in what TV teen drama?

3/12 ▷ The River Rhône begins in what alpine country?

3/13 ▷ Which Mexican painter did Salma Hayek play in the film *Frida*?

3/14 ▷ The 'red half of Merseyside' refers to what football team?

3/15 ▷ 'Endgame' is a song from what Tim Rice musical?

3/16 ▷ Most of ABBA's Number One singles were in what decade?

3/17 ▷ What sort of building would have a room called a 'snug'?

3/18 ▷ The 1814 Treaty of Ghent was between the UK and what country?

3/19 ▷ What material are squash balls made of?

3/20 ▷ Which of Victoria Beckham's sons was born in 2002?

3/21 ▷ Flying Officer is a rank in which of the armed forces?

3/22 ▷ What Terry's chocolate product is a ball divided into segments?

The Sinnerman Quiz 4: Contestant 1

Answer at least 5 questions correctly to progress on to the Final Chase.

4/1 ▶ Which of these sitcoms debuted on UK TV most recently?

> **A** *DAD'S ARMY* **B** *IT AIN'T HALF HOT MUM* **C** *2POINT4 CHILDREN*

4/2 ▶ Which US city boasts the world's largest library and the world's largest museum?

> **A** BOSTON **B** WASHINGTON DC **C** CHICAGO

4/3 ▶ Which skateboarding trick involves sliding sideways along a handrail or curb?

> **A** CRUSH **B** GRIND **C** SHRED

4/4 ▶ In 2007, who did Boris Johnson describe as having 'dyed blonde hair and pouty lips, and a steely blue stare'?

> **A** HILLARY CLINTON **B** ANGELA MERKEL **C** HIMSELF

4/5 ▶ In physics, which of these varies according to the strength of gravity?

> **A** MASS **B** WEIGHT **C** DENSITY

4/6 ▶ Opened in 1976, what was the first major enclosed shopping centre to be built in the UK?

> **A** METRO CENTRE **B** MEADOWHALL **C** BRENT CROSS

4/7 ▶ Europe's longest river flows entirely within what country?

> **A** FRANCE **B** GERMANY **C** RUSSIA

The Sinnerman Quiz 4: Contestant 2

Answer at least 5 questions correctly to progress on to the Final Chase.

4/1 ▶ Which of these scientists is NOT the subject of a 2014 film?

> **A** STEPHEN HAWKING **B** ALAN TURING **C** LINUS PAULING

4/2 ▶ In Greek myth, which goddess brought the statue of Galatea to life?

> **A** ARTEMIS **B** APHRODITE **C** ATHENA

4/3 ▶ What is defined in the *Oxford English Dictionary* as 'an unstimulating, low-paid job'?

> **A** TELEJOB **B** MCJOB **C** QUIZJOB

4/4 ▶ Which pop star headlined the half-time show at the 2015 Super Bowl?

> **A** KATY PERRY **B** TAYLOR SWIFT **C** RIHANNA

4/5 ▶ What beauty procedure was popularised by the silent film 'vamp' Pola Negri?

> **A** PAINTING TOENAILS **B** FAKE TANNING **C** BIKINI WAXING

4/6 ▶ In the musical *Evita*, what game is played by cast members during the song 'The Art of the Possible'?

> **A** MUSICAL CHAIRS **B** PASS THE PARCEL **C** PIN THE DONKEY'S TAIL

4/7 ▶ Instead of its annual 'Man of the Year', in 1982 *Time* magazine named what object 'Machine of the Year'?

> **A** PERSONAL COMPUTER **B** MOBILE PHONE **C** WALKMAN

The Sinnerman Quiz 4: Contestant 3

Answer at least 5 questions correctly to progress on to the Final Chase.

4/1 ▶ Which of these Italian artists was born in the 15th century?

> **A** BOTTICELLI **B** DONATELLO **C** TINTORETTO

4/2 ▶ In the film *Star Wars,* Princess Leia's hologram message says that which character is her 'only hope'?

> **A** LUKE SKYWALKER **B** OBI-WAN KENOBI **C** CHEWBACCA

4/3 ▶ Which of these items are students at Oxford University allowed to take into exams?

> **A** SWEETS **B** MOBILE PHONES **C** GOOD LUCK CHARMS

4/4 ▶ Which cocktail was declared Puerto Rico's 'official beverage' in 1978?

> **A** PIÑA COLADA **B** MOJITO **C** BELLINI

4/5 ▶ Which bear said 'My spelling is wobbly. It's good spelling but it wobbles, and the letters get in the wrong places'?

> **A** POOH **B** RUPERT **C** PADDINGTON

4/6 ▶ Which of these explorers was alive when Columbus set sail for the New World?

> **A** JAMES COOK **B** MARCO POLO **C** VASCO DA GAMA

4/7 ▶ Academy rules allow each Oscar winner how long on stage to make their acceptance speech?

> **A** 45 SECONDS **B** 90 SECONDS **C** 180 SECONDS

The Sinnerman Quiz 4: Contestant 4

Answer at least 5 questions correctly to progress on to the Final Chase.

4/1 ▶ Which of these cakes does NOT traditionally include currants?

> **A** ECCLES CAKE **B** UPSIDE DOWN CAKE **C** SIMNEL CAKE

4/2 ▶ Daniel Powter had a big 2005 hit with which of these songs?

> **A** 'OH HAPPY DAY' **B** 'HAVE A NICE DAY' **C** 'BAD DAY'

4/3 ▶ Which of these words appears in the titles of two plays by Oscar Wilde?

> **A** EARNEST **B** IDEAL **C** IMPORTANCE

4/4 ▶ What gas is produced if a diamond is burned?

> **A** AMMONIA **B** CARBON DIOXIDE **C** OXYGEN

4/5 ▶ Complete the title of the 2014 comic autobiography *We Need to Talk About...* who?

> **A** KEVIN BRIDGES **B** RUSSELL KANE **C** KEITH LEMON

4/6 ▶ The four surviving copies of which document went on display together in 2015?

> **A** DOMESDAY BOOK **B** SHAKESPEARE'S FIRST FOLIO **C** MAGNA CARTA

4/7 ▶ Which of these paintings in the National Gallery is unfinished?

> **A** *MR AND MRS ANDREWS* **B** *THE FIGHTING TEMERAIRE* **C** *THE HAY WAIN*

The Sinnerman Quiz 4: Final Chase

★ Prize fund in the Final Chase was £35,000

★ Your target is 19 correct

Three contestants reached the final in this programme. All contributed to their magnificent total of 26, the top scorer being Andrew, a 57-year-old copy editor from London. The Sinnerman was impeded in his chase by 6 executed push backs and was ultimately beaten by an astonishing 13-step margin.

4/1 ▶ What type of snack is a fig roll?

4/2 ▶ In what 1980s Dustin Hoffman film does Michael become Dorothy?

4/3 ▶ Bobcats are native to what continent?

4/4 ▶ Who was the longest lived man in the Bible?

4/5 ▶ What winter sport uses goals that are four feet by six feet?

4/6 ▶ What is the UK's largest budget airline?

4/7 ▶ The One Ring is a central feature in what trilogy of novels?

4/8 ▶ 'One Shot' was a 2010 hit for what boy band?

4/9 ▶ In what century was the Battle of Waterloo?

4/10 ▶ Tierra del Fuego is divided between Argentina and what country?

4/11 ▶ What is the only primate in the Chinese zodiac?

THE SINNERMAN

4/12 ▶ What flower is named after horticulturist William Forsyth?

4/13 ▶ The Grange B & B features in what TV soap?

4/14 ▶ Which woman became India's Prime Minister in 1966?

4/15 ▶ Tennis star Monica Seles was born what nationality?

4/16 ▶ What is added to a Pot Noodle prior to eating?

4/17 ▶ How many members were there in the original Sugababes line-up?

4/18 ▶ Which 19th century Pointillist painted *Circus Sideshow*?

4/19 ▶ 'Redmayniacs' are fans of which Oscar-winning actor?

4/20 ▶ What bone forms the upper arm in the human body?

4/21 ▶ 'Choo-choo' is a child's term for what form of transport?

4/22 ▶ Which king succeeded Henry VII in 1509?

4/23 ▶ Flora Poste is the heroine of what Stella Gibbons novel?

4/24 ▶ Shakira's hit 'Hips Don't Lie' featured which Fugees rapper?

4/25 ▶ The Celtic Sea is an inlet of what ocean?

4/26 ▶ Who won a Golden Globe for his role in *Doctor Zhivago*?

The Sinnerman Quiz 5: Contestant 1

Answer at least 5 questions correctly to progress on to the Final Chase.

5/1 ▶ Which of these TV shows was set in the Channel Islands?

> **A** *BERGERAC* **B** *BOON* **C** *BREAD*

5/2 ▶ In Greek myth, who was the wife of the blacksmith god Hephaestus?

> **A** APHRODITE **B** HERA **C** ATHENA

5/3 ▶ Which of these kings reigned the earliest?

> **A** EDWARD LONGSHANKS **B** JOHN LACKLAND **C** RICHARD THE LIONHEART

5/4 ▶ 'Rock the baby' and 'the sleeper' are classic tricks in which hobby?

> **A** SKATEBOARDING **B** JUGGLING **C** YO-YOING

5/5 ▶ How was Pepsi known when it was invented in 1893?

> **A** ADAM'S ALE **B** BRAD'S DRINK **C** CHARLIE'S COKE

5/6 ▶ An 'echinate' animal is covered with what?

> **A** SPINES **B** SCALES **C** SPOTS

5/7 ▶ In the financial abbreviations 'APR' and 'LIBOR' what does the 'R' mean?

> **A** RATE **B** RATIO **C** RELATIONSHIP

The Sinnerman Quiz 5: Contestant 2

Answer at least 5 questions correctly to progress on to the Final Chase.

5/1 ▶ Why was George Best shown a red card during a match on the first day they were used in English football?

> **A** USING BAD LANGUAGE **B** DELIBERATE HAND BALL **C** FLASHING HIS BOTTOM

5/2 ▶ Which of these songs was a hit for Girls Aloud?

> **A** 'UGLY' **B** 'UNPRETTY' **C** 'SEXY! NO NO NO'

5/3 ▶ The Bulgarian artist Christo is famous for doing what to buildings?

> **A** PHOTOGRAPHING THEM **B** WRAPPING THEM **C** LICKING THEM

5/4 ▶ An ergograph measures and records the work done by what part of the body?

> **A** BRAIN **B** MUSCLES **C** LUNGS

5/5 ▶ The 1954 film *Animal Farm* was partially funded by which organisation?

> **A** BBC **B** RSPCA **C** CIA

5/6 ▶ Which word was used to describe King Ludwig II, who ruled Bavaria from 1864 to 1886?

> **A** MAD **B** BAD **C** DANGEROUS

5/7 ▶ Which winner of *The X Factor* is the daughter of former Soul II Soul singer Melissa Bell?

> **A** ALEXANDRA BURKE **B** LEIGH-ANNE PINNOCK **C** LEONA LEWIS

The Sinnerman Quiz 5: Contestant 3

Answer at least 5 questions correctly to progress on to the Final Chase.

5/1 ▶ In cricket, which of these fielding positions is furthest from the batsman on strike?

> **A** LEG SLIP **B** SILLY POINT **C** THIRD MAN

5/2 ▶ Tea is native to which country?

> **A** JAPAN **B** TURKEY **C** CHINA

5/3 ▶ In what trade could you make English Bond and Monk Bond patterns?

> **A** BRICKLAYING **B** PIPEFITTING **C** SHOEMAKING

5/4 ▶ In which film did Marilyn Monroe's character say 'Real diamonds! They must be worth their weight in gold'?

> **A** *BUS STOP* **B** *SOME LIKE IT HOT* **C** *THE SEVEN YEAR ITCH*

5/5 ▶ As the crow flies, which of these places is closest to Liverpool?

> **A** BLACKPOOL **B** HARTLEPOOL **C** PONTYPOOL

5/6 ▶ What farm is the setting of the children's TV series *Shaun The Sheep*?

> **A** MOSSY BOTTOM **B** SOGGY BOTTOM **C** TOFFY BOTTOM

5/7 ▶ Which monarch initiated the Royal Ascot race meeting?

> **A** QUEEN ANNE **B** QUEEN MARY II **C** QUEEN VICTORIA

The Sinnerman Quiz 5: Contestant 4

Answer at least 5 questions correctly to progress on to the Final Chase.

5/1 ▶ What was the title of Dennis Waterman's autobiography?

> **A** *REMORSE* **B** *REMINDER* **C** *REMEMBRANCE*

5/2 ▶ A flying buttress is a common feature of which architectural style?

> **A** BAROQUE **B** GOTHIC **C** NEOCLASSICAL

5/3 ▶ Who appeared as the singer in a band in the film *Harry Potter and the Goblet of Fire*?

> **A** DAMON ALBARN **B** BRETT ANDERSON **C** JARVIS COCKER

5/4 ▶ What would you be using if you required an STD code?

> **A** CASHPOINT **B** TELEPHONE **C** OINTMENT

5/5 ▶ In 1932, who landed at Culmore, Northern Ireland after her solo flight across the Atlantic?

> **A** AMELIA EARHART **B** AMY JOHNSON **C** BERYL MARKHAM

5/6 ▶ Which medical condition is also called 'tinea'?

> **A** NETTLE RASH **B** CHICKENPOX **C** RINGWORM

5/7 ▶ Which of these characters from the children's TV programme *Rainbow* did NOT usually sit behind a desk?

> **A** GEORGE **B** ZIPPY **C** BUNGLE

The Sinnerman Quiz 5: Final Chase

★ Prize fund in the Final Chase was £35,000

★ Your target is 19 correct

In this programme 3 players reached the final. All members of the team made a valuable contribution to their highly creditable score of 19. Having been stalled by 5 push back opportunities, 3 of which were executed, The Sinnerman was unable to make up for lost time and missed catching the team by just one step when the clock ran out.

5/1 ▶ On what part of the body is a 'bowler' worn?

5/2 ▶ Cricketer Don Bradman played for what country?

5/3 ▶ Noel and Louise are A & E receptionists in what TV drama?

5/4 ▶ What Rembrandt painting has the Dutch title *De Nachtwacht*?

5/5 ▶ What's the maximum age of an octogenarian?

5/6 ▶ What was the first UK Number One for Bucks Fizz?

5/7 ▶ Treacle is produced when what foodstuff is refined?

5/8 ▶ What South African city was previously called Port Natal?

5/9 ▶ What liquid is added to sand and cement to make mortar?

5/10 ▶ In what 2011 film did John Sessions play Edward Heath?

THE SINNERMAN

5/11 ▶ 'O Fortuna' is a movement in what Carl Orff composition?

5/12 ▶ What word comes from the Latin for 'Middle Ages'?

5/13 ▶ Plymouth and London are varieties of what alcoholic drink?

5/14 ▶ Which cartoon duck has a name that means 'foolish'?

5/15 ▶ Leodegrance was the father-in-law of which legendary king?

5/16 ▶ A paediatrician specialises in treating what patients?

5/17 ▶ The coyote is native to what continent?

5/18 ▶ In 2014, which Cuban ballet dancer received a CBE?

5/19 ▶ How many of Henry the Eighth's wives were beheaded?

5/20 ▶ George Baker played which Ruth Rendell policeman on TV?

5/21 ▶ What confectionery company makes Creme Eggs and Mini Eggs?

5/22 ▶ NASA's Landsat program observes what planet?

The Sinnerman Quiz 6: Contestant 1

Answer at least 5 questions correctly to progress on to the Final Chase.

6/1 ▶ Julia Roberts played a single mother who becomes a legal assistant in which film?

> **A** *DUPLICITY* **B** *ERIN BROCKOVICH* **C** *THE PELICAN BRIEF*

6/2 ▶ Which of these EU countries has the largest population?

> **A** AUSTRIA **B** DENMARK **C** BELGIUM

6/3 ▶ In Greek myth, who is the twin brother of Thanatos, god of Death?

> **A** HELIOS **B** HADES **C** HYPNOS

6/4 ▶ What term is used to describe people in academic, artistic, or media circles who give their opinions freely?

> **A** CHATTERING CLASSES **B** GOSSIPING CLASSES **C** PRATTLING CLASSES

6/5 ▶ Between 1979 and 1985, three British runners broke the world record at which Olympic distance?

> **A** 100M **B** 400M **C** 1,500M

6/6 ▶ What element was discovered by chemist Clemens Winkler and named after his country of birth?

> **A** FRANCIUM **B** GERMANIUM **C** POLONIUM

6/7 ▶ 'Wouldn't Change a Thing' was a hit for which Australian?

> **A** NATALIE IMBRUGLIA **B** KYLIE MINOGUE **C** DAME EDNA EVERAGE

The Sinnerman Quiz 6: Contestant 2

Answer at least 5 questions correctly to progress on to the Final Chase.

6/1 ▶ Rebecca Shambaugh's book about women in business is entitled *It's Not a Glass Ceiling, It's a...* what?

> **A** STICKY FLOOR **B** STONE BASEMENT **C** SHAG PILE CARPET

6/2 ▶ Fred Casely is a murder victim in what stage and film musical?

> **A** *CHICAGO* **B** *SWEENEY TODD* **C** *WEST SIDE STORY*

6/3 ▶ What word is used to describe cooking that combines two or more styles of cuisine?

> **A** HYBRID **B** FUSION **C** MONGREL

6/4 ▶ Which of these *Doctor Who* actors has appeared in a *Harry Potter* film?

> **A** DAVID TENNANT **B** MATT SMITH **C** PETER CAPALDI

6/5 ▶ *The Museum at Le Havre* and *The Water-Lily Pond* are paintings in the National Gallery by which Frenchman?

> **A** GAUGUIN **B** MONET **C** RENOIR

6/6 ▶ What is the only British mammal with a prehensile tail?

> **A** HARVEST MOUSE **B** MOUNTAIN HARE **C** SIKA DEER

6/7 ▶ In 2003, Iepe Rubingh founded a sport which mixes boxing with what board game?

> **A** CHESS **B** MONOPOLY **C** LUDO

The Sinnerman Quiz 6: Contestant 3

Answer at least 5 questions correctly to progress on to the Final Chase.

6/1 ▶ Louis-Philippe, the last king of France, was a member of what royal house?

> **A BOURBON B VALOIS C ORLÉANS**

6/2 ▶ In the 1957 film *An Affair to Remember*, the two main characters agree to meet at the top of what?

> **A EMPIRE STATE BUILDING B EIFFEL TOWER C MOUNT EVEREST**

6/3 ▶ Which of these women succeeded her husband as leader of their country?

> **A CRISTINA KIRCHNER B ANGELA MERKEL C JULIA GILLARD**

6/4 ▶ Which psychiatrist coined the term 'collective unconscious'?

> **A R D LAING B SIGMUND FREUD C CARL JUNG**

6/5 ▶ On TV's *Monty Python*, which of these was used by Eric Idle's character with the catchphrase 'nudge-nudge, wink-wink'?

> **A HOW'S YOUR FATHER? B YOU ARE AWFUL C SAY NO MORE**

6/6 ▶ Which of these literary title characters appeared first?

> **A JANE EYRE B ANNA KARENINA C CHARLOTTE GRAY**

6/7 ▶ Which king died after failing to recover from a fall when his horse stumbled over a molehill?

> **A WILLIAM III B GEORGE III C EDWARD III**

The Sinnerman Quiz 6: Contestant 4

Answer at least 5 questions correctly to progress on to the Final Chase.

6/1 ▶ In 2007, cricketer Kevin Pietersen married a member of which pop group?

> **A** HEAR'SAY **B** SUGABABES **C** LIBERTY X

6/2 ▶ Christopher Plummer voiced the villainous explorer Charles Muntz in which Pixar film?

> **A** *BRAVE* **B** *THE INCREDIBLES* **C** *UP*

6/3 ▶ How many terms did the Duke of Wellington serve as Prime Minister?

> **A** ONE **B** TWO **C** THREE

6/4 ▶ Where is Billingsgate fish market located?

> **A** ISLE OF DOGS **B** ISLE OF ELY **C** ISLE OF WIGHT

6/5 ▶ Which of these is NOT a play by Neil Simon?

> **A** *CALIFORNIA SUITE* **B** *PLAZA SUITE* **C** *BATHROOM SUITE*

6/6 ▶ Trismus is the medical term for what condition?

> **A** FROZEN SHOULDER **B** LOCKJAW **C** TONGUE TIE

6/7 ▶ What name is given to a ball of dust and fluff, often found behind or beneath furniture?

> **A** DUST BIRDY **B** DUST PUPPY **C** DUST BUNNY

The Sinnerman Quiz 6: Final Chase

★ Prize fund in the Final Chase was £35,000

★ Your target is 19 correct

> *Three contestants qualified for the final. In the opening round in which they achieved an excellent 21 points, equal contributions were made by Jo, a 47-year-old learning mentor from Liverpool, and Andy, a 30-year-old actor. The team made the most of the push back opportunities, executing 4 out of 5, and preventing The Sinnerman from catching them.*

6/1 ▶ What dome-shaped nest is a home for bees?

6/2 ▶ What doll appears in the title of a Number One by Aqua?

6/3 ▶ How many of Enid Blyton's Famous Five were boys?

6/4 ▶ What multi-event sport was introduced at the 1912 Olympics?

6/5 ▶ William Walton wrote the cantata 'Belshazzar's...' what?

6/6 ▶ Which Bond girl starred in *Desperate Housewives*?

6/7 ▶ What meat is usually included in a cheeseburger?

6/8 ▶ Painter Willem de Kooning was born in what country?

6/9 ▶ The letters 'ScD' stand for 'Doctor of...' what subject?

6/10 ▶ In what film did Charlize Theron play killer Aileen Wuornos?

THE SINNERMAN

6/11 ▶ *The Death of Ivan Ilyich* is a novella by which Russian?

6/12 ▶ What type of boot is the official state footwear of Texas?

6/13 ▶ Guy Fawkes died in what century?

6/14 ▶ A 'sea elephant' is a species of what mammal?

6/15 ▶ What UK band had the 1990s hit 'Last Train To Trancentral'?

6/16 ▶ French navy is a shade of what colour?

6/17 ▶ In 2004, Letizia Ortiz married the prince of what country?

6/18 ▶ Which actress played Tauriel the Elf in *The Hobbit* films?

6/19 ▶ What is the baby offspring of a ram and a ewe called?

6/20 ▶ What beverage is the base of the apéritif Dubonnet?

6/21 ▶ In TV, 'soap' is a shortened version of what two-word phrase?

6/22 ▶ What Scottish city is in the lyrics of ABBA's 'Super Trouper'?

6/23 ▶ *The Decameron* was originally written in what language?

6/24 ▶ What leg muscles contract to straighten a bent knee?

6/25 ▶ Boudicca led a revolt against what overseas invaders?

The Sinnerman Quiz 7: Contestant 1

Answer at least 5 questions correctly to progress on to the Final Chase.

7/1 ▶ Which of these films did NOT win a Best Picture Oscar?

> **A** *THE ENGLISH PATIENT* **B** *THE FRENCH CONNECTION* **C** *THE ITALIAN JOB*

7/2 ▶ Which mythical hero was recognised, thanks to a scar on his leg, by his old nurse Eurycleia on returning from Troy?

> **A** AGAMEMNON **B** ODYSSEUS **C** ODYSSEUS

7/3 ▶ What was the name of the Chinese gymnast who won trampoline gold at the London Olympics?

> **A** DANG DANG **B** DING DING **C** DONG DONG

7/4 ▶ A person with hypermnesia has exceptionally exact what?

> **A** HEARING **B** MEMORY **C** SIGHT

7/5 ▶ What did David Cameron liken to Prime Ministerial terms, saying 'Two are wonderful, but three might just be too many'?

> **A** OATIBIX **B** SHREDDED WHEAT **C** WEETABIX

7/6 ▶ A group of Dutch engineers changed the name of a Cornish village from Nankersey to what?

> **A** DRIPPING **B** FLUSHING **C** PIDDLING

7/7 ▶ Where would you be most likely to wear items designed by Christian Louboutin?

> **A** ON YOUR HEAD **B** ROUND YOUR WAIST **C** ON YOUR FEET

The Sinnerman Quiz 7: Contestant 2

Answer at least 5 questions correctly to progress on to the Final Chase.

7/1 ▶ Chris Martin and Jonny Buckland of Coldplay had cameo roles in what zombie film?

> **A** *LAND OF THE DEAD* **B** *DAWN OF THE DEAD* **C** *SHAUN OF THE DEAD*

7/2 ▶ On a French restaurant menu, what are 'rognons'?

> **A** KIDNEYS **B** SWEETBREADS **C** TROTTERS

7/3 ▶ Which of these characters appeared on UK television first?

> **A** DAISY DUKE **B** HYACINTH BUCKET **C** LILY MUNSTER

7/4 ▶ A £2 coin issued in 2015 was criticised for a 'schoolboy error' because it showed King John holding what?

> **A** SWORD **B** QUILL **C** MOBILE PHONE

7/5 ▶ San Francisco's Golden Gate Bridge is designed in which architectural style?

> **A** ART DECO **B** GOTHIC REVIVAL **C** NEOCLASSICAL

7/6 ▶ The song 'Dedicated Follower of Fashion' is performed in which musical?

> **A** *SUNNY AFTERNOON* **B** *JERSEY BOYS* **C** *THRILLER LIVE*

7/7 ▶ What figure of speech would you be using if you described a massive dent in your car as a 'bit of a prang'?

> **A** MEIOSIS **B** ALLITERATION **C** SPOONERISM

The Sinnerman Quiz 7: Contestant 3

Answer at least 5 questions correctly to progress on to the Final Chase.

7/1 ▶ West Indian batsman Brian Lara scored 501 not out for which English county?

> **A** NOTTINGHAMSHIRE   **B** SURREY   **C** WARWICKSHIRE

7/2 ▶ Which of these drinks does NOT turn milky white when water is added?

> **A** ABSINTHE   **B** OUZO   **C** POTEEN

7/3 ▶ Reality TV star Vogue Williams married which former member of Westlife in 2012?

> **A** NICKY BYRNE   **B** KIAN EGAN   **C** BRIAN MCFADDEN

7/4 ▶ What is the world's heaviest lizard?

> **A** KOMODO DRAGON   **B** GILA MONSTER   **C** STUMP-TAILED SKINK

7/5 ▶ Which of these war films featured the notorious Burma Railway?

> **A** *A BRIDGE TOO FAR*   **B** *THE BRIDGE AT REMAGEN*   **C** *THE BRIDGE ON THE RIVER KWAI*

7/6 ▶ What substance is added to food to stop liquid and solid parts from separating?

> **A** EMULSIFIER   **B** PRESERVATIVE   **C** ANTIOXIDANT

7/7 ▶ Which of these phrases comes from John Donne's work 'Meditation XVII'?

> **A** FOOLS RUSH IN   **B** THE WAY OF ALL FLESH   **C** NO MAN IS AN ISLAND

The Sinnerman Quiz 7: Contestant 4

Answer at least 5 questions correctly to progress on to the Final Chase.

7/1 ▶ Rafael Nadal's winning percentage on which tennis court surface is the best of any player in the Open era?

> **A** CLAY **B** HARD **C** GRASS

7/2 ▶ What name was given to a sailor with a government commission authorising the capture of an enemy's shipping?

> **A** PRIVATEER **B** PIONEER **C** PROFITEER

7/3 ▶ Which of these characters was NOT the subject of a Verdi opera?

> **A** HAMLET **B** MACBETH **C** OTHELLO

7/4 ▶ White, old glory red and old glory blue are the official colours of what country's flag?

> **A** FRANCE **B** RUSSIA **C** USA

7/5 ▶ Of whom did Mary Peters say 'Hasn't she kept it clean?' when receiving the Sports Personality of the Year award in 1972?

> **A** ANN JONES **B** MARY RAND **C** PRINCESS ANNE

7/6 ▶ Which of these groups had a UK hit first?

> **A** SLY & THE FAMILY STONE **B** LIGHTHOUSE FAMILY **C** THE PARTRIDGE FAMILY

7/7 ▶ What is usually used to bind the pigments used for oil-painting?

> **A** LINSEED OIL **B** OLIVE OIL **C** SUNFLOWER OIL

The Sinnerman Quiz 7: Final Chase

★ Prize fund in the Final Chase was £35,000

★ Your target is 19 correct

In this programme 3 players reached the final. In an impressive opening round they notched up a total of 21. All contributed but the top scorer was Mickey, a 36-year-old X-ray operative from Hertfordshire. The Sinnerman was on good form and provided only 3 push back opportunities, but the team executed all of these to narrowly outrun their chaser.

7/1 ▷ In Asia, what type of geographical feature is K2?

7/2 ▷ *Danke schön* is 'thank you' in what language?

7/3 ▷ What Mel Brooks film features Sheriff Bart?

7/4 ▷ The song 'My Man's Gone Now' is from what Gershwin opera?

7/5 ▷ Which Tory MP was born Theresa Brasier in 1956?

7/6 ▷ What type of creature is an erne?

7/7 ▷ What burger chain took its name from a Popeye character?

7/8 ▷ 'Ego' was a 2009 hit for which girl group?

7/9 ▷ In 1967, what country won the Six Day War?

THE SINNERMAN

7/10 ▷ Carrie-Anne Moss played Trinity in what film trilogy?

7/11 ▷ In *The Tempest* who releases Ariel from a witch's spell?

7/12 ▷ The Caelian is one of what capital city's seven hills?

7/13 ▷ What was Nelson's flagship at the Battle of Trafalgar?

7/14 ▷ Boarding and roughing are offences in what Winter Olympic sport?

7/15 ▷ What gas is the main component of firedamp or mine gas?

7/16 ▷ What organs are chiefly affected by bronchitis?

7/17 ▷ Babies 'R' Us is a division of what retailer?

7/18 ▷ Who was the last French king to live at Versailles?

7/19 ▷ Canadian rye is a form of what alcoholic drink?

7/20 ▷ Who starred as Margaret Tate in the rom-com *The Proposal*?

7/21 ▷ The FIFA series of computer games is based on what sport?

7/22 ▷ The novel *The Brothers Karamazov* is set in what country?

7/23 ▷ *Live SOS* was a 2014 album by which Australian band?

THE SINNERMAN QUIZ 7: Final Chase

The Sinnerman Quiz 8: Contestant 1

Answer at least 5 questions correctly to progress on to the Final Chase.

8/1 ▶ Which of these Italian cheeses is classified as hard?

A MOZZARELLA B PARMESAN C RICOTTA

8/2 ▶ The Battle of Culloden was the last battle in what rebellion?

A BOXER REBELLION B JACOBITE REBELLION C RUM REBELLION

8/3 ▶ Who sings the first line on the USA for Africa 1985 hit 'We Are the World'?

A MICHAEL JACKSON B STEVIE WONDER C LIONEL RICHIE

8/4 ▶ What adjective describes animals that are said to have nine lives?

A CANINE B EQUINE C FELINE

8/5 ▶ When the Queen is in residence, how many guards stand at the front of Buckingham Palace?

A FOUR B SIX C EIGHT

8/6 ▶ Of all the countries to have hosted the Summer Olympics, which has the smallest population?

A BELGIUM B NETHERLANDS C FINLAND

8/7 ▶ Coconut oil is extracted from which part of a coconut palm tree?

A KERNEL B SHELL C LEAF

The Sinnerman Quiz 8: Contestant 2

Answer at least 5 questions correctly to progress on to the Final Chase.

8/1 ▶ What nickname was given to the Parliament of 1377 that met the year after the 'Good Parliament'?

> **A** BAD PARLIAMENT **B** GREAT PARLIAMENT **C** SO-SO PARLIAMENT

8/2 ▶ What was the first rap track to win an Academy Award for Best Original Song?

> **A** 'GANGSTA'S PARADISE' **B** 'MEN IN BLACK' **C** 'LOSE YOURSELF'

8/3 ▶ Which empire controlled much of the Andes of South America until it was conquered by the Spanish in 1532?

> **A** AZTEC **B** INCA **C** MAYA

8/4 ▶ In Greek mythology, who was the trusted companion of Odysseus?

> **A** MENTOR **B** TUTOR **C** SUPERVISOR

8/5 ▶ Which of these Jane Austen novels was published posthumously?

> **A** *MANSFIELD PARK* **B** *NORTHANGER ABBEY* **C** *SENSE AND SENSIBILITY*

8/6 ▶ Which artist used a four-poster bed to create the 2002 work *To Meet My Past*?

> **A** TRACEY EMIN **B** MARC QUINN **C** DAMIEN HIRST

8/7 ▶ Who played the title role in the TV series *I, Claudius*?

> **A** BRIAN BLESSED **B** JOHN HURT **C** DEREK JACOBI

The Sinnerman Quiz 8: Contestant 3

Answer at least 5 questions correctly to progress on to the Final Chase.

8/1 ▶ What would you do with a 'talma'?

A EAT IT B SING IT C WEAR IT

8/2 ▶ Which of these is a major road junction in the north of England?

A RUM POINT B SCOTCH CORNER C WHISKY CHASE

8/3 ▶ Which American woman once said 'I wish I had a twin so I could know what I'd look like without plastic surgery'?

A CAROL BURNETT B ELLEN DEGENERES C JOAN RIVERS

8/4 ▶ Dysphemia is another name for what disorder?

A STAMMERING B CHRONIC HICCUPS C LISP

8/5 ▶ In which musical has the title character spent 15 years in a penal colony?

A *SWEENEY TODD* B *BILLY ELLIOT* C *MISS SAIGON*

8/6 ▶ Which of these vegetables is a brassica?

A CARROT B CAULIFLOWER C COURGETTE

8/7 ▶ 2013 was the centenary of which British composer's birth?

A BENJAMIN BRITTEN B EDWARD ELGAR C GUSTAV HOLST

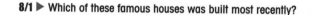

The Sinnerman Quiz 8: Contestant 4

Answer at least 5 questions correctly to progress on to the Final Chase.

8/1 ▶ Which of these famous houses was built most recently?

> **A** SANDRINGHAM HOUSE **B** THE WHITE HOUSE **C** SYDNEY OPERA HOUSE

8/2 ▶ The William Hill Sports Book of the Year for 2012, *The Secret Race,* is a whistle-blowing account of which sport?

> **A** ATHLETICS **B** CYCLING **C** SKIING

8/3 ▶ Which of these is a real medical condition?

> **A** MUD WRESTLER'S RASH **B** EXTREME IRONER'S WRIST **C** WORM CHARMER'S KNEE

8/4 ▶ Saying the line 'And don't call me Shirley', who played Dr Rumack in the spoof film *Airplane!?*

> **A** LESLIE NIELSEN **B** LEE J COBB **C** LEONARD NIMOY

8/5 ▶ The Judaeo-Galilean Highlands form part of which country?

> **A** IRAN **B** ISRAEL **C** INDIA

8/6 ▶ Graminology is the study of what?

> **A** GRASS **B** CONIFERS **C** FERNS

8/7 ▶ How old was Lady Diana Spencer when she married Prince Charles?

> **A** 20 **B** 25 **C** 30

THE SINNERMAN QUIZ 8: Contestant 4

The Sinnerman Quiz 8: Final Chase

★ Prize fund in the Final Chase was £35,000

★ Your target is 19 correct

All 4 contestants in this programme qualified for the final. In an impressive display, the team racked up a total of 24, 12 of the correct answers being provided by Andrew, a 25-year-old online banking advisor from Bangor. With the team taking advantage of all 4 push back opportunities, The Sinnerman was beaten in the Final Chase.

8/1 ▶ Flamenco and acoustic are types of what stringed instrument?

8/2 ▶ Thomas Seymour was brother-in-law to which monarch?

8/3 ▶ The actress Jane Fonda was born in what decade?

8/4 ▶ In *Toy Story 3*, what's the name of the triceratops toy?

8/5 ▶ What Shakespeare play is set in Scotland and England?

8/6 ▶ In 1982, what soft drinks giant introduced its Diet variety?

8/7 ▶ In the proverb, imitation is the sincerest form of what?

8/8 ▶ Who made his own novel *Blackeyes* into a 1980s TV drama?

8/9 ▶ What part of a car can be described as a V6 or V8?

8/10 ▶ Annie MacManus is the real name of which Radio One DJ?

THE SINNERMAN

8/11 ▷ Now called Zimbabwe, what was Rhodesia called before 1965?

8/12 ▷ In 1970, who left The Supremes to go solo?

8/13 ▷ The June bug is a leaf-eating type of what insect?

8/14 ▷ What single letter is the chemical symbol for boron?

8/15 ▷ Which acting Dame played Lilli in the film musical *Nine*?

8/16 ▷ What country of the UK comes last alphabetically?

8/17 ▷ The Yanks is a short name for what famous baseball team?

8/18 ▷ What's the fourth book of the Bible?

8/19 ▷ Morrissey was a founder member of what Manchester band?

8/20 ▷ What number is added to 37 to make 100?

8/21 ▷ Lillet Blanc is an apéritif made with what colour wine?

8/22 ▷ What first name links Hollywood actors Cagney and Coburn?

8/23 ▷ The Out Skerries are part of which British island group?

8/24 ▷ Theresa May retained what senior Cabinet position in 2015?

8/25 ▷ The national flag of Denmark features what two colours?

The Sinnerman Quiz 9: Contestant 1

Answer at least 5 questions correctly to progress on to the Final Chase.

9/1 ▶ Complete the intro: 'If you have a problem, if no one else can help, and if you can find them, maybe you can hire...'

> **A** THE GHOSTBUSTERS **B** THE A-TEAM **C** THE WILD BUNCH

9/2 ▶ In 2003, who ended Catherine Cookson's 17-year reign as the most borrowed author from UK libraries?

> **A** JACQUELINE WILSON **B** ROALD DAHL **C** J K ROWLING

9/3 ▶ Which US player defeated Steffi Graf to win the 1992 Olympic Women's Singles title?

> **A** JENNIFER CAPRIATI **B** KATHY JORDAN **C** LINDSAY DAVENPORT

9/4 ▶ What are a policeman in a Charles Penrose song and a cavalier in the title of a Frans Hals painting both doing?

> **A** WHISTLING **B** SINGING **C** LAUGHING

9/5 ▶ Which actress played Bruce Banner's love interest in the film *The Incredible Hulk*?

> **A** JENNIFER ANISTON **B** NATALIE PORTMAN **C** LIV TYLER

9/6 ▶ Peniaphobia is the fear of what?

> **A** POVERTY **B** PRISONS **C** PENS

9/7 ▶ Which of these is NOT a rank in the Royal Navy?

> **A** COMMANDER **B** COMMODORE **C** COMMISSIONER

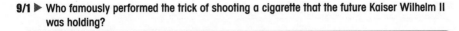

THE SINNERMAN

The Sinnerman Quiz 9: Contestant 2

Answer at least 5 questions correctly to progress on to the Final Chase.

9/1 ▶ Who famously performed the trick of shooting a cigarette that the future Kaiser Wilhelm II was holding?

A ANNIE OAKLEY **B** BELLE STARR **C** CALAMITY JANE

9/2 ▶ In which song does the singer want three staircases: one going up, one coming down and one 'just for show'?

A 'WOULDN'T IT BE LOVERLY?' **B** 'BIG SPENDER' **C** 'IF I WERE A RICH MAN'

9/3 ▶ In which US state is Lei Day traditionally celebrated on 1 May?

A HAWAII **B** GEORGIA **C** FLORIDA

9/4 ▶ In Greek legend, the Muse Terpsichore was the patron of what?

A DANCING **B** HISTORY **C** COMEDY

9/5 ▶ Coruscant and Naboo are planets in which sci-fi franchise?

A *DOCTOR WHO* **B** *BATTLESTAR GALACTICA* **C** *STAR WARS*

9/6 ▶ In championship darts, which score can a player NOT finish on?

A BULL **B** DOUBLE **C** TREBLE

9/7 ▶ Which girls' name has featured in Top 10 singles by both The Vamps and Suggs?

A VALERIE **B** DELILAH **C** CECILIA

The Sinnerman Quiz 9: Contestant 3

Answer at least 5 questions correctly to progress on to the Final Chase.

9/1 ▶ Which of these shipping forecast areas lies immediately off the coast of Ireland?

> **A** FASTNET **B** FITZROY **C** FORTIES

9/2 ▶ 'The Big One' is a phrase used to describe a huge future natural disaster of what type that will hit California?

> **A** EARTHQUAKE **B** VOLCANIC ERUPTION **C** FLOOD

9/3 ▶ In what decade was Kenneth Tynan's controversial theatre review *Oh! Calcutta!* first performed in London?

> **A** 1950S **B** 1960S **C** 1970S

9/4 ▶ Who said 'I never worry about diets. The only carrots that interest me are the number you get in a diamond'?

> **A** MARILYN MONROE **B** MAE WEST **C** ZSA ZSA GABOR

9/5 ▶ The name of which of these chemical elements begins with the same letter as its symbol?

> **A** COPPER **B** GOLD **C** SILVER

9/6 ▶ What was Take That's first UK Number One single?

> **A** 'COULD IT BE MAGIC' **B** 'PRAY' **C** 'RELIGHT MY FIRE'

9/7 ▶ The Olmec civilisation has a name meaning what?

> **A** RUBBER PEOPLE **B** WOODEN PEOPLE **C** SHINY HAPPY PEOPLE

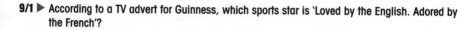

The Sinnerman Quiz 9: Contestant 4

Answer at least 5 questions correctly to progress on to the Final Chase.

9/1 ▶ According to a TV advert for Guinness, which sports star is 'Loved by the English. Adored by the French'?

> **A** DAVID BECKHAM **B** JONNY WILKINSON **C** ANDY MURRAY

9/2 ▶ A reading of one on the pH scale indicates that a liquid is what?

> **A** ACIDIC **B** ALKALINE **C** NEUTRAL

9/3 ▶ Who starred in the 2015 time-travelling film *Predestination*?

> **A** ETHAN HAWKE **B** JAKE GYLLENHAAL **C** NICK FROST

9/4 ▶ Which of these earthenware dishes is traditionally used in Spanish cooking?

> **A** TAGINE **B** CAZUELA **C** TANDOOR

9/5 ▶ The semi-autobiographical TV comedy *Moone Boy* stars which comedy actor as imaginary friend Sean?

> **A** ED BYRNE **B** DYLAN MORAN **C** CHRIS O'DOWD

9/6 ▶ The Cenotaph in Whitehall was built at the request of which Prime Minister?

> **A** DAVID LLOYD GEORGE **B** RAMSAY MACDONALD **C** STANLEY BALDWIN

9/7 ▶ Which of these fictional doctors makes a deal with the Devil in return for knowledge and power?

> **A** DR FAUSTUS **B** DR FOSTER **C** DR FINLAY

The Sinnerman Quiz 9: Final Chase

★ Prize fund in the Final Chase was £35,000

★ Your target is 19 correct

Four players reached the final in this programme. With Benjamin, a 23-year-old philosophy graduate from London leading the scoring, the team achieved an excellent 21. The Sinnerman conceded 6 push back opportunities, of which the team executed 4, stalling his pursuit and giving them victory in the Final Chase.

9/1 ▶ An Irish Terrier is a breed of what animal?

9/2 ▶ What branch of Germany's armed forces is the Luftwaffe?

9/3 ▶ A so-called 'mystery' house features in what BBC property show?

9/4 ▶ What famous statue was donated to the Louvre in 1821?

9/5 ▶ Which TV cook wrote the 1980s book *One is Fun*?

9/6 ▶ Lupita Nyong'o won an Oscar for her role in what film?

9/7 ▶ What was Princess Diana's maiden name?

9/8 ▶ What San Antonio landmark now has World Heritage Site status?

9/9 ▶ A *karateka* practises what Japanese martial art?

THE SINNERMAN

9/10 ▶ What James Bond theme was sung by Morten Harket?

9/11 ▶ The Chakri dynasty rules what Asian country?

9/12 ▶ Gandalf first appeared in what J R R Tolkien novel?

9/13 ▶ What is the longest relay race in Olympic athletics?

9/14 ▶ The term '*memento mori*' comes from what ancient language?

9/15 ▶ What Asian river's name means 'The son of Brahma'?

9/16 ▶ What's half of 250?

9/17 ▶ Who played the title character in the film *Zoolander*?

9/18 ▶ The world of Earthsea was created by which fantasy author?

9/19 ▶ Which exiled French emperor lived his last days at Longwood?

9/20 ▶ What Japanese car company makes the Auris model?

9/21 ▶ What is the first book of the Bible?

9/22 ▶ What major park in Manhattan first opened in 1857?

9/23 ▶ Which Czech player won the Wimbledon Men's Singles in 1973?

9/24 ▶ The patellar tendon is just below what joint?

The Sinnerman Quiz 10: Contestant 1

Answer at least 5 questions correctly to progress on to the Final Chase.

10/1 ▶ How many times did Fred Perry win the Wimbledon Singles title?

> **A** ONE **B** TWO **C** THREE

10/2 ▶ Which poet wrote the verse for the 1936 documentary film *Night Mail,* about the London to Glasgow postal train?

> **A** W H AUDEN **B** JOHN BETJEMAN **C** PHILIP LARKIN

10/3 ▶ Which disgraced MP was Chief Secretary to the Treasury in John Major's Cabinet?

> **A** JONATHAN AITKEN **B** NEIL HAMILTON **C** JEFFREY ARCHER

10/4 ▶ Which of these countries is NOT in Africa?

> **A** GHANA **B** GUINEA **C** GUYANA

10/5 ▶ Which of these British athletes won Olympic gold in Los Angeles and Moscow?

> **A** DALEY THOMPSON **B** ALLAN WELLS **C** STEVE OVETT

10/6 ▶ The Oscar-winning director of the Russell Crowe film *A Beautiful Mind* was a star of which US sitcom?

> **A** *HAPPY DAYS* **B** *M*A*S*H** **C** *CHEERS*

10/7 ▶ In which sport can you make screw shots, draw shots and safety shots?

> **A** FOOTBALL **B** BADMINTON **C** SNOOKER

The Sinnerman Quiz 10: Contestant 2

Answer at least 5 questions correctly to progress on to the Final Chase.

10/1 ▶ Which shipwreck lies off the Old Head of Kinsale in over 300 feet of water?

> **A** *LUSITANIA* **B** *BISMARCK* **C** *TITANIC*

10/2 ▶ Which of these was a major British defeat in the American War of Independence?

> **A** BATTLE OF HARVARD **B** BATTLE OF YALE **C** BATTLE OF PRINCETON

10/3 ▶ In a 1940s film, which actress says 'Play it, Sam. Play "As Time Goes By"'?

> **A** INGRID BERGMAN **B** JAYNE MANSFIELD **C** LANA TURNER

10/4 ▶ In the novel *Nineteen Eighty-Four*, who does Winston Smith work for?

> **A** MINISTRY OF JUSTICE **B** MINISTRY OF PEOPLE **C** MINISTRY OF TRUTH

10/5 ▶ Which of these artists is depicted in portraits with a broken nose?

> **A** LEONARDO DA VINCI **B** TITIAN **C** MICHELANGELO

10/6 ▶ Which ancient city is the setting for the musical *A Funny Thing Happened On The Way To The Forum*?

> **A** ROME **B** CARTHAGE **C** TROY

10/7 ▶ Who said 'In my time... we said we had the best two teams on Merseyside – Liverpool and Liverpool reserves'?

> **A** BILL SHANKLY **B** GRAEME SOUNESS **C** BOB PAISLEY

The Sinnerman Quiz 10: Contestant 3

Answer at least 5 questions correctly to progress on to the Final Chase.

10/1 ▶ *Stone Mattress* is a 2014 short story collection by which Canadian author?

A ALICE MUNRO B YANN MARTEL C MARGARET ATWOOD

10/2 ▶ The TV series *Prisoner: Cell Block H* was set in what facility?

A WENTWORTH DETENTION CENTRE B STONE PARK C SLADE PRISON

10/3 ▶ Which cricketing knight played football for Antigua in the qualifiers for the 1974 FIFA World Cup?

A GARY SOBERS B VIV RICHARDS C WES HALL

10/4 ▶ Which King excluded his wife Caroline from his coronation?

A EDWARD IV B GEORGE IV C HENRY IV

10/5 ▶ Which cartoon bird first appeared in newspapers in April 1967?

A DAFFY DUCK B FOGHORN LEGHORN C WOODSTOCK

10/6 ▶ Which of these politicians is NOT known by a first name based on his initials?

A RAB BUTLER B NYE BEVAN C JEB BUSH

10/7 ▶ Which song from the *Toy Story* films won the Oscar for Best Original Song?

A 'YOU'VE GOT A FRIEND IN ME' B 'WHEN SHE LOVED ME' C 'WE BELONG TOGETHER'

The Sinnerman Quiz 10: Contestant 4

Answer at least 5 questions correctly to progress on to the Final Chase.

10/1 ▶ 'Natality' is another name for what rate?

> **A** PULSE RATE **B** INFLATION RATE **C** BIRTH RATE

10/2 ▶ Associated with a legend about rain, St Swithin was the Bishop of what city?

> **A** DURHAM **B** LONDON **C** WINCHESTER

10/3 ▶ What legendary creature is mentioned in the first line of the hit song 'Get Lucky' by Daft Punk and Pharrell Williams?

> **A** PHOENIX **B** UNICORN **C** YETI

10/4 ▶ Footballer Matt Le Tissier was born where?

> **A** CHANNEL ISLANDS **B** ISLES OF SCILLY **C** SHETLAND ISLANDS

10/5 ▶ In Greek myth, the Graeae were sisters who had how many teeth between them?

> **A** 1 **B** 15 **C** 500

10/6 ▶ Which work by Shakespeare is a play within a play, performed for a drunken tinker called Christopher Sly?

> **A** *MEASURE FOR MEASURE* **B** *LOVE'S LABOUR'S LOST* **C** *THE TAMING OF THE SHREW*

10/7 ▶ Which fictional TV chat show host ran Pear Tree Productions?

> **A** KEITH LEMON **B** ALAN PARTRIDGE **C** MRS MERTON

The Sinnerman Quiz 10: Final Chase

★ Prize fund in the Final Chase was £35,000

★ Your target is 19 correct

In this programme 3 contestants reached the final. The top scorer, Liz, a 49-year-old science technician from Buckinghamshire, secured an incredible 14 out of the 18 correct answers achieved by the team. Their total of 21 proved too difficult for The Sinnerman to overtake, having been reined in by 2 successfully executed push backs.

10/1 ▷ What colour gloves are worn by the Nintendo character Mario?

10/2 ▷ What precedes Antonio and Diego in the names of two US cities?

10/3 ▷ In the medical term 'path lab', what is 'path' short for?

10/4 ▷ The composer Antonio Salieri was born in what century?

10/5 ▷ The Sailor's Arms is a pub in what Dylan Thomas play?

10/6 ▷ Which synthesiser-based pop star was born Gary Webb?

10/7 ▷ Who was elected leader of the Labour Party in 2015?

10/8 ▷ Sören Sörensen invented what two-letter chemical scale in 1909?

10/9 ▷ The female Spanish title '*infanta*' means what in English?

THE SINNERMAN

10/10 ▷ Which American travel author edited the book *Icons of England*?

10/11 ▷ Rosamund Pike was Oscar nominated for her role in what 2014 film?

10/12 ▷ What character did Eartha Kitt play in the TV show *Batman*?

10/13 ▷ What London ground is the Surrey Lions cricket team's home?

10/14 ▷ Sonny Corleone is a character in what Mario Puzo novel?

10/15 ▷ Which famous painter was born in 1727 in Sudbury, Suffolk?

10/16 ▷ Mandy is a short form of what girl's name?

10/17 ▷ Which sisters have won more than 100 tennis Singles titles?

10/18 ▷ Joss Stone played Anne of Cleves in what TV show?

10/19 ▷ The St George's Channel links the Irish Sea to what ocean?

10/20 ▷ What's thought to be the most venomous snake in the 'mamba' family?

10/21 ▷ The film *Hook* was based on what famous story?

10/22 ▷ Astolat is an English town in the legends of which king?

10/23 ▷ *Cyber* is a 2015 spin-off from what US TV crime show?

The
VIXEN

The Vixen

Flame-haired Jenny Ryan, known on the show as The Vixen, has also been labelled the Bolton Brainiac by Bradley Walsh. And she certainly brings impressive intellectual resources to *The Chase*. On screen the youngest Chaser appears calm and unruffled, her demeanour concealing a steely determination to win. The Vixen confidently powers her way through questions from chart-topping music to classical mythology, and is always ready to expand on her answers to display her encyclopaedic knowledge.

Naturally competitive, she relishes a challenging target and has been responsible for the highest offers accepted by a contestant (£100,000). Like her namesake, The Vixen is a ruthless hunter, and she has been responsible for *The Chase*'s fastest catch in the Final Chase, having caught her opponent in 1 minute 36 seconds.

The high standards she sets herself are apparent in her visible disappointment with her performance when she loses. While readily conceding the quality of the opposition, she will blame herself for failing to overcome the challenge.

The Vixen Quiz 1: Contestant 1

Answer at least 5 questions correctly to progress on to the Final Chase.

1/1 ▶ What record label, named after a London nightclub, has sold over 50 million albums since its launch in the 1990s?

> **A** NOW! **B** MINISTRY OF SOUND **C** POP PARTY

1/2 ▶ How long is the Khyber Pass?

> **A** 3 MILES **B** 33 MILES **C** 330 MILES

1/3 ▶ The fruit of fig trees are pollinated by what insects?

> **A** ANTS **B** BUTTERFLIES **C** WASPS

1/4 ▶ What was the name of the captain of HMS *Victory* at the Battle of Trafalgar?

> **A** ANTHONY TROLLOPE **B** ROBERT LOUIS STEVENSON **C** THOMAS HARDY

1/5 ▶ Which Wonder of the Ancient World was located in the Dodecanese islands?

> **A** COLOSSUS OF RHODES **B** TEMPLE OF ARTEMIS **C** STATUE OF ZEUS

1/6 ▶ Which of these singers did NOT appear on the official film soundtrack of *Grease*?

> **A** FRANKIE AVALON **B** FRANKIE LAINE **C** FRANKIE VALLI

1/7 ▶ Which TV drama features the pubs The Dog & Duck and The Grantham Arms?

> **A** *MR SELFRIDGE* **B** *LEWIS* **C** *DOWNTON ABBEY*

The Vixen Quiz 1: Contestant 2

Answer at least 5 questions correctly to progress on to the Final Chase.

1/1 ▶ How many even prime numbers are there?

> **A** ONE **B** TWO **C** THREE

1/2 ▶ The first woman to win a Nobel Prize did so in which category?

> **A** PEACE **B** MEDICINE **C** PHYSICS

1/3 ▶ In legend, Mizaru, Kikazaru and Iwazaru are the names of the 'Three wise...' what?

> **A** MEN **B** MONKEYS **C** AMIGOS

1/4 ▶ Orson Welles claimed which of the deadly sins was 'not a secret vice'?

> **A** ENVY **B** GLUTTONY **C** PRIDE

1/5 ▶ The playing time in a full match of which of these sports lasts the longest?

> **A** AMERICAN FOOTBALL **B** HOCKEY **C** RUGBY UNION

1/6 ▶ The M5 motorway terminates east of what National Park?

> **A** DARTMOOR **B** PEAK DISTRICT **C** YORKSHIRE DALES

1/7 ▶ In which movie franchise do characters give a three-fingered salute?

> **A** *THE TWILIGHT SAGA* **B** *HARRY POTTER* **C** *THE HUNGER GAMES*

The Vixen Quiz 1: Contestant 3

Answer at least 5 questions correctly to progress on to the Final Chase.

1/1 ▶ What was the first man-made object to break the sound barrier?

> **A** AEROPLANE **B** BULLET **C** WHIP

1/2 ▶ Which Old Testament leader's name follows 'Holy' in an exclamation of surprise?

> **A** ABRAHAM **B** GIDEON **C** MOSES

1/3 ▶ Which of these British athletes won Olympic gold before the others?

> **A** DENISE LEWIS **B** KELLY HOLMES **C** SALLY GUNNELL

1/4 ▶ Which of these Nordic alphabets has the most letters?

> **A** ICELANDIC **B** SWEDISH **C** DANISH

1/5 ▶ How many sides do a triangle, square and pentagon have in total?

> **A** 10 **B** 12 **C** 14

1/6 ▶ In 2015, the probe *Beagle 2* was found on what planet, 11 years after losing contact?

> **A** MARS **B** VENUS **C** JUPITER

1/7 ▶ Used in the making of perfume, the strong-smelling substance 'castoreum' comes from what animal?

> **A** BEAVER **B** OTTER **C** BADGER

The Vixen Quiz 1: Contestant 4

Answer at least 5 questions correctly to progress on to the Final Chase.

1/1 ▶ Which of these sportsmen is a pugilist?

> **A** CARL FROCH **B** CARL FOGARTY **C** CARL LEWIS

1/2 ▶ In 2014, who became the first British female to have five UK Number One singles?

> **A** ADELE **B** CHERYL **C** JESSIE J

1/3 ▶ Which of these Balkan countries does NOT have a coastline on the Adriatic?

> **A** CROATIA **B** MONTENEGRO **C** SERBIA

1/4 ▶ What name is given to elements, such as iodine and cobalt, that the body only needs in minute amounts?

> **A** TOKEN ELEMENT **B** TRACE ELEMENT **C** TRAIL ELEMENT

1/5 ▶ In 2014, Harry Reid became the fifth actor to play which EastEnders character?

> **A** BEN MITCHELL **B** LIAM BUTCHER **C** PETER BEALE

1/6 ▶ Which US President and First Lady have both won Grammy awards?

> **A** THE CLINTONS **B** THE FORDS **C** THE REAGANS

1/7 ▶ What's another way to describe an 'effervescent' drink?

> **A** ALCOHOLIC **B** HOT **C** FIZZY

The Vixen Quiz 1: Final Chase

⭐ Prize fund in the Final Chase was £12,000

⭐ Your target is 17 correct

In this programme 3 contestants were in the team for the final. All three contributed to a creditable score of 17, but the top scorer was Ayo, a 51-year-old accountant from London. In the Final Chase there were 6 push back opportunities and the team managed to execute 3 of these. The Vixen, however, put on a real spurt in the closing half minute and was only beaten by a single step.

1/1 ▶ Maundy Thursday can be in March or what other month?

1/2 ▶ The Darjeeling Himalayan Railway is in what country?

1/3 ▶ Alexis Sanchez left Barcelona for what London football club?

1/4 ▶ Which US President was the only one to be a five-star general?

1/5 ▶ What compass direction is at 180 degrees from south?

1/6 ▶ 'Axel F' was the theme tune to what Eddie Murphy film?

1/7 ▶ What sport is most associated with the Rod Laver Arena?

THE VIXEN

1/8 ▷ Bolivia fought the Gran Chaco war against what country?

1/9 ▷ Mavis Wilton was a character on what TV soap?

1/10 ▷ The choral hymn 'Glory to Egypt' is from what Verdi opera?

1/11 ▷ Privé is the haute couture line of what Italian fashion house?

1/12 ▷ The art or science of designing buildings is called what?

1/13 ▷ 'Work' was a 2009 hit for which girl band?

1/14 ▷ Willy Brandt was the Mayor of which city?

1/15 ▷ Sybil Vane is in love with which Oscar Wilde title character?

1/16 ▷ The egg in a Scotch egg is cooked by what method?

1/17 ▷ The name of what flatfish is also a word meaning 'alone'?

1/18 ▷ Which mezzo-soprano released the 2014 album *Home Sweet Home*?

1/19 ▷ How many chairs did Goldilocks sit on in the fairy tale?

The Vixen Quiz 2: Contestant 1

Answer at least 5 questions correctly to progress on to the Final Chase.

2/1 ▶ The karahi is a cooking utensil most commonly used in which cuisine?

> **A** IRISH **B** INDIAN **C** THAI

2/2 ▶ Which of these recording artists has won an Academy Award?

> **A** COOLIO **B** DIDO **C** EMINEM

2/3 ▶ What is the most reactive chemical element?

> **A** FLUORINE **B** BORON **C** VANADIUM

2/4 ▶ Which actress returned to *EastEnders* in its 30th anniversary episode?

> **A** ANITA DOBSON **B** PAM ST CLEMENT **C** GILLIAN TAYLFORTH

2/5 ▶ In 1950, what circuit hosted the inaugural Grand Prix of the Formula One World Drivers' Championship?

> **A** SILVERSTONE **B** BRANDS HATCH **C** GOODWOOD

2/6 ▶ In what book series does the President announce a so-called 'Quarter Quell'?

> **A** *A SONG OF ICE AND FIRE* **B** *THE HUNGER GAMES* **C** *TWILIGHT*

2/7 ▶ Which of these is a symbol of the Mormon faith?

> **A** ANTHILL **B** BEEHIVE **C** SPIDER'S WEB

The Vixen Quiz 2: Contestant 2

Answer at least 5 questions correctly to progress on to the Final Chase.

2/1 ▶ In *A Grand Day Out*, Wallace and Gromit travel to the Moon because they are desperate for 'a nice bit' of which cheese?

> **A** EMMENTAL **B** ROQUEFORT **C** GORGONZOLA

2/2 ▶ Great Britain fought in which of these wars?

> **A** SEVEN YEARS' WAR **B** THIRTY YEARS' WAR **C** HUNDRED YEARS' WAR

2/3 ▶ The use of what item was banned by the National Gallery in 2015?

> **A** MOBILE PHONES **B** SKETCHBOOKS **C** SELFIE STICKS

2/4 ▶ Not published in full in the UK until 1960, in what decade was *Lady Chatterley's Lover* written?

> **A** 1920S **B** 1930S **C** 1940S

2/5 ▶ Who said 'Not only does God definitely play dice, but… confuses us by throwing them where they can't be seen'?

> **A** MARIE CURIE **B** ALBERT EINSTEIN **C** STEPHEN HAWKING

2/6 ▶ What species of animal was Washoe, who used over 150 signs to communicate with humans?

> **A** CHIMPANZEE **B** DOG **C** HAMSTER

2/7 ▶ 'FourFiveSeconds' was a 2015 hit for Kanye West, Paul McCartney and which female singer?

> **A** RIHANNA **B** BEYONCÉ **C** ALICIA KEYS

The Vixen Quiz 2: Contestant 3

Answer at least 5 questions correctly to progress on to the Final Chase.

2/1 ▶ Which of these Commonwealth capitals is yet to host the Commonwealth Games?

> **A** CARDIFF **B** KUALA LUMPUR **C** WELLINGTON

2/2 ▶ The Union flag introduced by King James I combined the cross of St. George with the cross of which saint?

> **A** ST ANDREW **B** ST DAVID **C** ST PATRICK

2/3 ▶ The name of what pasta means 'little bells'?

> **A** CAMPANELLE **B** CAVATELLI **C** CORZETTI

2/4 ▶ Hugo A-Go-Go was the arch enemy of which cartoon hero?

> **A** ROGER RAMJET **B** SECRET SQUIRREL **C** BATFINK

2/5 ▶ As of 2015, what was the approximate height difference between the world's tallest and shortest living men?

> **A** 96CM **B** 196CM **C** 296CM

2/6 ▶ Which of these has been the name of several Popes?

> **A** INNOCENT **B** HONEST **C** PURE

2/7 ▶ Until his death, for 14 years Ivan V was joint Tsar of Russia with which other ruler?

> **A** IVAN THE TERRIBLE **B** BORIS GODUNOV **C** PETER THE GREAT

The Vixen Quiz 2: Contestant 4

Answer at least 5 questions correctly to progress on to the Final Chase.

2/1 ▶ A testator has written or created what legal document?

> **A** WILL **B** LEASE **C** PRENUPTIAL AGREEMENT

2/2 ▶ Which of these is the name of a national currency?

> **A** AFGHANI **B** TAJIKI **C** UZBEKI

2/3 ▶ 'Alevin' is a name given to the newly hatched young of which fish?

> **A** SALMON **B** TUNA **C** CARP

2/4 ▶ Which Shakespeare play opens 'Two households, both alike in dignity'?

> **A** *ROMEO AND JULIET* **B** *ANTONY AND CLEOPATRA* **C** *TROILUS AND CRESSIDA*

2/5 ▶ Which of these astronomers was NOT a heliocentrist?

> **A** PTOLEMY **B** COPERNICUS **C** GALILEO

2/6 ▶ Which actor plays the private military contractor Jonathan Irons in the 2014 game 'Call of Duty: Advanced Warfare'?

> **A** BEN KINGSLEY **B** MATTHEW MCCONAUGHEY **C** KEVIN SPACEY

2/7 ▶ Traditionally, how many of Santa's reindeer have names beginning with 'D'?

> **A** ONE **B** TWO **C** THREE

The Vixen Quiz 2: Final Chase

★ Prize fund in the Final Chase was £16,000

★ Your target is 18 correct

Four contestants reached the final in this programme. They all contributed to their score of 18 – a real team effort. In the Final Chase The Vixen stumbled on 7 questions and the team took advantage of these chances to execute 4 push backs, enough to outrun the chaser by 4 steps.

2/1 ▷ Rubens painted a religious picture of *Cain Slaying...* who?

2/2 ▷ What surname links teen idol David and outlaw Butch?

2/3 ▷ In which building is Charles Dickens buried?

2/4 ▷ Who played Velma Von Tussle in the 2007 film *Hairspray*?

2/5 ▷ What animal was Queen Victoria's pet Dash?

2/6 ▷ What European language is an official language of Chad?

2/7 ▷ What spirit's the main ingredient in a Kremlin Colonel cocktail?

2/8 ▷ The Guru Granth Sahib is the holy scripture of what religion?

THE VIXEN

2/9 ▶ Torremolinos is a resort on what Spanish Costa?

2/10 ▶ The abdominal thrust is another name for what manoeuvre?

2/11 ▶ Cesar Romero played which villain in the TV series *Batman*?

2/12 ▶ What is the youngest of the three UK armed forces?

2/13 ▶ Which *Ben-Hur* star wrote the autobiography *In the Arena*?

2/14 ▶ Mauna Kea is the highest peak in what American state?

2/15 ▶ Geoffrey Hughes played Onslow in what sitcom?

2/16 ▶ Which of the four Gospel writers' names starts with a 'J'?

2/17 ▶ Highgrove House is the home of what royal duchess?

2/18 ▶ The name of what Titan of Greek myth means 'forethought'?

2/19 ▶ Gatwick Airport has how many main runways?

2/20 ▶ Totland Bay is a feature of what English island?

2/21 ▶ What major Chinese political party was founded in 1921?

The Vixen Quiz 3: Contestant 1

Answer at least 5 questions correctly to progress on to the Final Chase.

3/1 ▶ What name is given to a thin coating of gold applied to the surface of another metal?

> **A** FOOL'S GOLD **B** WHITE GOLD **C** ROLLED GOLD

3/2 ▶ What gives Thai green and red curries their colour?

> **A** CHILLIES **B** LENTILS **C** TOMATOES

3/3 ▶ Which of these actresses has a twin brother named Hunter?

> **A** NATALIE PORTMAN **B** SCARLETT JOHANSSON **C** ANNE HATHAWAY

3/4 ▶ The two-way traffic system on one carriageway of a main road, to allow for road works, is called what?

> **A** CONTRABAND **B** CONTRAFLOW **C** CONTRADICTION

3/5 ▶ Which of these is named after its inventor?

> **A** ASPHALT **B** VELCRO **C** JACUZZI

3/6 ▶ Which king was on the English throne in the year 1200?

> **A** JOHN **B** HENRY II **C** STEPHEN

3/7 ▶ Usually attached at each end to a natural tooth, what device is used to replace one or several missing teeth?

> **A** BRIDGE **B** DAM **C** RAIL

The Vixen Quiz 3: Contestant 2

Answer at least 5 questions correctly to progress on to the Final Chase.

3/1 ▶ Which of these American states does NOT have a coastline?

> **A** CONNECTICUT **B** DELAWARE **C** VERMONT

3/2 ▶ What sort of creature is a 'dung chafer'?

> **A** INSECT **B** BIRD **C** FISH

3/3 ▶ Which of these seasons appears in the title of a Shakespeare play?

> **A** SPRING **B** AUTUMN **C** WINTER

3/4 ▶ As featured in the film *Glengarry Glen Ross*, the name of the sales strategy ABC stands for 'Always Be...' what?

> **A** CHEAP **B** CLEVER **C** CLOSING

3/5 ▶ What name is shared by the bells that ring the hours at Christ Church, Oxford and St Paul's Cathedral, London?

> **A** GREAT TOM **B** GREAT DICK **C** GREAT HARRY

3/6 ▶ A Welsh dresser was a traditional piece of furniture for what room in the home?

> **A** BATHROOM **B** BEDROOM **C** KITCHEN

3/7 ▶ In the TV show, who was the youngest member of the Waltons?

> **A** ELIZABETH **B** JIM-BOB **C** MARY ELLEN

The Vixen Quiz 3: Contestant 3

Answer at least 5 questions correctly to progress on to the Final Chase.

3/1 ▶ In which of these sports did Britain NOT win a gold medal at London 2012?

> **A** CANOEING **B** JUDO **C** SHOOTING

3/2 ▶ Which Conservative Prime Minister was born the year before the Queen?

> **A** ANTHONY EDEN **B** EDWARD HEATH **C** MARGARET THATCHER

3/3 ▶ What novel ends with the line 'And the ashes blew towards us with the salt wind from the sea'?

> **A** *JANE EYRE* **B** *WUTHERING HEIGHTS* **C** *REBECCA*

3/4 ▶ Denzel Washington won an Oscar for his role in which American Civil War film?

> **A** *GLORY* **B** *COLD MOUNTAIN* **C** *GETTYSBURG*

3/5 ▶ Velvet-collared jackets, drain-pipe trousers and sideburns were worn by members of what youth subculture?

> **A** MODS **B** TEDDY BOYS **C** HIPPIES

3/6 ▶ In 2015, who did *Forbes* magazine name as the world's richest person for the 16th time?

> **A** BILL GATES **B** SULTAN OF BRUNEI **C** CARLOS SLIM

3/7 ▶ Which group had a US Number One hit with a James Bond film song?

> **A** A-HA **B** DURAN DURAN **C** WINGS

The Vixen Quiz 3: Contestant 4

Answer at least 5 questions correctly to progress on to the Final Chase.

3/1 ▶ Which of these is NOT a correct anagram of 'Chaser'?

> **A** REACHES **B** SEARCH **C** ARCHES

3/2 ▶ Which golfer won the 1979 Open despite sending one tee shot into a car park?

> **A** SEVE BALLESTEROS **B** JACK NICKLAUS **C** TOM WATSON

3/3 ▶ In Greek mythology, Phoebe was one of which group?

> **A** THE FATES **B** THE MUSES **C** THE TITANS

3/4 ▶ Who sang 'Furry Happy Monsters' on *Sesame Street* to the tune of one of their hits?

> **A** TALKING HEADS **B** R.E.M. **C** THE SMITHS

3/5 ▶ Leonardo da Vinci's *Last Supper* was painted onto what surface?

> **A** CANVAS **B** PLASTER **C** WOOD PANEL

3/6 ▶ Which of these acids is made up of only two elements?

> **A** SULPHURIC **B** NITRIC **C** HYDROCHLORIC

3/7 ▶ 'Look into my eyes' is a catchphrase of which *Little Britain* character?

> **A** KENNY CRAIG **B** BUBBLES DEVERE **C** MARJORIE DAWES

The Vixen Quiz 3: Final Chase

★ Prize fund in the Final Chase was £11,000

★ Your target is 17 correct

Only 2 contestants made the final in this programme. Mark, a 54-year-old practice manager born in Slough, took the top scorer honours in the opening round, providing 11 of the pair's 15 correct answers. The Vixen slipped up on 7 questions, providing the opportunity for the pair to slow her progress. They executed 4 push backs and outran her by 3 steps.

3/1 ▶ Which of the Minogue sisters had a UK hit single first?

3/2 ▶ What fashion magazine's name means 'she' in French?

3/3 ▶ In 1999, Hungary and Poland joined what military alliance?

3/4 ▶ Ian Wright joined Arsenal from what London football club?

3/5 ▶ How many ulna bones does the human body have?

3/6 ▶ The London Gateway services are on what motorway?

3/7 ▶ What German sportswear brand makes the 'Originals' range?

3/8 ▶ Templeton the rat appears in what E B White novel?

3/9 ▶ In the phrase 'to dis someone' what word is 'dis' short for?

THE VIXEN

3/10 ▷ The Roman numerals DCCC represent what number?

3/11 ▷ What's the national currency of Namibia?

3/12 ▷ Liesl von Trapp appears in what stage and film musical?

3/13 ▷ On which river does Bishop's Stortford stand?

3/14 ▷ What human blood group was originally called C?

3/15 ▷ In 1994, Paula Abdul divorced which US actor?

3/16 ▷ What type of percussion instrument is a tom-tom?

3/17 ▷ The lemato fruit is a hybrid of a tomato and what else?

3/18 ▷ What New York skyscraper features decorative hubcaps?

3/19 ▷ Leia and Luke are reunited siblings in what film series?

3/20 ▷ In what decade was the first nuclear submarine launched?

3/21 ▷ The word 'pancreatic' refers to what organ?

3/22 ▷ In rhyming slang, what are your 'dinky doos'?

3/23 ▷ The Cabot Tower is a landmark in what English city?

The Vixen Quiz 4: Contestant 1

Answer at least 5 questions correctly to progress on to the Final Chase.

4/1 ▶ Which of these songs spent the longest time at Number One in the UK charts?

> A 'IT'S RAINING MEN' B 'JUST WALKIN' IN THE RAIN' C 'UMBRELLA'

4/2 ▶ In Greek myth, who was punished by being immersed up to his neck in water, which drained away when he tried to drink it?

> A MIDAS B PRIAM C TANTALUS

4/3 ▶ The ephemera is another name for which insect?

> A BLOWFLY B MAYFLY C FRUIT FLY

4/4 ▶ In 1987, the Mr Potato Head toy lost which accessory after pressure from campaigners?

> A BEER CAN B REVOLVER C SMOKING PIPE

4/5 ▶ Which of these countries joined the United Nations most recently?

> A MACEDONIA B MONTENEGRO C MOLDOVA

4/6 ▶ Which US actress starred in the films *The Help*, *Zero Dark Thirty* and *Interstellar*?

> A JESSICA CHASTAIN B EMMA STONE C ANNE HATHAWAY

4/7 ▶ In the novel *The Day of the Triffids*, the humans become vulnerable after most of them have been made what?

> A BLIND B DEAF C MUTE

The Vixen Quiz 4: Contestant 2

Answer at least 5 questions correctly to progress on to the Final Chase.

4/1 ▶ Patrick and Pippa were the neighbours of which sitcom character?

> **A** DEL BOY TROTTER **B** REGGIE PERRIN **C** VICTOR MELDREW

4/2 ▶ The Golden Horde was an empire founded by which people?

> **A** HUNS **B** TURKS **C** MONGOLS

4/3 ▶ Who designed the bridesmaid dress worn by Pippa Middleton at her sister's wedding?

> **A** SARAH BURTON **B** VIVIENNE WESTWOOD **C** GEORGE AT ASDA

4/4 ▶ Who wrote the line 'What a beautiful Pussy you are!'?

> **A** EDWARD LEAR **B** ALFRED, LORD TENNYSON **C** BARBARA CARTLAND

4/5 ▶ In 2013, which boy band had a Top 10 hit with the song 'We Own The Night'?

> **A** ONE DIRECTION **B** THE WANTED **C** UNION J

4/6 ▶ In what Olympic discipline might an athlete be marked for a flic-flac?

> **A** ARCHERY **B** GYMNASTICS **C** THREE-DAY EVENTING

4/7 ▶ The Aire Gap is a wide break in which English range of hills?

> **A** CHILTERNS **B** MENDIPS **C** PENNINES

The Vixen Quiz 4: Contestant 3

Answer at least 5 questions correctly to progress on to the Final Chase.

4/1 ▶ According to Ernest Hemingway, 'All modern American literature comes from...' which book?

> **A** *HUCKLEBERRY FINN* **B** *THE GREAT GATSBY* **C** *TO KILL A MOCKINGBIRD*

4/2 ▶ Which endangered animal can grip food, thanks to an enlarged wrist bone that functions like a thumb?

> **A** GIANT PANDA **B** SNOW LEOPARD **C** ASIAN ELEPHANT

4/3 ▶ Which of these Broadway musicals is NOT based on an opera by Puccini?

> **A** *A LITTLE NIGHT MUSIC* **B** *MISS SAIGON* **C** *RENT*

4/4 ▶ The Levant is the name given to the eastern coast of which sea?

> **A** BLACK SEA **B** CASPIAN SEA **C** MEDITERRANEAN SEA

4/5 ▶ What name was given to a dance in which one was allowed to 'cut in'?

> **A** EXCUSE ME **B** PARDON ME **C** FORGIVE ME

4/6 ▶ Which of these was a 2010 hit single for Katy Perry?

> **A** 'TEENAGE KICKS' **B** 'TEENAGE DREAM' **C** 'TEENAGE DIRTBAG'

4/7 ▶ What day is also known as 'Gowkie Day' in Scotland?

> **A** BOXING DAY **B** HALLOWE'EN **C** APRIL FOOLS' DAY

The Vixen Quiz 4: Contestant 4

Answer at least 5 questions correctly to progress on to the Final Chase.

4/1 ▶ Which politician caused controversy in 2015 by launching a pink campaign bus to appeal to female voters?

> **A** ESTHER MCVEY **B** HARRIET HARMAN **C** NIGEL FARAGE

4/2 ▶ What group had a cameo as the 'town band' in *Back To The Future Part III*?

> **A** AEROSMITH **B** METALLICA **C** ZZ TOP

4/3 ▶ Released 46 years before his death in 1970, what was E M Forster's last novel to be published in his lifetime?

> **A** *A ROOM WITH A VIEW* **B** *HOWARDS END* **C** *A PASSAGE TO INDIA*

4/4 ▶ On a boat, the galley is what type of room?

> **A** BEDROOM **B** KITCHEN **C** TOILET

4/5 ▶ The soundtrack to which 1958 film musical topped the UK charts for 70 consecutive weeks?

> **A** *FIDDLER ON THE ROOF* **B** *CAMELOT* **C** *SOUTH PACIFIC*

4/6 ▶ In astrology, what animal comes between the Archer and the Water Bearer?

> **A** GOAT **B** LION **C** RAM

4/7 ▶ Cheek, claw, face and neck are parts of which hand tool?

> **A** HAMMER **B** SCREWDRIVER **C** HACKSAW

The Vixen Quiz 4: Final Chase

★ Prize fund in the Final Chase was £35,000

★ Your target is 19 correct

Three contestants reached the final. The team's top scorer was Rosie, a 24-year-old medical student. She supplied 8 of the team's 13 correct answers. The team needed to capitalise on push backs to keep the Chaser at bay. They executed 5 of the 7 opportunities offered and squeaked in ahead of The Vixen by a margin of one.

4/1 ▶ Lasagne sheets are a variety of what foodstuff?

4/2 ▶ The Manhattan Project took place during what war?

4/3 ▶ Who played Helen in the 1990s film *Sliding Doors*?

4/4 ▶ What Italian fashion house makes the perfume 'Sicily'?

4/5 ▶ Grizzly bears live on what continent?

4/6 ▶ What Scottish band had a 1990s hit with 'Julia Says'?

4/7 ▶ Who was the first of the Queen's children to re-marry?

4/8 ▶ Jing-mei Woo is a character in what Amy Tan novel?

4/9 ▶ What city is located in the Australian Capital Territory?

THE VIXEN

4/10 ▷ Which puppeteer created the TV show *Fraggle Rock*?

4/11 ▷ 'Scene by the Brook' is a part of what Beethoven symphony?

4/12 ▷ Edward the Sixth succeeded which Tudor king?

4/13 ▷ Gynocracy is rule by what group of people?

4/14 ▷ Copacabana beach lies on what ocean?

4/15 ▷ In what film did Johnny Depp play the author of *Peter Pan*?

4/16 ▷ Chopsticks are used in what activity?

4/17 ▷ '*De profundis*' is an expression from what language?

4/18 ▷ Who won Best British Female at the 2015 BRIT Awards?

4/19 ▷ What number on a dartboard is furthest from the floor?

4/20 ▷ Ammonium sulphate is a salt of what acid?

4/21 ▷ What letter is not pronounced in the word 'thumb'?

4/22 ▷ What Manchester train station has the code MCV?

THE VIXEN QUIZ 4: Final Chase

The Vixen Quiz 5: Contestant 1

Answer at least 5 questions correctly to progress on to the Final Chase.

5/1 ▶ Complete the famous TV opening sequence: '5-4-3-2-1 Thunderbirds are...' what?

> **A** READY **B** GO **C** LAUNCHED

5/2 ▶ Which woman was US Open Mixed Doubles champion three times over a period of 21 years?

> **A** BILLIE JEAN KING **B** CHRIS EVERT **C** MARTINA NAVRATILOVA

5/3 ▶ *The Unexpected Virtue of Ignorance* is the alternative title of what Oscar-winning film?

> **A** *ARGO* **B** *BIRDMAN* **C** *CRASH*

5/4 ▶ Which part of the Earth forms the solid surface?

> **A** CORE **B** MANTLE **C** CRUST

5/5 ▶ The Sugarhill Gang are credited with the first UK Top 40 hit for what style of music?

> **A** GRIME **B** NORTHERN SOUL **C** RAP

5/6 ▶ Which of these kings of England was NOT born in Wales?

> **A** HENRY V **B** HENRY VI **C** HENRY VII

5/7 ▶ Hippotherapy is a form of physiotherapy that involves riding what animal?

> **A** HYENA **B** HORSE **C** HIPPO

The Vixen Quiz 5: Contestant 2

Answer at least 5 questions correctly to progress on to the Final Chase.

5/1 ▶ Which of these was NOT a British backing band of the 1960s?

> **A** BRUVVERS **B** LUVVERS **C** MUVVERS

5/2 ▶ On a Monopoly board, the Electric Company sits between two properties of what colour?

> **A** YELLOW **B** GREEN **C** PINK

5/3 ▶ Which chestnut is commonly used in Chinese cooking?

> **A** WATER CHESTNUT **B** SWEET CHESTNUT **C** HORSE CHESTNUT

5/4 ▶ Which TV series was mentioned by the Queen in her 2014 Christmas broadcast?

> **A** *BREAKING BAD* **B** *MAD MEN* **C** *GAME OF THRONES*

5/5 ▶ Which of these acids does NOT contain oxygen molecules?

> **A** HYDROCHLORIC ACID **B** NITRIC ACID **C** SULPHURIC ACID

5/6 ▶ The Greenwich Meridian is also called the what?

> **A** Home Meridian **B** Basic Meridian **C** Prime Meridian

5/7 ▶ Who sang 'Rainbow Connection' in *The Muppet Movie*?

> **A** KERMIT THE FROG **B** FOZZIE BEAR **C** MISS PIGGY

The Vixen Quiz 5: Contestant 3

Answer at least 5 questions correctly to progress on to the Final Chase.

5/1 ▶ The Bath Comedy Festival gives which award for services to comedy?

> **A** BATH PLUG AWARD **B** BATH TOWEL AWARD **C** BATH WATER AWARD

5/2 ▶ New Hampshire is in what US time zone?

> **A** MOUNTAIN **B** EASTERN **C** PACIFIC

5/3 ▶ How many albums need to be sold to earn a gold disc in the UK?

> **A** 10,000 **B** 100,000 **C** 1,000,000

5/4 ▶ Which of these original founders of the Football League has never won the FA Cup?

> **A** BOLTON WANDERERS **B** NOTTS COUNTY **C** STOKE CITY

5/5 ▶ What does the best-selling mobile phone app Shazam help the user to identify?

> **A** MUSIC **B** ILLNESSES **C** TELEPHONE NUMBERS

5/6 ▶ Nice Guy Eddie was a character in which Quentin Tarantino film?

> **A** *PULP FICTION* **B** *RESERVOIR DOGS* **C** *TRUE ROMANCE*

5/7 ▶ Monkeys from what continent have flat, as opposed to long, noses?

> **A** SOUTH AMERICA **B** AFRICA **C** ASIA

The Vixen Quiz 5: Contestant 4

Answer at least 5 questions correctly to progress on to the Final Chase.

5/1 ▶ What road sign is a blue circle, with a red rim and single diagonal line running from upper left to lower right?

> **A** NO WAITING **B** NO U-TURNS **C** NO TOWED CARAVANS

5/2 ▶ What bird of prey gives its name to the highest rank attainable in the Boy Scouts of America?

> **A** HAWK **B** BUZZARD **C** EAGLE

5/3 ▶ Which singer duetted with U2 on the 2006 re-release of their hit single 'One'?

> **A** MARY J BLIGE **B** ALICIA KEYS **C** MACY GRAY

5/4 ▶ What is oil called before it is refined?

> **A** STRUDE **B** CRUDE **C** PRUDE

5/5 ▶ Which children's game shares its name with a famous boxing style?

> **A** PEEK-A-BOO **B** HIDE AND SEEK **C** DOCTORS AND NURSES

5/6 ▶ 'Chaos and the Calm' was a 2015 Number One album for which singer?

> **A** JAMES BLUNT **B** JAMES BAY **C** JAMES MORRISON

5/7 ▶ What is made by the villagers of Denby Dale when they want to celebrate a major event?

> **A** GIANT PIE **B** GIANT KEBAB **C** GIANT PORK SCRATCHING

The Vixen Quiz 5: Final Chase

★ Prize fund in the Final Chase was £14,000

★ Your target is 16 correct

The final featured 3 contestants, who racked up a creditable score of 16. Mary, a 51-year-old customer service advisor from Milton Keynes was their top scorer. The team showed their quality in the Final Chase, executing 5 push back opportunities. With The Vixen stumbling on a medical question, the team achieved a 2-step victory.

5/1 ▶ 'Botham's Ashes' was a famous series in what sport?

5/2 ▶ Zepheads are fans of which English rock band?

5/3 ▶ El Salvador has a coastline on what ocean?

5/4 ▶ The anti-heroine of the novel *Vanity Fair* is Becky... who?

5/5 ▶ What star sign is someone born on Christmas Eve?

5/6 ▶ The Morgan Arcade is a shopping area in what UK capital city?

5/7 ▶ On a dashboard, a dipswitch operates what parts of the car?

5/8 ▶ A nephron is a blood-filtering unit found in what organ?

5/9 ▶ Growl Tiger is a character in what Lloyd Webber musical?

THE VIXEN

5/10 ▷ With his wife, Gordon Roddick co-founded what retail chain?

5/11 ▷ Which Dame played Katherine in the film *The English Patient*?

5/12 ▷ With reference to vehicles, what does 'LGV' stand for?

5/13 ▷ What two colours are the stripes on Cuba's flag?

5/14 ▷ The so-called 'Darnley portrait' is of which Tudor queen?

5/15 ▷ Wilmington is the largest city in what American state?

5/16 ▷ The abbreviation 'sat fat' refers to what type of fat?

5/17 ▷ Who presented the food campaign TV show *Hugh's Fish Fight*?

5/18 ▷ Jarvis Cocker's band Pulp was formed in what decade?

5/19 ▷ By seating capacity, what's the largest stadium in the UK?

5/20 ▷ The economic term FDI stands for 'Foreign Direct...' what?

5/21 ▷ What is half of 80?

5/22 ▷ The red wine grape Syrah is known by what name in Australia?

The Vixen Quiz 6: Contestant 1

Answer at least 5 questions correctly to progress on to the Final Chase.

6/1 ▶ In 1969, Peter Cushing starred in the film *Frankenstein Must Be...* what?

> **A** DESTROYED **B** DERANGED **C** DEBAGGED

6/2 ▶ What company was set up in 1600 to import spices?

> **A** EAST INDIA COMPANY **B** HUDSON'S BAY COMPANY **C** THE LONDON COMPANY

6/3 ▶ Which of these footballers won the most caps playing for his country in official international matches?

> **A** PELÉ **B** MARADONA **C** BECKENBAUER

6/4 ▶ Which apostle was the 'rock' on which Jesus built his church?

> **A** SIMON PETER **B** MATTHEW **C** ANDREW

6/5 ▶ Patricia Arquette won the Best Supporting Actress Oscar in 2015 for her role in what film?

> **A** *BIRDMAN* **B** *WHIPLASH* **C** *BOYHOOD*

6/6 ▶ The word 'distaff' describes what branch of a family?

> **A** OVERSEAS **B** ILLEGITIMATE **C** FEMALE

6/7 ▶ The Horatio Hornblower novels are set at the time of what conflict?

> **A** NAPOLEONIC WARS **B** WARS OF THE ROSES **C** ENGLISH CIVIL WAR

The Vixen Quiz 6: Contestant 2

Answer at least 5 questions correctly to progress on to the Final Chase.

6/1 ▶ The plot of which Shakespeare play inspired the Taylor Swift song 'Love Story'?

> **A** *THE TAMING OF THE SHREW* **B** *A MIDSUMMER NIGHT'S DREAM* **C** *ROMEO AND JULIET*

6/2 ▶ Lusus was the legendary founder of which European country?

> **A** BELGIUM **B** PORTUGAL **C** ROMANIA

6/3 ▶ 'Cynology' is the study of which animals?

> **A** DOGS **B** CATS **C** MICE

6/4 ▶ In what film comedy is a Tom Jones stage performance interrupted by aliens?

> **A** *MARS ATTACKS!* **B** *GALAXY QUEST* **C** *GUARDIANS OF THE GALAXY*

6/5 ▶ During the First World War, the ruling house of which empire collapsed first?

> **A** RUSSIAN **B** GERMAN **C** AUSTRO-HUNGARIAN

6/6 ▶ Sashimi is most likely to be eaten with which of these sauces?

> **A** BÉCHAMEL SAUCE **B** SOY SAUCE **C** TOMATO SAUCE

6/7 ▶ Daenerys Targaryen is a character in what series of fantasy novels?

> **A** *THE CHRONICLES OF NARNIA* **B** *A SONG OF ICE AND FIRE* **C** *THE LORD OF THE RINGS*

The Vixen Quiz 6: Contestant 3

Answer at least 5 questions correctly to progress on to the Final Chase.

6/1 ▶ Which TV personality was a best man at Benedict Cumberbatch's wedding?

> **A** JUDGE RINDER **B** JEREMY KYLE **C** DAVID DICKINSON

6/2 ▶ What word of hesitation can be typed using adjacent keys on a standard computer keyboard?

> **A** AH **B** ER **C** UM

6/3 ▶ The *Mary Celeste* was found abandoned near what island group in 1872?

> **A** AZORES **B** BAHAMAS **C** CAYMAN ISLANDS

6/4 ▶ Kate Bush's first hit was based on a novel by which writer?

> **A** EMILY DICKINSON **B** ENID BLYTON **C** EMILY BRONTË

6/5 ▶ What is sounded when the 60 seconds are up in a round of the radio show *Just A Minute*?

> **A** BUZZER **B** GONG **C** WHISTLE

6/6 ▶ Which composer's music was once famously described as 'rather too much like a cow looking over a gate'?

> **A** RALPH VAUGHAN WILLIAMS **B** EDWARD ELGAR **C** WILLIAM WALTON

6/7 ▶ Which of these gases is NOT flammable?

> **A** METHANE **B** HYDROGEN **C** HELIUM

The Vixen Quiz 6: Contestant 4

Answer at least 5 questions correctly to progress on to the Final Chase.

6/1 ▶ In the *Mr Men* books, what colour is Mr Bump?

> **A** BLUE **B** RED **C** YELLOW

6/2 ▶ Liza Minnelli married Jack Haley Junior, whose father played which character in the 1939 film *The Wizard of Oz*?

> **A** THE COWARDLY LION **B** THE SCARECROW **C** THE TIN MAN

6/3 ▶ Which of these German cities has NOT hosted an Olympic Games?

> **A** BERLIN **B** HAMBURG **C** MUNICH

6/4 ▶ Which of these numbers is an 'integer'?

> **A** PI **B** THREE-QUARTERS **C** MINUS THREE

6/5 ▶ What is the official currency of Panama?

> **A** BALBOA **B** RAMBO **C** TANGO

6/6 ▶ What song was a 2009 Number One hit for La Roux?

> **A** 'BULLETPROOF' **B** 'GREASEPROOF' **C** 'RAINPROOF'

6/7 ▶ Which football club has two seahorses on its badge?

> **A** NEWCASTLE UNITED **B** NORTHAMPTON TOWN **C** NORWICH CITY

The Vixen Quiz 6: Final Chase

★ Prize fund in the Final Chase was £4,000

★ Your target is 12 correct

Just 1 contestant made it to the final: Scott a 33-year-old bar manager from Hampshire. With only a single step advantage he did well to amass a final score of 12. This looked to be a do-able target for The Vixen, but she slipped up to provide 7 push back opportunities, of which Scott executed 4, heroically outrunning the Chaser.

6/1 ▷ 'Potterheads' are fans of what J K Rowling franchise?

6/2 ▷ The sauce called a 'coulis' gets its name from what language?

6/3 ▷ Laila Rouass played WAG Amber Gates in what TV drama?

6/4 ▷ Habichtsburg Castle was the ancestral seat of which dynasty?

6/5 ▷ 1978 is known as the year of how many Popes?

6/6 ▷ Which *Twilight* actress played Lydia in the film *Still Alice*?

6/7 ▷ Bayer Leverkusen is a top football team in what country?

6/8 ▷ Which Italian composed the opera *La Forza del Destino*?

6/9 ▷ In publishing, what does the 'B' in ISBN stand for?

THE VIXEN

6/10 ▷ Leucoderma is a condition of what part of the body?

6/11 ▷ 'When I was a Youngster' was a 2011 hit for what duo?

6/12 ▷ Who was first re-elected as Russian President in 2004?

6/13 ▷ What's the English title held by Tarzan?

6/14 ▷ What are the two on-pitch officials in a game of cricket called?

6/15 ▷ The play *Peer Gynt* is based on a folk hero from what country?

6/16 ▷ What colour is the fruit produced by cranberry plants?

6/17 ▷ 'Civitas' was the status of citizenship in what ancient empire?

6/18 ▷ Cobie Smulders played Robin Scherbatsky in what US sitcom?

6/19 ▷ On what continent is the Malay Peninsula?

6/20 ▷ Which singer and actress played Kira in the film *Xanadu*?

6/21 ▷ Kingsmill is a major brand of what staple foodstuff?

6/22 ▷ Whose abdication did Queen Mary call 'a pretty kettle of fish'?

The Vixen Quiz 7: Contestant 1

Answer at least 5 questions correctly to progress on to the Final Chase.

7/1 ▶ What pen name is used by American author Daniel Handler?

> **A** LEMONY SNICKET **B** PLUMMY GINNELL **C** QUINCY ALLEY

7/2 ▶ Which of these men has held the world land and water speed records at the same time?

> **A** DONALD CAMPBELL **B** JOHN COBB **C** ANDY GREEN

7/3 ▶ Which female UK performer sang on David Guetta's hit 'What I Did For Love'?

> **A** LILY ALLEN **B** JESSIE J **C** EMELI SANDÉ

7/4 ▶ Which Disney character is told 'Prove yourself brave, truthful and unselfish, and someday you will be a real boy'?

> **A** MOWGLI **B** PETER PAN **C** PINOCCHIO

7/5 ▶ What was the first name of the Prince Regent played by Hugh Laurie in TV's *Blackadder the Third*?

> **A** FREDERICK **B** GEORGE **C** WILLIAM

7/6 ▶ The great enemy of the Norse god Thor, what creature is Jörmungand?

> **A** DRAGON **B** SERPENT **C** WOLF

7/7 ▶ The French dessert croquembouche is usually made with what type of pastry?

> **A** CHOUX **B** FILO **C** PUFF

The Vixen Quiz 7: Contestant 2

Answer at least 5 questions correctly to progress on to the Final Chase.

7/1 ▶ Stilwater and Steelport are settings in the video game series called what?

> A 'SAINTS ROW'   B 'VILLAINS ROW'   C 'HEATH ROW'

7/2 ▶ Rizzio, the secretary of Mary, Queen of Scots, was murdered in what Scottish landmark?

> A EDINBURGH CASTLE   B HOLYROODHOUSE   C BALMORAL CASTLE

7/3 ▶ Which of these countries has a white cross on its flag?

> A DENMARK   B FINLAND   C SWEDEN

7/4 ▶ The coat of which of these British mammals turns white for winter?

> A RED DEER   B PINE MARTEN   C MOUNTAIN HARE

7/5 ▶ In *Twelfth Night*, which character says 'If music be the food of love, play on'?

> A SEBASTIAN   B SIR TOBY BELCH   C DUKE ORSINO

7/6 ▶ Which of these is NOT a character in the *Mr Men* books?

> A MR SILLY   B MR AVERAGE   C MR CLEVER

7/7 ▶ How many African countries are members of the Commonwealth?

> A 8   B 18   C 28

The Vixen Quiz 7: Contestant 3

Answer at least 5 questions correctly to progress on to the Final Chase.

7/1 ▶ Which of these is the real name of the founder of a luxury fashion house?

> **A** VERSACCIO VERSACE **B** PRADIO PRADA **C** GUCCIO GUCCI

7/2 ▶ Which member of the band D:Ream became a Professor at the University of Manchester?

> **A** PETER CUNNAH **B** CIAN MCCARTHY **C** BRIAN COX

7/3 ▶ Which of these is a Tiger Barb most likely to be seen in?

> **A** AQUARIUM **B** KENNEL **C** HUTCH

7/4 ▶ Who was Pope throughout the Second World War?

> **A** BENEDICT XV **B** JOHN XXIII **C** PIUS XII

7/5 ▶ Which of these British sports stars won Olympic gold at the shortest distance?

> **A** DUNCAN GOODHEW **B** MO FARAH **C** STEVE REDGRAVE

7/6 ▶ Emmet Brickowski is the protagonist in what animated film?

> **A** *DESPICABLE ME* **B** *THE LEGO MOVIE* **C** *THE INCREDIBLES*

7/7 ▶ Murray Walker once said in a commentary 'There's nothing wrong with the car except it's...' what?

> **A** CRASHED **B** FALLING APART **C** ON FIRE

THE VIXEN

The Vixen Quiz 7: Contestant 4

Answer at least 5 questions correctly to progress on to the Final Chase.

7/1 ▶ 'Pandemonium' is a collective noun for what type of animals?

> **A** PORPOISES **B** PANDAS **C** PARROTS

7/2 ▶ What modern country gets its name from former inhabitants of ancient Gaul?

> **A** LUXEMBOURG **B** NETHERLANDS **C** BELGIUM

7/3 ▶ The Island of Reil is found in what part of the body?

> **A** BRAIN **B** PANCREAS **C** SOLES OF FEET

7/4 ▶ What nationality is the children's TV character Fireman Sam?

> **A** IRISH **B** SCOTTISH **C** WELSH

7/5 ▶ What number did Charles de Gaulle give to the new republic he established in France in 1958?

> **A** FIRST REPUBLIC **B** THIRD REPUBLIC **C** FIFTH REPUBLIC

7/6 ▶ Which of these was a battle in the Korean War?

> **A** PORK CHOP HILL **B** BEEFSTEAK RIDGE **C** CHICKEN WING HEIGHTS

7/7 ▶ How did Madonna describe her 1990 greatest hits collection?

> **A** *IMMEDIATE* **B** *IMMACULATE* **C** *IMMORAL*

THE VIXEN QUIZ 7: Contestant 4

The Vixen Quiz 7: Final Chase

★ Prize fund in the Final Chase was £75,000

★ Your target is 17 correct

With 3 contestants reaching the final, their top scorer, providing 13 out of 14 correct answers was Jonathan, a 30-year-old marketing consultant from Leeds. The Vixen was doing well until she began to lose her way with 7 questions to go. In all she conceded 7 push back opportunities of which the team executed 5, winning the Chase.

7/1 ▶ South Korea's only land border is with what country?

7/2 ▶ Which Brontë sister shared her first name with a Stuart monarch?

7/3 ▶ Frenchy and Cha-Cha are characters in what Broadway musical?

7/4 ▶ What chemical element has the symbol Ac?

7/5 ▶ The Tien Shan mountain range is on what continent?

7/6 ▶ Who played coughing Bob Fleming on *The Fast Show*?

7/7 ▶ Muscle fatigue is caused by an excess of what acid?

7/8 ▶ What sport is played by the Dallas Mavericks?

7/9 ▶ In the USA in what month does Veterans Day fall?

THE VIXEN

7/10 ▷ In the early 1990s, which US rapper famously wore harem pants?

7/11 ▷ *Any Objections?* was a book by which Peruvian photographer?

7/12 ▷ What planet shares its name with a liquid metal?

7/13 ▷ What name is given to the ant that lays eggs in a colony?

7/14 ▷ Redcar and Ripon are venues for what professional sport?

7/15 ▷ *In My Shoes* is the memoir of a co-founder of what shoe brand?

7/16 ▷ What deadly sin is also the name for a group of lions?

7/17 ▷ The *Apollo* moon missions stopped in what decade?

7/18 ▷ Which artist sold the painting *The Red Vineyard* to Anna Boch?

7/19 ▷ What name is given to a female seal?

7/20 ▷ The song 'I Want to Break Free' features in what stage musical?

7/21 ▷ 'Crow's feet' are found around what part of the face?

7/22 ▷ The company Fujifilm is based in what country?

7/23 ▷ Which American hosts the TV show *Man Finds Food*?

THE VIXEN QUIZ 7: Final Chase

The Vixen Quiz 8: Contestant 1

Answer at least 5 questions correctly to progress on to the Final Chase.

8/1 ▶ Which TV cartoon character's sidekick was a dog called Muttley?

> **A** DICK DASTARDLY **B** FRED FLINTSTONE **C** PORKY PIG

8/2 ▶ Which Chelsea footballer won the PFA Player of the Year Award for 2015?

> **A** EDEN HAZARD **B** GARY CAHILL **C** JOHN TERRY

8/3 ▶ What is the real first name of Australian rapper Iggy Azalea?

> **A** AMETHYST **B** RUBY **C** SAPPHIRE

8/4 ▶ The name of what food item comes from the Latin meaning 'to season with salt'?

> **A** SANDWICH **B** SOUP **C** SALAD

8/5 ▶ In terms of population, the largest city in the southern hemisphere is in what country?

> **A** ARGENTINA **B** CHILE **C** BRAZIL

8/6 ▶ Ben McKenzie starred as Ryan Atwood in which US TV teen drama?

> **A** *ONE TREE HILL* **B** *DAWSON'S CREEK* **C** *THE O.C.*

8/7 ▶ Which royal was demoted to fifth in line to the throne by the birth of Princess Charlotte?

> **A** PRINCE HARRY **B** PRINCE ANDREW **C** PRINCESS BEATRICE

The Vixen Quiz 8: Contestant 2

Answer at least 5 questions correctly to progress on to the Final Chase.

8/1 ▶ The leader of both the Welsh and Scottish devolved governments has what title?

> **A** FIRST MINISTER **B** LEAD MEMBER **C** PRESIDING OFFICER

8/2 ▶ Which future poet laureate was taught at school by T S Eliot and at university by C S Lewis?

> **A** CECIL DAY-LEWIS **B** TED HUGHES **C** JOHN BETJEMAN

8/3 ▶ What NFL football team play their home games in Phoenix?

> **A** ARIZONA BISHOPS **B** ARIZONA CARDINALS **C** ARIZONA POPES

8/4 ▶ Which of these countries does NOT have a red, white and blue flag

> **A** CZECH REPUBLIC **B** RUSSIA **C** HUNGARY

8/5 ▶ In *The Godfather* films, what is the name of Don Corleone's daughter?

> **A** CONNIE **B** CATARINA **C** CLAUDIA

8/6 ▶ A large piece of flat stone used for making a garden path is called a what?

> **A** BRIMSTONE **B** FLAGSTONE **C** MILESTONE

8/7 ▶ In what music video did Cheryl Cole wear a red military-style jacket and hat?

> **A** 'FIGHT FOR THIS LOVE' **B** 'PROMISE THIS' **C** 'CALL MY NAME'

The Vixen Quiz 8: Contestant 3

Answer at least 5 questions correctly to progress on to the Final Chase.

8/1 ▶ Which part of the human body receives oxygen, despite not having a blood supply?

> **A** CORNEA **B** KIDNEY **C** BONES

8/2 ▶ Which of these is a farm implement used to break up clods of soil and cover seed?

> **A** ETON **B** HARROW **C** WINCHESTER

8/3 ▶ Which Pop Art artist created a series of *Fright Wig* self-portraits?

> **A** JASPER JOHNS **B** ROY LICHTENSTEIN **C** ANDY WARHOL

8/4 ▶ In 2015, who set up a theatre company with one year's residency at London's Garrick Theatre?

> **A** IAN MCKELLEN **B** BENEDICT CUMBERBATCH **C** KENNETH BRANAGH

8/5 ▶ What term is used to describe a wine with a pleasing sense of acidity?

> **A** CRISP **B** OAKY **C** FRUITY

8/6 ▶ Which of these terms for a horse is NOT the name of a Ford car model?

> **A** BRONC **B** MUSTANG **C** STEED

8/7 ▶ Which US President was assassinated in the same year that Queen Victoria died?

> **A** JAMES GARFIELD **B** ABRAHAM LINCOLN **C** WILLIAM MCKINLEY

The Vixen Quiz 8: Contestant 4

Answer at least 5 questions correctly to progress on to the Final Chase.

8/1 ▶ What name is given to a small or misshapen hen's egg?

> **A** BRUMMIES **B** COCKNEY **C** GEORDIE

8/2 ▶ In the first aid abbreviation ABC, what does the 'B' stand for?

> **A** BEAT **B** BONE **C** BREATHING

8/3 ▶ Written as Roman numerals, the numbers 9, 10, 11 and 12 have how many Xs in total?

> **A** FOUR **B** FIVE **C** SIX

8/4 ▶ 'Coco by Karl' is a short video in a series about what fashion house?

> **A** CHANEL **B** GUCCI **C** PRADA

8/5 ▶ Which character has been played on screen by both Leslie Howard and Rex Harrison?

> **A** DOCTOR DOLITTLE **B** HENRY HIGGINS **C** MARK ANTONY

8/6 ▶ Which of these African countries straddles the Tropic of Capricorn?

> **A** ALGERIA **B** BOTSWANA **C** RWANDA

8/7 ▶ Which of these wars was NOT ended by a Treaty of Paris?

> **A** US WAR OF INDEPENDENCE **B** SPANISH-AMERICAN WAR **C** FIRST BOER WAR

The Vixen Quiz 8: Final Chase

⭐ Prize fund in the Final Chase was £16,000

⭐ Your target is 16 correct

Three contestants qualified for the final in this programme. Eight of the team's 13 correct answers were contributed by Melika, a 21-year-old psychology student from Wiltshire. With a start of 16 steps, the team needed to make the most of any push back chances. The Vixen conceded 9 and, executing 4 push backs, the team secured a victory.

8/1 ▶ What's the large pip in a cherry called?

8/2 ▶ The Tour de Suisse is an event in what sport?

8/3 ▶ What chemical element is named after Scandinavia?

8/4 ▶ Which *Peep Show* actor played Dan in *Fresh Meat*?

8/5 ▶ How many letter Ps are in the word 'hippopotamus'?

8/6 ▶ What 1975 Broadway musical is set in 1920s Illinois?

8/7 ▶ Snooker champions Joe, Fred and Steve share what surname?

8/8 ▶ In the 5th century BC, the Thirty Tyrants ruled what city?

8/9 ▶ Helen Daniels was a character in what Australian soap?

THE VIXEN

8/10 ▷ The Large Munsterlander is a breed of what domestic animal?

8/11 ▷ Braque and Picasso created cubism in what capital city?

8/12 ▷ Two internal angles of a square add up to how many degrees?

8/13 ▷ 'Bootie Call' was a Number One single for what girl group?

8/14 ▷ Which English monarch died during Shakespeare's lifetime?

8/15 ▷ In 1806, which Royal Navy officer proposed his wind force scale?

8/16 ▷ The United States has what two-letter internet domain?

8/17 ▷ Marshmallow is a giant snowman in what 2013 Disney film?

8/18 ▷ Which rapper starred as Nick in the film comedy *Are We There Yet?*?

8/19 ▷ What's the longest bone in the human leg?

8/20 ▷ Nicolas Cage won a Best Actor Oscar for what 1990s film?

8/21 ▷ How many decimetres in one metre?

8/22 ▷ In 1860, who founded a school of nursing in London?

The Vixen Quiz 9: Contestant 1

Answer at least 5 questions correctly to progress on to the Final Chase.

9/1 ▶ Which of these is NOT the subject of a Harry Potter novel?

A *THE GOBLET OF FIRE* B *THE CHAMBER OF SECRETS* C *THE TEMPLE OF DOOM*

9/2 ▶ American heiress Christine Colgate is the subject of the attention of two con men in what stage musical?

A *THE COMMITMENTS* B *THE PAJAMA GAME* C *DIRTY ROTTEN SCOUNDRELS*

9/3 ▶ Before Prince Edward, which royal was the last to hold the title Earl of Wessex?

A GEORGE II B RICHARD II C HAROLD II

9/4 ▶ What is commonly used to stop avocados from turning brown once cut open?

A LEMON JUICE B MILK C GINGER

9/5 ▶ Which of these animals is NOT the symbol of either of the two main political parties of the United States?

A DONKEY B ELEPHANT C HAWK

9/6 ▶ The TV sitcom *House of Fools* stars which comedy duo?

A REEVES AND MORTIMER B MITCHELL AND WEBB C CANNON AND BALL

9/7 ▶ Leading players in what sport are given an ATP ranking?

A TENNIS B CRICKET C GOLF

The Vixen Quiz 9: Contestant 2

Answer at least 5 questions correctly to progress on to the Final Chase.

9/1 ▶ In 1520, which Portuguese explorer discovered the strait that bears his name?

> **A** VASCO DE GAMA **B** FERDINAND MAGELLAN **C** ALFONSO DE ALBUQUERQUE

9/2 ▶ In the traditional song 'A Frog Went a-Courtin'', what animal did the frog marry?

> **A** MOUSE **B** HORSE **C** BADGER

9/3 ▶ Which of these is NOT a nickname for a helicopter?

> **A** CHOPPER **B** EGGBEATER **C** GRATER

9/4 ▶ ''Cause the players gonna play' and 'the haters gonna hate' are lyrics in what Taylor Swift hit?

> **A** 'LOVE STORY' **B** 'I KNEW YOU WERE TROUBLE' **C** 'SHAKE IT OFF'

9/5 ▶ Devil-in-the-bush is an alternative name for a plant usually known by what name?

> **A** DELIA **B** NIGELLA **C** GORDON

9/6 ▶ TV detective Kojak sucked lollies to stop him doing what?

> **A** SINGING **B** SMOKING **C** SUCKING HIS THUMB

9/7 ▶ Who completed snooker's 'Triple Crown' when he won the Masters title in 2015?

> **A** SHAUN MURPHY **B** GRAEME DOTT **C** RICKY WALDEN

The Vixen Quiz 9: Contestant 3

Answer at least 5 questions correctly to progress on to the Final Chase.

9/1 ▶ Which of these German composers was born first?

> **A** J S BACH **B** BEETHOVEN **C** BRAHMS

9/2 ▶ *Travelling to Infinity: My Life with Stephen* is Jane Wilde's memoir of life with which former husband?

> **A** STEPHEN KING **B** STEPHEN HAWKING **C** STEPHEN FRY

9/3 ▶ Which of these capital cities is situated on an island of the West Indies?

> **A** BRIDGETOWN **B** CAPE TOWN **C** FREETOWN

9/4 ▶ In 1905, Alf Common became the first footballer transferred for how much money?

> **A** £100 **B** £1,000 **C** £10,000

9/5 ▶ Which of these is the name of an American actress born in 1978?

> **A** MAY MITCHELL **B** APRIL ALLEN **C** JANUARY JONES

9/6 ▶ All postcodes in Northern Ireland start with what two letters?

> **A** NI **B** DR **C** BT

9/7 ▶ In 2012, who won the Oscar for Best Actor in a Supporting Role for his performance in the film *Beginners*?

> **A** CHRISTOPHER PLUMMER **B** BURT REYNOLDS **C** ROBERT DUVALL

The Vixen Quiz 9: Contestant 4

Answer at least 5 questions correctly to progress on to the Final Chase.

9/1 ▶ Which of these Olympians did NOT win a gold medal at the 2012 Games in London?

> **A** MO FARAH **B** STEVE REDGRAVE **C** BRADLEY WIGGINS

9/2 ▶ In what school lesson would you be most likely to use a petri dish?

> **A** PHYSICS **B** CHEMISTRY **C** BIOLOGY

9/3 ▶ The Castle of Mey is a royal residence close to where?

> **A** SNOWDONIA **B** JOHN O'GROATS **C** LAND'S END

9/4 ▶ Which writer provides us with the earliest recorded example of the verb 'to twitter'?

> **A** CHAUCER **B** SHAKESPEARE **C** MILTON

9/5 ▶ Which Hollywood actress reputedly said 'Some of my best leading men have been dogs and horses'?

> **A** ELIZABETH TAYLOR **B** AUDREY HEPBURN **C** MARILYN MONROE

9/6 ▶ Which of these dwarf planets in our Solar System is the largest?

> **A** MAKEMAKE **B** CERES **C** ERIS

9/7 ▶ The young boy in Millais' painting *Bubbles* grew up to become a what?

> **A** JUDGE **B** BISHOP **C** ADMIRAL

The Vixen Quiz 9: Final Chase

★ Prize fund in the Final Chase was £19,000

★ Your target is 17 correct

Four contestants made it through to the final. All contributed to the total of 17 that they set for the Chaser. Push backs would be vital, as indeed they proved to be. The Vixen failed to answer 7 questions and the team capitalised, executing 5 push backs to enable them to comfortably stave off her challenge.

9/1 ▶ Who was the first wife of Prince Charles?

9/2 ▶ The Light Infantry was part of which of the armed forces?

9/3 ▶ Who wrote the children's book *The Giraffe and the Pelly and Me*?

9/4 ▶ Who plays the title character in the 2015 film *Danny Collins*?

9/5 ▶ A heptangular object has how many points?

9/6 ▶ Jacksonian Democrats were named after which US President?

9/7 ▶ Blue Cod and Bluenose are New Zealand species of what?

9/8 ▶ Matt Damon played Dr Mann in what 2014 sci-fi film?

9/9 ▶ What Tower of London guards wear scarlet and gold uniforms?

THE VIXEN

9/10 ▷ In what sequel did Paul Newman play 'Fast Eddie' Felson?

9/11 ▷ In 1285, Philip the Fair became king of what country?

9/12 ▷ 'Never Too Late' was an 1980s hit for which Australian pop star?

9/13 ▷ What green pigment is needed in photosynthesis?

9/14 ▷ In 2006, Tom Jones was knighted for services to what?

9/15 ▷ Golden Dawn is a far-right political party in what country?

9/16 ▷ 'Lauren' is a women's line by what American fashion brand?

9/17 ▷ Who wrote the short story 'Octopussy', published in 1966?

9/18 ▷ Defensive end is a position in what ball sport?

9/19 ▷ The islands of Jersey and Sark are in what stretch of water?

9/20 ▷ In what decade did China hold its first nuclear test?

9/21 ▷ What type of creature is a jackdaw?

9/22 ▷ Santos is a football team in what South American country?

THE VIXEN QUIZ 9: Final Chase

The Vixen Quiz 10: Contestant 1

Answer at least 5 questions correctly to progress on to the Final Chase.

10/1 ▶ An economic cycle with alternating periods of prosperity and recession is called boom and what?

> **A** BREAK **B** BANKRUPT **C** BUST

10/2 ▶ '(I Just) Died in Your Arms' was the only Top 10 single for what band?

> **A** CUTTING CREW **B** ROCK STEADY CREW **C** SO SOLID CREW

10/3 ▶ Which of these islands is NOT in the Hebrides?

> **A** JURA **B** MUCK **C** ARRAN

10/4 ▶ According to a famous line in *The War of the Worlds*, 'the chances against anything manlike on Mars are...' what?

> **A** A HUNDRED TO ONE **B** A THOUSAND TO ONE **C** A MILLION TO ONE

10/5 ▶ Which of these materials is obtained through mining?

> **A** ASBESTOS **B** FIBREGLASS **C** CELLOPHANE

10/6 ▶ What is it called in baseball when a runner is stranded between two bases and is at risk of being tagged out?

> **A** A STEW **B** A JAM **C** A PICKLE

10/7 ▶ The actors who played which of these TV duos married each other in real life?

> **A** DEMPSEY AND MAKEPEACE **B** MULDER AND SCULLY **C** GEORGE AND MILDRED

The Vixen Quiz 10: Contestant 2

Answer at least 5 questions correctly to progress on to the Final Chase.

10/1 ▶ What does the 'U' stand for in the acronym UAV when referring to remote controlled aircrafts?

> **A** UNIDENTIFIED **B** UTILITY **C** UNMANNED

10/2 ▶ The city of Persepolis was founded by which leader?

> **A** DARIUS THE GREAT **B** SULEIMAN THE MAGNIFICENT **C** IVAN THE TERRIBLE

10/3 ▶ What name is given to the person who conducts a séance?

> **A** LARGE **B** MEDIUM **C** SMALL

10/4 ▶ Which of these singers had a UK Number One single first?

> **A** DAVID BOWIE **B** DAVID CASSIDY **C** DAVID ESSEX

10/5 ▶ The name of what water lily is derived from the alcoholic smell given off by its flowers?

> **A** BRANDY BOTTLE **B** CHAMPAGNE FLUTE **C** WHISKY FLASK

10/6 ▶ What is the name of the penguin in *Toy Story 2*?

> **A** SQUEEZY **B** WHEEZY **C** CHEEZEY

10/7 ▶ Which of these famous battles took place first?

> **A** BUNKER HILL **B** EDGEHILL **C** PORK CHOP HILL

The Vixen Quiz 10: Contestant 3

Answer at least 5 questions correctly to progress on to the Final Chase.

10/1 ▶ 'Mezzanine' is a 1998 album released by which trip-hop group?

> **A** AIR **B** MASSIVE ATTACK **C** PORTISHEAD

10/2 ▶ Findus specialises in what sector of the food industry?

> **A** CANNING **B** PICKLING **C** FREEZING

10/3 ▶ What range of hills crosses Buckinghamshire and western Hertfordshire?

> **A** CHILTERNS **B** COTSWOLDS **C** QUANTOCKS

10/4 ▶ Which Prime Minister was the first commoner to be portrayed on a British coin?

> **A** STANLEY BALDWIN **B** WINSTON CHURCHILL **C** DAVID LLOYD GEORGE

10/5 ▶ The 2014 cinema box-office flop *United Passions* is about which organisation?

> **A** FIFA **B** OPEC **C** UNICEF

10/6 ▶ In a beehive, which of these bees is male?

> **A** DRONE **B** QUEEN **C** WORKER

10/7 ▶ In musical notation, what major scale has no sharps?

> **A** A MAJOR **B** B MAJOR **C** C MAJOR

The Vixen Quiz 10: Contestant 4

Answer at least 5 questions correctly to progress on to the Final Chase.

10/1 ▶ What is the more common name of the Roma tomato?

> **A** PEACH TOMATO **B** PEAR TOMATO **C** PLUM TOMATO

10/2 ▶ New Zealand was originally settled by people from where?

> **A** MICRONESIA **B** MELANESIA **C** POLYNESIA

10/3 ▶ Which pop star removed her entire catalogue of music from streaming service Spotify in 2014?

> **A** BEYONCÉ **B** TAYLOR SWIFT **C** KATY PERRY

10/4 ▶ In what film directed by Tim Burton did Michael Sheen provide the voice of the White Rabbit?

> **A** *ALICE IN WONDERLAND* **B** *CORPSE BRIDE* **C** *EDWARD SCISSORHANDS*

10/5 ▶ The regions of the ocean ranging from 1,000 metres to 4,000 metres are called what?

> **A** MIDDAY ZONE **B** TWILIGHT ZONE **C** MIDNIGHT ZONE

10/6 ▶ Someone who is an 'FRCR' has what medical speciality?

> **A** DENTISTRY **B** RADIOLOGY **C** SURGERY

10/7 ▶ The name of what musical completes each verse of the rhyme 'London Bridge Is Falling Down'?

> **A** *MY FAIR LADY* **B** *THE MUSIC MAN* **C** *GUYS AND DOLLS*

The Vixen Quiz 10: Final Chase

★ Prize fund in the Final Chase was £11,000

★ Your target is 16 correct

Only 2 contestants reached the final in this programme. With both contributing in almost equal measure, they achieved a creditable score of 16, but a win would need success with push backs. The duo failed to convert 5 of the 9 opportunities The Vixen provided, but the 4 they executed were sufficient to secure victory.

10/1 ▷ The word 'journo' is short for what job title?

10/2 ▷ Bungle was a bear in what children's TV show?

10/3 ▷ The Heineken Experience beer museum is in what capital city?

10/4 ▷ Which English king invaded Scotland in 1296?

10/5 ▷ How many musicians make up a dectet?

10/6 ▷ In physics, what sort of energy is abbreviated to 'KE'?

10/7 ▷ *Minions* is a spin-off movie from what animated film?

10/8 ▷ Politician Ming Campbell was an Olympian in what sport?

10/9 ▷ In 2010, what TV soap killed off Ashley Peacock?

THE VIXEN

10/10 ▷ Buzz Aldrin took part in what number *Apollo* moon mission?

10/11 ▷ Which actress was the first wife of Tom Cruise?

10/12 ▷ Daniel F Malan instituted apartheid in what country?

10/13 ▷ What two main colours make up the current Starbucks logo?

10/14 ▷ What is the stage name of the comedian born Mark Bailey?

10/15 ▷ What German title was used by Holy Roman Emperors from 962?

10/16 ▷ Monmouth is a market town in what Welsh county?

10/17 ▷ In what month is Royal Ascot held each year?

10/18 ▷ Oxford Sandy and Black is a breed of what farm animal?

10/19 ▷ Who said 'The lady's not for turning' in a speech of 1980?

10/20 ▷ Which of Dickens' novels is semi-autobiographical?

10/21 ▷ The term 'stellar structure' refers to the structure of what?

10/22 ▷ The Goring Hotel is adjacent to which royal residence?

10/23 ▷ In 2006, which female singer had a Top 10 hit with 'Who Knew'?

The
BARRISTER

The Barrister

The Barrister Shaun Wallace, also known as The Dark Destroyer, is perhaps the most inscrutable of the Chasers. He shows little emotion and rarely smiles as he focuses on the job in hand – namely the destruction of any challenge that the contestants may offer. His famous deadpan put-downs are designed to remind contestants of the scale of the task ahead. He couples an astute legal mind and broad general knowledge with a possibly unexpected expertise in the subject of football.

The Barrister holds a number of programme records. He was the Chaser involved in the Cashbuilder round that included the highest number of questions – an amazing 14 (on this occasion the player was caught). He has succeeded in catching a target of 23 in the Final Chase. Two of the three Final Chases with the highest prize money involved him. And he holds the record for the longest run of correct questions (21), offering no push back opportunities. Unsurprisingly, this achievement helped him to catch his opponents.

It can come as a surprise when his chilling persona sometimes gives way to the warmer side to his character. On the rare occasions when he is thwarted in his mission, he is quick to be generous in his acknowledgement of the skill of his opponents.

The Barrister Quiz 1: Contestant 1

Answer at least 5 questions correctly to progress on to the Final Chase.

1/1 ▶ Eustace Scrubb is a character in what book series?

> A *HARRY POTTER* B *THE LORD OF THE RINGS* C *NARNIA*

1/2 ▶ Who did the conductor Sir Thomas Beecham describe as 'drooling, drivelling, doleful, depressing, dropsical drips'?

> A CRITICS B VIOLINISTS C PROM-GOERS

1/3 ▶ In the animated film, what sort of creature is the title character Turbo?

> A JAGUAR B GOAT C SNAIL

1/4 ▶ From 1949 to 1951, the future Queen and Prince Philip lived together on what island?

> A SKYE B CYPRUS C MALTA

1/5 ▶ What chemical element can be obtained from the decay of radium?

> A URANIUM B PLUTONIUM C POLONIUM

1/6 ▶ What is the title of Geoff Hurst's autobiography?

> A *1066 AND ALL THAT* B *1666 AND ALL THAT* C *1966 AND ALL THAT*

1/7 ▶ Which of these bands was founded the earliest?

> A BEAUTIFUL SOUTH B GO WEST C EAST 17

The Barrister Quiz 1: Contestant 2

Answer at least 5 questions correctly to progress on to the Final Chase.

1/1 ▶ What is the most expensive property on the *Coronation Street* version of Monopoly?

> **A** THE KABIN **B** THE ROVERS RETURN **C** THE RED REC

1/2 ▶ Complete the *Animal Farm* quote 'Four legs good, two legs…' what?

> **A** BAD **B** WRONG **C** BANDY

1/3 ▶ What is the traditional religion of the Sherpas?

> **A** HINDUISM **B** ISLAM **C** BUDDHISM

1/4 ▶ How large was Wordsworth's host of daffodils?

> **A** ONE THOUSAND **B** TEN THOUSAND **C** FIFTY THOUSAND

1/5 ▶ Which of these months does NOT have a bank holiday in it?

> **A** JANUARY **B** MAY **C** SEPTEMBER

1/6 ▶ In what industry could a person once be employed as a saggar maker's bottom knocker?

> **A** THE POTTERY INDUSTRY **B** THE STEEL INDUSTRY **C** THE COTTON INDUSTRY

1/7 ▶ The Queensland Red Claw is a freshwater species of which crustacean?

> **A** CRAYFISH **B** KRILL **C** SHRIMP

The Barrister Quiz 1: Contestant 3

Answer at least 5 questions correctly to progress on to the Final Chase.

1/1 ▶ What is the usual nickname for the bingo call 44?

> **A** DROOPY DRAWERS **B** SNOOPY'S PAWS **C** SCOOBY SNORES

1/2 ▶ How would you play an ocarina?

> **A** BLOW IT **B** PLUCK IT **C** BEAT IT

1/3 ▶ Which singer's 'Meow' fragrance was sold in a cat-shaped bottle?

> **A** JESSIE J **B** KATY PERRY **C** BRITNEY SPEARS

1/4 ▶ The legal term 'alibi' comes from the Latin for what?

> **A** ELSEWHERE **B** INNOCENT **C** OVERSEAS

1/5 ▶ Which of these was first introduced as a medal sport at the 1964 Olympics?

> **A** BASEBALL **B** WATER SKIING **C** JUDO

1/6 ▶ The Composite order of architecture combines the Ionic order with what other?

> **A** CORINTHIAN **B** DORIC **C** TUSCAN

1/7 ▶ What is the currency of the Falkland Islands?

> **A** FALKLAND PESO **B** FALKLAND PESETA **C** FALKLAND POUND

The Barrister Quiz 1: Contestant 4

Answer at least 5 questions correctly to progress on to the Final Chase.

1/1 ▶ The Statue of Zeus, a Wonder of the Ancient World, held a sceptre with what bird perched upon it?

> **A** DOVE **B** EAGLE **C** RAVEN

1/2 ▶ *Child Whispers* was the first published book by which children's author?

> **A** ENID BLYTON **B** ROALD DAHL **C** BEATRIX POTTER

1/3 ▶ A narrow valley or ravine with steep sides, made by a fast-flowing stream, is called what?

> **A** GULLY **B** DEEP POINT **C** SQUARE LEG

1/4 ▶ In the musical *Oliver!* which character is the 'he' in Nancy's song 'As Long as He Needs Me'?

> **A** FAGIN **B** ARTFUL DODGER **C** BILL SIKES

1/5 ▶ What did Einstein predict the Fourth World War would be fought with?

> **A** FOOD AND WATER **B** STICKS AND STONES **C** WOMEN AND CHILDREN

1/6 ▶ The musical *Hairspray* is based on a film by which director?

> **A** DAVID LYNCH **B** ALAN PARKER **C** JOHN WATERS

1/7 ▶ Which of these actresses played the role of Lois Lane on screen first?

> **A** AMY ADAMS **B** TERI HATCHER **C** MARGOT KIDDER

The Barrister Quiz 1: Final Chase

★ Prize fund in the Final Chase was £35,000

★ Your target is 19 correct

In this programme 4 contestants made the final. With an impressive 14 correct answers they slowed the Chaser with 3 push backs. Ian, a 29-year-old lettings officer from London correctly answered 9 of the contestants' 14 answers with The Barrister falling after failing to give buttermilk as a by-product of the butter-making process.

1/1 ▶ 'Bart the Genius' was a season one episode of what cartoon?

1/2 ▶ What big cats are the nickname of Millwall Football Club?

1/3 ▶ In TV ads, which Kid was 'strong and tough'?

1/4 ▶ In what year were the first modern Olympic Games held?

1/5 ▶ Which singer and actress was born Cherilyn Sarkisian?

1/6 ▶ What type of sea creature is a 'stargazer'?

1/7 ▶ What nationality is golfer John Daly?

1/8 ▶ What Midlands county town stands on the River Sow?

1/9 ▶ In the film *Dr No* what colour was Honey Rider's bikini?

1/10 ▶ Voting by ballot was adopted in Britain in what century?

THE BARRISTER

1/11 ▷ Which Russian-born composer wrote the opera *The Rake's Progress*?

1/12 ▷ Which royal received his RAF wings in 1971?

1/13 ▷ Who sold Fulham Football Club to Shahid Khan in 2013?

1/14 ▷ Which former glamour model designed the KP Equestrian range?

1/15 ▷ *English Rain* is the debut album by which British female singer?

1/16 ▷ Which month starts with the letter 'D'?

1/17 ▷ David Mellor was an MP for what party?

1/18 ▷ Film director Sam Mendes is the son of which author?

1/19 ▷ What song was an 1980s Number One for Renee and Renato?

1/20 ▷ The Goliath is the largest species of what amphibian?

1/21 ▷ What aniseed-flavour sweet shares its name with a card game?

1/22 ▷ What European capital is commonly called 'The City of Light'?

1/23 ▷ What's the brightest star in the constellation Gemini?

1/24 ▷ What halogen is present in the compound chloroform?

1/25 ▷ What film industry's name is a blend of Bombay and Hollywood?

The Barrister Quiz 2: Contestant 1

Answer at least 5 questions correctly to progress on to the Final Chase.

2/1 ▶ Which of these is the title of a film co-written by Meera Syal?

> **A** *BHAJI ON THE BEACH* **B** *SAMOSA AT THE SEASIDE* **C** *PAKORA IN THE PARK*

2/2 ▶ Which animal secretes an oily red fluid on its skin that acts as a sunblock?

> **A** HIPPOPOTAMUS **B** RHINOCEROS **C** ELEPHANT

2/3 ▶ In 2014, who became the first woman to be voted 'Rear of The Year' twice?

> **A** FELICITY KENDALL **B** FIONA BRUCE **C** CAROL VORDERMAN

2/4 ▶ In Japanese cookery, deep-fried pieces of fish and vegetables are called what?

> **A** TEMPURA **B** WASABI **C** GYOZA

2/5 ▶ Which city did Brasilia replace as the federal capital of Brazil in 1960?

> **A** RIO DE JANEIRO **B** SÃO PAULO **C** SALVADOR

2/6 ▶ Which of these religions is 'non-theistic'?

> **A** ZOROASTRIANISM **B** SHINTO **C** BUDDHISM

2/7 ▶ Tatooine is the home planet of which fictional character?

> **A** LUKE SKYWALKER **B** SPOCK **C** SUPERMAN

The Barrister Quiz 2: Contestant 2

Answer at least 5 questions correctly to progress on to the Final Chase.

2/1 ▶ As well as writing and producing the song, who sang on the 2013 Robin Thicke hit 'Blurred Lines'?

> **A** ALOE BLACC **B** JASON DERULO **C** PHARRELL WILLIAMS

2/2 ▶ Which language is called 'Ivrit' by its own speakers?

> **A** MANX **B** ESTONIAN **C** HEBREW

2/3 ▶ The sitcom *Dinnerladies* was set in what type of establishment?

> **A** FACTORY **B** POLICE STATION **C** SCHOOL

2/4 ▶ Which of these countries is NOT a federal republic?

> **A** FRANCE **B** GERMANY **C** RUSSIA

2/5 ▶ Which tennis player won the Wimbledon Women's Singles title when she was just 17 years old?

> **A** SERENA WILLIAMS **B** MARIA SHARAPOVA **C** CONCHITA MARTÍNEZ

2/6 ▶ Which of these does the average adult human have the greatest number of?

> **A** TEETH **B** RIBS **C** FINGERNAILS

2/7 ▶ Who created the fictional character Katniss Everdeen?

> **A** JACKIE COLLINS **B** SUZANNE COLLINS **C** WILKIE COLLINS

The Barrister Quiz 2: Contestant 3

Answer at least 5 questions correctly to progress on to the Final Chase.

2/1 ▶ Which of these foods does NOT have protected geographical status within the EU?

> **A** CORNISH PASTY **B** CUMBERLAND SAUSAGE **C** CHESHIRE CHEESE

2/2 ▶ Which lively dance became an American craze after its appearance in the 1923 musical *Runnin' Wild*?

> **A** BLOW IT **B** PLUCK IT **C** BEAT IT

2/3 ▶ On TV, what was the nickname of *Grange Hill* PE teacher Dai Jones?

> **A** DAI HARD **B** DAI ANOTHER DAY **C** LIVE AND LET DAI

2/4 ▶ Which of these models is the youngest?

> **A** AGYNESS DEYN **B** LILY COLE **C** DAISY LOWE

2/5 ▶ The constellation Orion is also known by what name?

> **A** THE SHEPHERD **B** THE FARMER **C** THE HUNTER

2/6 ▶ *The Slightly Annoying Elephant* is the first children's picture book by which TV star?

> **A** ROWAN ATKINSON **B** JOANNA LUMLEY **C** DAVID WALLIAMS

2/7 ▶ Which of these is a village in Norfolk?

> **A** LITTLE SLEEPING **B** LITTLE SLUMBERING **C** LITTLE SNORING

THE BARRISTER

The Barrister Quiz 2: Contestant 4

Answer at least 5 questions correctly to progress on to the Final Chase.

2/1 ▶ Jessica Simpson's version of 'These Boots Are Made for Walkin'' was for the soundtrack to which of her films?

> **A** *BLONDE AMBITION* **B** *THE DUKES OF HAZZARD* **C** *THE LOVE GURU*

2/2 ▶ The salad ingredient cress is a member of the same family as which of these?

> **A** SPINACH **B** LETTUCE **C** MUSTARD

2/3 ▶ Henry VIII was the third husband of which woman?

> **A** CATHERINE OF ARAGON **B** CATHERINE HOWARD **C** CATHERINE PARR

2/4 ▶ Which of these FA Cup-winning teams plays its home games closest to Wembley?

> **A** BRADFORD CITY **B** COVENTRY CITY **C** MANCHESTER CITY

2/5 ▶ What mode of transport features in The Seekers' hit 'Morningtown Ride'?

> **A** BUS **B** SHIP **C** TRAIN

2/6 ▶ The city of Carthage was founded by which ancient people?

> **A** EGYPTIANS **B** GREEKS **C** PHOENICIANS

2/7 ▶ Which of these TV comedies was set in the UK?

> **A** *DUTY FREE* **B** *FATHER TED* **C** *WAITING FOR GOD*

The Barrister Quiz 2: Final Chase

★ Prize fund in the Final Chase was £35,000

★ Your target is 19 correct

In this programme 2 contestants made the final. Having achieved only 12 correct answers, they had to work hard to impede the Chaser. With 4 successful push backs, they beat The Barrister after he was unable to name cocoa as the main ingredient of chocolate.

2/1 ▶ Beehive and bob are both types of what?

2/2 ▶ What dance is usually performed to 'The Blue Danube'?

2/3 ▶ Sue Johnston joined what TV period drama series in 2014?

2/4 ▶ The coastline of Eritrea is on what sea?

2/5 ▶ What type of club did TV's Richard and Judy launch in 2004?

2/6 ▶ London and Dutch are types of what alcoholic spirit?

2/7 ▶ The bugle belongs to what group of wind instruments?

2/8 ▶ Which historical fiction author wrote the *Tudor Court* series?

2/9 ▶ 'Earth Song' was a Christmas Number One for which singer?

2/10 ▶ What's the official language of the Azores?

THE BARRISTER

2/11 ▷ Which 18th-century British artist painted *Mr and Mrs Andrews*?

2/12 ▷ Singer Olly Murs found fame on what TV talent show?

2/13 ▷ Which Spanish golfer won the Masters twice in the 1990s?

2/14 ▷ A porterhouse is a cut of which meat?

2/15 ▷ Who plays Gale Hawthorne in *The Hunger Games* film series?

2/16 ▷ What animal is known as the 'ship of the desert'?

2/17 ▷ Blake Carrington was a principle character in what TV series?

2/18 ▷ Which English composer wrote 'The Dream of Gerontius'?

2/19 ▷ What's the first vowel in the Greek alphabet?

2/20 ▷ Who wrote the children's book *Horton Hears A Who!*?

2/21 ▷ Fire extinguishers are normally what colour?

2/22 ▷ What Lloyd Webber musical features 'King Herod's Song'?

2/23 ▷ Who did Mary McAleese succeed as President of Ireland?

2/24 ▷ Which American author created the Corleone family?

2/25 ▷ The lachrymal glands produce what bodily fluid?

The Barrister Quiz 3: Contestant 1

Answer at least 5 questions correctly to progress on to the Final Chase.

3/1 ▶ The UK's two biggest-selling duets of all time are songs from which film?

A *GREASE* **B** *HAIRSPRAY* **C** *WEST SIDE STORY*

3/2 ▶ Which of these actresses did NOT marry a tennis player?

A BROOKE SHIELDS **B** TATUM O'NEAL **C** EVA LONGORIA

3/3 ▶ A lusophone is most likely to live in which of these countries?

A BRAZIL **B** KENYA **C** POLAND

3/4 ▶ Tom and Daisy Buchanan appear in what F Scott Fitzgerald novel?

A *TENDER IS THE NIGHT* **B** *THE GREAT GATSBY* **C** *THIS SIDE OF PARADISE*

3/5 ▶ The Banksy work *Heavy Weaponry* features what animal carrying a rocket bomb?

A ELEPHANT **B** GIANT PANDA **C** MEERKAT

3/6 ▶ Which British monarch suffered the so-called 'Bedchamber Crisis'?

A HENRY VIII **B** GEORGE III **C** VICTORIA

3/7 ▶ In Germany, what is a 'Fleischer'?

A BUTCHER **B** BAKER **C** CANDLESTICK MAKER

The Barrister Quiz 3: Contestant 2

Answer at least 5 questions correctly to progress on to the Final Chase.

3/1 ▶ What surname is shared by authors who created the soldier Sharpe and the sleuth Kay Scarpetta?

> **A** CORNWELL **B** HARRIS **C** MORTIMER

3/2 ▶ In 2014, which singer became the first person to have over 100 million 'likes' on Facebook?

> **A** ENRIQUE IGLESIAS **B** SHAKIRA **C** SELENA GOMEZ

3/3 ▶ A netball match begins with what?

> **A** CENTRE PASS **B** BULLY OFF **C** TEE OFF

3/4 ▶ Which of these films did Steven Spielberg produce but NOT direct?

> **A** *RAIDERS OF THE LOST ARK* **B** *HOOK* **C** *POLTERGEIST*

3/5 ▶ Sir Humphrey Gilbert, who annexed Newfoundland, was the half-brother of which other explorer?

> **A** JAMES COOK **B** FRANCIS DRAKE **C** WALTER RALEIGH

3/6 ▶ Which of these medical specialists practises 'odontology'?

> **A** MIDWIFE **B** PSYCHOLOGIST **C** DENTIST

3/7 ▶ Which newsreader featured on the 1982 fitness album *Shape Up and Dance*?

> **A** SELINA SCOTT **B** ANGELA RIPPON **C** TREVOR MCDONALD

The Barrister Quiz 3: Contestant 3

Answer at least 5 questions correctly to progress on to the Final Chase.

3/1 ▶ Which of these is the name of one of the Knights of the Round Table in Arthurian legend?

> **A** JAY **B** KAY **C** ROWLING

3/2 ▶ In a 1942 speech, who said 'It is not even the beginning of the end. But it is, perhaps, the end of the beginning'?

> **A** WINSTON CHURCHILL **B** FRANKLIN D ROOSEVELT **C** ADOLF HITLER

3/3 ▶ The Greek alphabet contains how many vowels?

> **A** FIVE **B** SEVEN **C** NINE

3/4 ▶ What Disney bears were 'dashing and daring, courageous and caring'?

> **A** CARE BEARS **B** HAIR BEAR BUNCH **C** GUMMI BEARS

3/5 ▶ Which of these currencies is spent furthest south?

> **A** KRONA **B** RAND **C** YEN

3/6 ▶ In astronomy, what is Betelgeuse?

> **A** PLANET **B** STAR **C** GALAXY

3/7 ▶ Which of these books was published the earliest?

> **A** *MOBY DICK* **B** *GULLIVER'S TRAVELS* **C** *ROBINSON CRUSOE*

The Barrister Quiz 3: Contestant 4

Answer at least 5 questions correctly to progress on to the Final Chase.

3/1 ▶ Which baddie was played in the same film by David Prowse, Sebastian Shaw and James Earl Jones?

> **A** LEX LUTHER **B** FREDDY KRUEGER **C** DARTH VADER

3/2 ▶ What was banned in Albania in 1967?

> **A** CINEMA **B** MINI-SKIRTS **C** RELIGIOUS WORSHIP

3/3 ▶ What was the title of an autobiography by disgraced former MP Jonathan Aitken?

> **A** *PRIDE AND PERJURY* **B** *SENSE AND NONSENSE* **C** *PERVERSION*

3/4 ▶ Edinburgh rock is a type of what?

> **A** MUSIC **B** STONE **C** CONFECTIONERY

3/5 ▶ Which of these cricket fielders stands closest to the batsman?

> **A** SILLY MID OFF **B** POINT **C** FINE LEG

3/6 ▶ Which country lies the closest to mainland Australia?

> **A** FIJI **B** NEW ZEALAND **C** PAPUA NEW GUINEA

3/7 ▶ The scientific name for which of these animals is exactly the same as its name in English?

> **A** FENNEC FOX **B** ARGENTINE PUMA **C** BOA CONSTRICTOR

The Barrister Quiz 3: Final Chase

★ Prize fund in the Final Chase was £35,000

★ Your target is 19 correct

Four contestants made the final in this programme and added a commendable 15 correct answers to their 4-step head start. Their top scorer was Ian, a 35-year-old Magazine Production Manager from London, who correctly answered 8 questions. With 4 successful push backs the contestants outran The Barrister.

3/1 ▶ Hollywood Boulevard is in what American city?

3/2 ▶ Which Spice Girl had a surname that was a colour?

3/3 ▶ What Spanish word for 'sauce' comes from the Latin for 'salty'?

3/4 ▶ In what decade was the Booker Prize first awarded?

3/5 ▶ Margate and Minster are coastal towns in what county?

3/6 ▶ The tam-tam belongs to what section of the orchestra?

3/7 ▶ Which Italian was twice champion jockey in the 1990s?

3/8 ▶ Which John Buchan character has a servant called Paddock?

3/9 ▶ 'Poor Jerusalem' is a song from what Lloyd Webber musical?

3/10 ▶ Peri Gilpin played radio producer Roz Doyle in what US sitcom?

3/11 ▶ What Moroccan port is known in Arabic as Dar el-Beida?

THE BARRISTER

3/12 ▶ What's the highest odd number on a standard roulette wheel?

3/13 ▶ Who was the second US President to be assassinated?

3/14 ▶ Which playwright wrote 'The fool doth think he is wise'?

3/15 ▶ In 1973, who won a Best Supporting Actor Oscar for *Cabaret*?

3/16 ▶ Other than humans, what animals take part in the Olympics?

3/17 ▶ The annual Order of the Garter service is held at what castle?

3/18 ▶ What online retailer produced the 'Fire TV'?

3/19 ▶ The play *Cyrano de Bergerac* is set in what city?

3/20 ▶ What famous South American falls are on the Churun River?

3/21 ▶ What colour was the bus in the film *Summer Holiday*?

3/22 ▶ Which Italian leader signed the 1938 Munich agreement?

3/23 ▶ Harbourne Blue cheese is made from what animal's milk?

3/24 ▶ Which Real Madrid footballer is nicknamed the 'Prince of Wales'?

3/25 ▶ Roland Browning was a pupil at what fictional TV school?

3/26 ▶ How many in a long dozen?

The Barrister Quiz 4: Contestant 1

Answer at least 5 questions correctly to progress on to the Final Chase.

4/1 ▶ Which pop star patented shoes that connected to bolts in the stage, enabling a gravity-defying lean in one of his dances?

> **A** MICHAEL JACKSON **B** JUSTIN TIMBERLAKE **C** ELVIS PRESLEY

4/2 ▶ Which of these months is NOT named after a female deity?

> **A** MAY **B** JUNE **C** JULY

4/3 ▶ Which animal was thought to be extinct in England until it was sighted in Devon in 2014?

> **A** WOLF **B** LEMMING **C** BEAVER

4/4 ▶ Which woman has been the wife and daughter-in-law of an American president?

> **A** ELEANOR ROOSEVELT **B** ABIGAIL ADAMS **C** LAURA BUSH

4/5 ▶ Which of these prison films is NOT based on a Stephen King story?

> **A** *MIDNIGHT EXPRESS* **B** *THE GREEN MILE* **C** *THE SHAWSHANK REDEMPTION*

4/6 ▶ What can be measured in units of sones?

> **A** PAPER SIZE **B** TEMPERATURE **C** LOUDNESS

4/7 ▶ Queen Marlena is the mother of which fictional hero?

> **A** HE-MAN **B** IRON MAN **C** BANANAMAN

The Barrister Quiz 4: Contestant 2

Answer at least 5 questions correctly to progress on to the Final Chase.

4/1 ▶ Which men's athletics field event world record has only been broken twice since 1965?

> **A** LONG JUMP **B** HIGH JUMP **C** TRIPLE JUMP

4/2 ▶ Actress Je'taime Morgan Hanley played pupil Shaznay Montrose in which TV series?

> **A** *BAD EDUCATION* **B** *BIG SCHOOL* **C** *WATERLOO ROAD*

4/3 ▶ When rolling two regular six-sided dice, what total number has the most combinations?

> **A** SEVEN **B** NINE **C** ELEVEN

4/4 ▶ Which of these authors published their novels using their original name?

> **A** AGATHA CHRISTIE **B** GEORGE ORWELL **C** DAPHNE DU MAURIER

4/5 ▶ Which captain of the brig *Rebecca* had his ear cut off by a Spaniard in 1731?

> **A** HAWKINS **B** JENKINS **C** WILKINS

4/6 ▶ An endodontist specialises in what part of the body?

> **A** MOUTH **B** HANDS **C** FEET

4/7 ▶ In what 1980s TV show did a female private eye invent a male boss to attract more clients?

> **A** *SPENSER: FOR HIRE* **B** *MATT HOUSTON* **C** *REMINGTON STEELE*

The Barrister Quiz 4: Contestant 3

Answer at least 5 questions correctly to progress on to the Final Chase.

4/1 ▶ Which of these stages comes earliest in the life cycle of a salmon?

> **A** PARR **B** SMOLT **C** GRILSE

4/2 ▶ Which cricketer has a map of the world tattoo with red stars marking where he has scored an international century?

> **A** ALEC STEWART **B** KEVIN PIETERSEN **C** GEOFFREY BOYCOTT

4/3 ▶ Which of these locations is NOT a British Overseas Territory?

> **A** ARUBA **B** BERMUDA **C** CAYMAN ISLANDS

4/4 ▶ Mark Twain once said whose music was 'better than it sounds'?

> **A** MOZART **B** BEETHOVEN **C** WAGNER

4/5 ▶ Which of these Olivier Award-winning actresses was born furthest from the West End?

> **A** HELEN MIRREN **B** SHERIDAN SMITH **C** ZOË WANAMAKER

4/6 ▶ Which tennis player was Australian Mixed Doubles Champion in 2015, 16 years after her last Singles title there?

> **A** JENNIFER CAPRIATI **B** LINDSAY DAVENPORT **C** MARTINA HINGIS

4/7 ▶ In Shakespeare's play *Henry VIII*, what is the name of the king's physician?

> **A** DOCTOR BUMS **B** DOCTOR BOTTOMS **C** DOCTOR BUTTS

The Barrister Quiz 4: Contestant 4

Answer at least 5 questions correctly to progress on to the Final Chase.

4/1 ▶ The fashion website 'whatkatewore.com' was launched to follow whose sartorial choices?

> **A** KATE WINSLET **B** KATE BECKINSALE **C** KATE MIDDLETON

4/2 ▶ Indra is an ancient god of the sky in which religion?

> **A** SHINTOISM **B** HINDUISM **C** JUDAISM

4/3 ▶ What is the title of Meghan Trainor's 2015 Number One debut album?

> **A** *DEBUT* **B** *ALBUM* **C** *TITLE*

4/4 ▶ Which technology company developed the 'FaceTime' video calling app?

> **A** APPLE **B** MICROSOFT **C** SAMSUNG

4/5 ▶ In how many films has Sir Ian McKellen played Gandalf?

> **A** TWO **B** FOUR **C** SIX

4/6 ▶ An animal described as 'benthic' lives where?

> **A** ON A MOUNTAINSIDE **B** IN THE JUNGLE **C** ON THE SEA-FLOOR

4/7 ▶ Which TV villain was shot dead 33 years after an earlier attempt didn't kill him?

> **A** J R EWING **B** NICK COTTON **C** MR BURNS

The Barrister Quiz 4: Final Chase

★ Prize fund in the Final Chase was £35,000

★ Your target is 19 correct

In this programme 3 contestants made it to the Final Chase and achieved a fantastic total score of 21. Fifty nine-year-old supply teacher Lee provided an astonishing 13 of their correct answers. Two successful push backs were enough to stall The Barrister, who failed by 2 steps to match their total.

4/1 ▷ The word 'dental' refers to what parts of the body?

4/2 ▷ Which actress played 'M' in the Bond film *Tomorrow Never Dies*?

4/3 ▷ How many times was Red Rum Grand National runner-up?

4/4 ▷ What university has its headquarters at Milton Keynes?

4/5 ▷ Consanguinity describes people that are 'related by...' what?

4/6 ▷ 'Four Minute Warning' was a hit for which Take That member?

4/7 ▷ The Kerry Blue is a breed of what dog?

4/8 ▷ In 1820, which English poet published *Prometheus Unbound*?

4/9 ▷ What country made the *Soyuz* and *Proton* space launchers?

4/10 ▷ On TV, which puppet title character worked for Spectrum?

THE BARRISTER

4/11 ▷ The Battle of Marston Moor took place in what century?

4/12 ▷ What colour is an 'Incredible Hulk' cocktail?

4/13 ▷ Luis Figo played football for what European country?

4/14 ▷ Which rapper featured on Rihanna's Number One 'Umbrella'?

4/15 ▷ Who was the Dutch queen between Wilhelmina and Beatrix?

4/16 ▷ What name is given to the long hair on a lion's neck?

4/17 ▷ Which Pope visited the UK in 1982?

4/18 ▷ What gas is named after the Greek word for 'hidden'?

4/19 ▷ What Paris airport is also known as Roissy?

4/20 ▷ Which member of The Monkees appeared on *Coronation Street*?

4/21 ▷ Where on the body are loafers worn?

4/22 ▷ An animal that eats only meat is known by what name?

4/23 ▷ What Nordic city hosted the 1952 Winter Olympics?

4/24 ▷ Who directed the Western *For a Few Dollars More*?

The Barrister Quiz 5: Contestant 1

Answer at least 5 questions correctly to progress on to the Final Chase.

5/1 ▶ Which of these films was NOT directed by Tim Burton?

> **A** *ED WOOD* **B** *TED* **C** *EDWARD SCISSORHANDS*

5/2 ▶ What colour is Euston Road on a Monopoly board?

> **A** RED **B** YELLOW **C** BLUE

5/3 ▶ What name is given to the top maths candidate at Cambridge University?

> **A** SENIOR BOSS **B** SENIOR LEVI **C** SENIOR WRANGLER

5/4 ▶ Travelling is NOT a foul in which of these sports?

> **A** BASKETBALL **B** VOLLEYBALL **C** NETBALL

5/5 ▶ Which inventor features on the US $100 banknote?

> **A** THOMAS EDISON **B** BENJAMIN FRANKLIN **C** ELI WHITNEY

5/6 ▶ Which public school was founded in 1440 to provide free education for 70 poor boys?

> **A** ETON **B** HARROW **C** RUGBY

5/7 ▶ What did the two female members lose when Bucks Fizz sang 'Making Your Mind Up' at the 1981 Eurovision Song Contest?

> **A** THEIR SKIRTS **B** THEIR MICROPHONES **C** THEIR BOYFRIENDS

The Barrister Quiz 5: Contestant 2

Answer at least 5 questions correctly to progress on to the Final Chase.

5/1 ▶ Which of these is a worm that is used as bait by sea anglers?

> **A** LUGWORM **B** JUGWORM **C** MUGWORM

5/2 ▶ Histology is a branch of what science?

> **A** PHYSICS **B** CHEMISTRY **C** BIOLOGY

5/3 ▶ Approximately what percentage of the keys on a standard piano are black?

> **A** 40% **B** 50% **C** 60%

5/4 ▶ Which snooker player wrote the 2015 book *Interesting: My Autobiography*?

> **A** JIMMY WHITE **B** DENNIS TAYLOR **C** STEVE DAVIS

5/5 ▶ The Golden Spurtle is awarded at what annual event?

> **A** WORLD BLACK PUDDING DAY **B** WORLD TRIPE DAY **C** WORLD PORRIDGE DAY

5/6 ▶ The 'black garden' is Britain's most commonly seen variety of what insect?

> **A** BEE **B** ANT **C** GRASSHOPPER

5/7 ▶ In 2014, which US pop star had a hit single with 'Blank Space'?

> **A** KATY PERRY **B** DEMI LOVATO **C** TAYLOR SWIFT

The Barrister Quiz 5: Contestant 3

Answer at least 5 questions correctly to progress on to the Final Chase.

5/1 ▶ What was the first country to host the Summer Olympics twice?

> **A** GERMANY **B** FRANCE **C** USA

5/2 ▶ Which of these can be classed as a 'plastic curd' cheese?

> **A** PARMESAN **B** CHEDDAR **C** MOZZARELLA

5/3 ▶ Which British monarch was born in Hanover in 1683?

> **A** EDWARD II **B** GEORGE II **C** HENRY II

5/4 ▶ 'Hard Work' and 'Think of Meryl Streep' are songs from what stage musical?

> **A** *FAME* **B** *A CHORUS LINE* **C** *42ND STREET*

5/5 ▶ Which of these digits has one bone fewer than the other two?

> **A** LITTLE FINGER **B** RING FINGER **C** THUMB

5/6 ▶ Which British actor got married on Valentine's Day 2015?

> **A** BENEDICT CUMBERBATCH **B** EDDIE REDMAYNE **C** DAVID TENNANT

5/7 ▶ Which of these words is sometimes used as a collective noun for a group of pugs?

> **A** JUMBLE **B** GRUMBLE **C** FUMBLE

The Barrister Quiz 5: Contestant 4

Answer at least 5 questions correctly to progress on to the Final Chase.

5/1 ▶ In the opening sequence of *The Simpsons,* which character is scanned at the supermarket checkout?

> **A** MAGGIE **B** BART **C** LISA

5/2 ▶ The figure in the logo of the company Bic is holding what item behind its back?

> **A** PEN **B** LIGHTER **C** RAZOR

5/3 ▶ In what year did England first play in the FIFA World Cup?

> **A** 1938 **B** 1950 **C** 1962

5/4 ▶ What is the name of the sister store to the high street chain Accessorize?

> **A** HURRICANE **B** MONSOON **C** TYPHOON

5/5 ▶ Tatting is a technique used in the making of what?

> **A** POTTERY **B** WICKER BASKETS **C** LACE

5/6 ▶ What river flows through Greenlaw in Berwickshire?

> **A** BALDRICK **B** BLACKADDER **C** MELCHETT

5/7 ▶ Boy George was a prominent figure in what youth subculture?

> **A** GOTHS **B** NEW ROMANTICS **C** ROCKERS

The Barrister Quiz 5: Final Chase

⭐ Prize fund in the Final Chase was £35,000

⭐ Your target is 19 correct

In this Final Chase 4 contestants beat The Barrister by a decisive 7 steps, greatly aided by 7 successful push backs. Bobby, a 51-year-old foster carer from Dumbarton, was the top-scoring member of the team, contributing 8 correct answers out of their total score of 19.

5/1 ▶ The planet Saturn orbits what star?

5/2 ▶ In 1620, the Pilgrim Fathers sailed to what continent?

5/3 ▶ How many different colours appear on the Twister game mat?

5/4 ▶ Geb was an earth god in what ancient mythology?

5/5 ▶ Dorking and Sussex are breeds of what farmyard bird?

5/6 ▶ Which female singer had the 1980s hit 'Self Control'?

5/7 ▶ Football pundit Robbie Savage played for what country?

5/8 ▶ Don John is a villain in what Shakespeare play?

5/9 ▶ Darth Vader dies in which film of the *Star Wars* series?

5/10 ▶ Guinea has a coastline on what ocean?

THE BARRISTER

5/11 ▷ Calamine is an ore of what metal?

5/12 ▷ The VXR8 is made by what British car manufacturer?

5/13 ▷ Death-watch and clown are types of what insect?

5/14 ▷ Who is heir to the Canadian throne?

5/15 ▷ 'Ambitions' was a Top Ten hit for which *X Factor* winner?

5/16 ▷ What UK city's police force is known as 'the Met'?

5/17 ▷ What credit-card brand makes the Maestro debit card?

5/18 ▷ What's the largest of the Republic of Ireland's four provinces?

5/19 ▷ Paddy Houlihan plays Dermot Brown in what sitcom?

5/20 ▷ A scorpion has how many pairs of legs?

5/21 ▷ What tropical fruit is sold tinned in rings and chunks?

5/22 ▷ Dot AU is the internet domain code for what country?

5/23 ▷ Which First World War poet wrote the collection *Counterattack*?

5/24 ▷ Which Scottish DJ had a hit with 'Feel So Close'?

5/25 ▷ Kitty Bennet is a character in what Jane Austen novel?

The Barrister Quiz 6: Contestant 1

Answer at least 5 questions correctly to progress on to the Final Chase.

6/1 ▶ Which food chain's first restaurant opened in San Bernardino in California in 1948?

> **A** MCDONALD'S **B** KENTUCKY FRIED CHICKEN **C** PIZZA HUT

6/2 ▶ Which of these countries does NOT have territory on the island of Borneo?

> **A** INDONESIA **B** MALAYSIA **C** PHILIPPINES

6/3 ▶ Which British singer won four MOBO awards in 2014?

> **A** SAM SMITH **B** ED SHEERAN **C** CALVIN HARRIS

6/4 ▶ In the board game Operation, what is removed from the throat?

> **A** TOAD **B** FROG **C** NEWT

6/5 ▶ In 1960 which American pilot was captured when his U-2 spy plane was shot down over Russia?

> **A** JUDD BRAWNY **B** HAL STRONG **C** GARY POWERS

6/6 ▶ Who was the first England footballer to be sent off at the World Cup?

> **A** DAVID BECKHAM **B** PAUL INCE **C** RAY WILKINS

6/7 ▶ Which of these materials is NOT made from plant fibre?

> **A** SILK **B** FLANNELETTE **C** LINEN

The Barrister Quiz 6: Contestant 2

Answer at least 5 questions correctly to progress on to the Final Chase.

6/1 ▶ By population, which capital city is the largest metropolitan area in the western hemisphere?

> **A** BUENOS AIRES **B** HAVANA **C** MEXICO CITY

6/2 ▶ What name was given to the last pitched battle to be fought between the kingdoms of England and Scotland?

> **A** BROWNIE **B** GREENIE **C** PINKIE

6/3 ▶ A person with no hair is sometimes said to be 'as bald as...' what bird?

> **A** COOT **B** CRANE **C** CUCKOO

6/4 ▶ Lines by which poet appear above the players' entrance to Centre Court at Wimbledon?

> **A** RUDYARD KIPLING **B** WILFRED OWEN **C** WILLIAM WORDSWORTH

6/5 ▶ Which of these is NOT a transition element?

> **A** TITANIUM **B** IRON **C** CARBON

6/6 ▶ Which of these geographical lines is the longest?

> **A** ANTARCTIC CIRCLE **B** TROPIC OF CANCER **C** EQUATOR

6/7 ▶ The title of the Soviet Communist newspaper *Pravda* means what in Russian?

> **A** TRUTH **B** PROPAGANDA **C** REVOLUTION

The Barrister Quiz 6: Contestant 3

Answer at least 5 questions correctly to progress on to the Final Chase.

6/1 ▶ The longest-known family tree in the world, descendants of the philosopher Confucius have what family name?

> **A** KONG **B** FU **C** SHI

6/2 ▶ The Devil and the Greek god Pan are both depicted with cloven what?

> **A** HOOVES **B** TAILS **C** HORNS

6/3 ▶ Which boxer's fight with Muhammad Ali is the subject of the documentary *When We Were Kings*?

> **A** GEORGE FOREMAN **B** JOE FRAZIER **C** SONNY LISTON

6/4 ▶ In the classic TV sitcom *Porridge*, how long was Fletcher's sentence?

> **A** THREE YEARS **B** FIVE YEARS **C** SEVEN YEARS

6/5 ▶ John Merrick is the Victorian title character of which play by Bernard Pomerance?

> **A** *THE BEST MAN* **B** *THE MUSIC MAN* **C** *THE ELEPHANT MAN*

6/6 ▶ What name was given to the clouds of thin aluminium strips dropped by bomber planes to confuse radar signals?

> **A** CHIFF **B** CHAFF **C** CHUFF

6/7 ▶ Which British pop star played Mia in the 2015 film *Fifty Shades of Grey*?

> **A** RITA ORA **B** JESSIE J **C** PIXIE LOTT

The Barrister Quiz 6: Contestant 4

Answer at least 5 questions correctly to progress on to the Final Chase.

6/1 ▶ Which of these colours does NOT feature on a traditional Rubik's Cube?

> **A** PURPLE **B** WHITE **C** YELLOW

6/2 ▶ The future Edward VII was heir to the throne for almost how many years?

> **A** 40 YEARS **B** 50 YEARS **C** 60 YEARS

6/3 ▶ Which musical opened in London's West End one day after the abolition of theatrical censorship?

> **A** *HAIR* **B** *OH! CALCUTTA!* **C** *THE ROCKY HORROR SHOW*

6/4 ▶ What drink is repeatedly mentioned in the lyrics to the Bernard Cribbins hit 'Right Said Fred'?

> **A** CUP OF COFFEE **B** CUP OF COCOA **C** CUP OF TEA

6/5 ▶ What is the only South American country to have had a winner of golf's Open Championship?

> **A** ARGENTINA **B** PERU **C** VENEZUELA

6/6 ▶ The so-called '4 Ps' of marketing are 'Product, Price, Place and...' what?

> **A** POSITIONING **B** PEOPLE **C** PROMOTION

6/7 ▶ In heraldry, what name is given to the surface of the shield?

> **A** FIELD **B** YIELD **C** WIELD

The Barrister Quiz 6: Final Chase

★ Prize fund in the Final Chase was £35,000

★ Your target is 19 correct

Three contestants made it to this Final Chase. Racking up a creditable score of 19 with Brian, a 34-year-old wedding photographer, just nicking the top scorer honours ahead of David, a 40-year-old football trader. In the end, The Barrister was soundly beaten, having conceded 10 push backs, of which the contestants won 4.

6/1 ▶ Dovedale is a blue-veined variety of what dairy product?

6/2 ▶ In 2001, Zinedine Zidane joined what Spanish football club?

6/3 ▶ 'Warriors of Rock' is a version of what music video game?

6/4 ▶ Which religious figure rode a white horse called Kanthaka?

6/5 ▶ The George Cross medal appears on what country's flag?

6/6 ▶ Which French shoe designer created the 'So Kate' pumps?

6/7 ▶ Who sang lead vocals on the Number One hit 'Sunday Girl'?

6/8 ▶ In 2014, Haider al-Abadi became what country's Prime Minister?

6/9 ▶ What nationality was the writer Cyrano de Bergerac?

THE BARRISTER

6/10 ▷ The brachial artery is in what part of the body?

6/11 ▷ What William Styron novel features a refugee called Sophie?

6/12 ▷ Karl Howman played Buster Briggs in what TV soap?

6/13 ▷ How many crowned Tudor monarchs were women?

6/14 ▷ What colour is the resin known as dragon's blood?

6/15 ▷ Which of the 12 disciples comes first alphabetically?

6/16 ▷ 'Boss Bottled' is a fragrance by which German fashion house?

6/17 ▷ Dame Vera Lynn was born during what World War?

6/18 ▷ Cupid is a moon of what planet?

6/19 ▷ 'VF Agenda' is an online blog run by what American magazine?

6/20 ▷ What species is the largest of South America's big cats?

6/21 ▷ What date is New Year's Eve?

6/22 ▷ 'Gethsemane' is a song in what Andrew Lloyd Webber musical?

6/23 ▷ Which queen described Balmoral as 'this dear paradise'?

6/24 ▷ Who is Prince Andrew's younger brother?

The Barrister Quiz 7: Contestant 1

Answer at least 5 questions correctly to progress on to the Final Chase.

7/1 ▶ Which Frank Sinatra hit includes the lyrics 'If I can make it there, I'll make it anywhere'?

> **A** 'FLY ME TO THE MOON' **B** 'NEW YORK, NEW YORK' **C** 'STRANGERS IN THE NIGHT'

7/2 ▶ Which of these books was published most recently?

> **A** *THE REMAINS OF THE DAY* **B** *DEATH IN THE AFTERNOON* **C** *TENDER IS THE NIGHT*

7/3 ▶ 'Oscitation' is the act of doing what?

> **A** YELLING **B** YAWNING **C** YODELLING

7/4 ▶ A 'hacking jacket' is tailored to be worn for what activity?

> **A** RIDING **B** FELL-WALKING **C** SKIING

7/5 ▶ Who played opposite Rock Hudson in the TV series *McMillan & Wife*?

> **A** SUSAN SAINT JAMES **B** JILL ST JOHN **C** PAM ST CLEMENT

7/6 ▶ Which European people are known in their own language as the 'Euskaldunak'?

> **A** MALTESE **B** ALBANIANS **C** BASQUES

7/7 ▶ During the 2015 election campaign, David Cameron claimed he was related to which reality TV star?

> **A** KIM KARDASHIAN **B** MILLIE MACKINTOSH **C** OZZY OSBOURNE

The Barrister Quiz 7: Contestant 2

Answer at least 5 questions correctly to progress on to the Final Chase.

7/1 ▶ In the Bible, Benjamin was the youngest of whose twelve sons?

> **A** JACOB **B** JEREMIAH **C** JOB

7/2 ▶ 'Left Outside Alone' and 'Sick and Tired' were hits for which singer?

> **A** SHAKIRA **B** ANASTACIA **C** KESHA

7/3 ▶ The book *Fantastic Beasts and Where to Find Them* is a spin-off from what franchise?

> **A** HARRY POTTER **B** TWILIGHT **C** THE HUNGER GAMES

7/4 ▶ Who is the only British actress to have won Oscars in both acting categories?

> **A** HELEN MIRREN **B** JUDI DENCH **C** MAGGIE SMITH

7/5 ▶ Which of these American cities is NOT a state capital?

> **A** TUCSON **B** JACKSON **C** MADISON

7/6 ▶ In a French restaurant, what will you get if you order '*fruits de mer*'?

> **A** BERRIES **B** RIBS **C** SHELLFISH

7/7 ▶ What is supermodel Elle Macpherson's full first name?

> **A** ELEANOR **B** GABRIELLE **C** ELOISE

The Barrister Quiz 7: Contestant 3

Answer at least 5 questions correctly to progress on to the Final Chase.

7/1 ▶ Former military dictator Muhammadu Buhari was democratically elected as the new President of what country in 2015?

> **A** NIGERIA **B** SENEGAL **C** GHANA

7/2 ▶ What title is shared by hits for Radiohead and TLC?

> **A** 'CRAWL' **B** 'CROUCH' **C** 'CREEP'

7/3 ▶ What is the alternative name for the puffin?

> **A** SEA PARROT **B** SEA PEACOCK **C** SEA PIGEON

7/4 ▶ Which actress voiced Shira the smilodon in the film *Ice Age: Continental Drift*?

> **A** JENNIFER CONNELLY **B** JENNIFER GARNER **C** JENNIFER LOPEZ

7/5 ▶ Which of these countries is NOT landlocked?

> **A** ANDORRA **B** LUXEMBOURG **C** MONACO

7/6 ▶ The Battle of Agincourt was fought on which saint's day?

> **A** ST GEORGE **B** ST CRISPIN **C** ST DENIS

7/7 ▶ In Greek myth, Prometheus gave fire to mortals after stealing it from where?

> **A** HADES **B** MOUNT ETNA **C** OLYMPUS

The Barrister Quiz 7: Contestant 4

Answer at least 5 questions correctly to progress on to the Final Chase.

7/1 ▶ Which footballer scored 79 seconds into his England debut against Lithuania in 2015?

> **A** HARRY KANE **B** ANDROS TOWNSEND **C** ROSS BARKLEY

7/2 ▶ Which of these songs was a UK hit first?

> **A** 'BIG YELLOW TAXI' **B** 'PINK CADILLAC' **C** 'LITTLE RED CORVETTE'

7/3 ▶ What cut of veal is used in the Italian dish osso buco?

> **A** SHOULDER **B** RIBS **C** SHIN

7/4 ▶ What personal pronoun can be typed using adjacent keys on a keyboard?

> **A** HE **B** ME **C** WE

7/5 ▶ Which of these is an American supermarket chain founded in 1916?

> **A** HENNY PENNY **B** FOXY LOXY **C** PIGGLY WIGGLY

7/6 ▶ On a children's TV show, how were Brains, Billie, Sticks, Scooper, Spring, Tiger and Doughnut collectively known?

> **A** THE DOUBLE DECKERS **B** PRESS GANG **C** S CLUB 7

7/7 ▶ Which of these orchestral instruments can produce the loudest noise?

> **A** TROMBONE **B** BASSOON **C** VIOLA

The Barrister Quiz 7: Final Chase

★ Prize fund in the Final Chase was £35,000

★ Your target is 19 correct

In this programme 4 players won a place in the final. They answered 15 questions correctly, giving them a total of 19 steps for the Chaser to pursue. Lacksley, a 54-year-old IT security advisor from Bedfordshire was the team's top scorer. Executing 5 out of 5 push back opportunity, the team thwarted The Barrister.

7/1 ▶ The four gospels appear in what religious work?

7/2 ▶ Who starred as Brian Flanagan in the 1980s film *Cocktail*?

7/3 ▶ What type of creature is a Greater Pewee?

7/4 ▶ What team did Brazil beat in the 1958 FIFA World Cup Final?

7/5 ▶ What shape are the coloured segments on a chequered flag?

7/6 ▶ Which biscuit brand makes Boasters?

7/7 ▶ How was the Australian TV drama *Prisoner* known in the UK?

7/8 ▶ Which Egyptian queen was the Great Wife of Amenhotep the Fourth?

7/9 ▶ What's the most populous city in Hungary?

THE BARRISTER

7/10 ▷ In what decade was the Liberal Democrat party founded?

7/11 ▷ Someone with FRCVS after their name has what job?

7/12 ▷ Which Greek sea god was the father of Orion?

7/13 ▷ Peter Tork was the oldest member of which 1960s pop group?

7/14 ▷ The cerebral fissure is a groove in what human organ?

7/15 ▷ Stephen Guest courts Lucy Deane in what George Eliot novel?

7/16 ▷ St Nicholas is famously associated with what festival?

7/17 ▷ Who did Sean Connery play in the film *Never Say Never Again*?

7/18 ▷ What Belgian football team has won the most national titles?

7/19 ▷ If it's four o'clock in London, what time is it in Frankfurt?

7/20 ▷ What 1970s sitcom featured transport inspector Cyril Blake?

7/21 ▷ What four letters represent the New York Police Force?

7/22 ▷ Which is the largest of the big cats in the wild?

The Barrister Quiz 8: Contestant 1

Answer at least 5 questions correctly to progress on to the Final Chase.

8/1 ▶ Coloured black, what was the value of the first adhesive postage stamp issued in 1840?

> **A** ONE PENNY **B** SIXPENCE **C** ONE SHILLING

8/2 ▶ In TV, Jim Phelps was a leader of what group?

> **A** CTU **B** IMF **C** MIB

8/3 ▶ Which of these birds is the smallest?

> **A** NIGHTINGALE **B** CHAFFINCH **C** WREN

8/4 ▶ What weekly music show from Nashville claims to be 'The Show That Made Country Music Famous'?

> **A** *GRAND OLE MILL* **B** *GRAND OLE OPRY* **C** *GRAND OLE BARN*

8/5 ▶ What name was given to the revolution that resulted in King James II being deposed?

> **A** GLORIOUS REVOLUTION **B** MARVELLOUS REVOLUTION **C** WONDROUS REVOLUTION

8/6 ▶ Founded in the Netherlands, the sport of 'korfball' has a name meaning what?

> **A** HAND BALL **B** DODGE BALL **C** BASKET BALL

8/7 ▶ In the film *Monsters, Inc.*, Celia the receptionist has hair made from what?

> **A** BATS **B** HEDGEHOGS **C** SNAKES

THE BARRISTER

The Barrister Quiz 8: Contestant 2

Answer at least 5 questions correctly to progress on to the Final Chase.

8/1 ▶ Which *EastEnders* character has been played by six different actors?

> **A** BEN MITCHELL **B** LIAM BUTCHER **C** PETER BEALE

8/2 ▶ In 1941, art collector Peggy Guggenheim married which surrealist?

> **A** ANDRÉ BRETON **B** MAX ERNST **C** RENÉ MAGRITTE

8/3 ▶ The Bank of England £20 note used in the 1970s and 1980s featured Shakespeare and a scene from which of his plays?

> **A** *ROMEO AND JULIET* **B** *THE TEMPEST* **C** *HAMLET*

8/4 ▶ Which actress said in a film 'Between two evils, I always pick the one I never tried before'?

> **A** ELIZABETH TAYLOR **B** KATHARINE HEPBURN **C** MAE WEST

8/5 ▶ The point in the Pacific Ocean furthest from land is named after which fictional character?

> **A** HORATIO HORNBLOWER **B** CAPTAIN NEMO **C** LONG JOHN SILVER

8/6 ▶ The episode titles of the third series of which sitcom parodied the works of Jane Austen?

> **A** *BLACKADDER* **B** *DAD'S ARMY* **C** *GOODNIGHT SWEETHEART*

8/7 ▶ As part of their 'Message for Mars' project, NASA invited members of the public to submit poems in what form?

> **A** LIMERICK **B** HAIKU **C** SONNET

The Barrister Quiz 8: Contestant 3

Answer at least 5 questions correctly to progress on to the Final Chase.

8/1 ▶ King Henry I was part of what royal house?

> **A** NORMANDY **B** WESSEX **C** PLANTAGENET

8/2 ▶ Abibliophobia is the fear of running out of what?

> **A** THINGS TO DRINK **B** THINGS TO READ **C** THINGS TO THINK

8/3 ▶ Which of these is NOT a US state capital?

> **A** COLUMBIA **B** COLUMBUS **C** COLUMBO

8/4 ▶ Which of these famous plays was staged the earliest?

> **A** *ABIGAIL'S PARTY* **B** *THE BIRTHDAY PARTY* **C** *THE COCKTAIL PARTY*

8/5 ▶ Caddies work at which of these sporting venues?

> **A** ANFIELD **B** SOLDIER FIELD **C** MUIRFIELD

8/6 ▶ The actor who played Doug Willis in *Neighbours* is the real-life father of which other star of the show?

> **A** KYLIE MINOGUE **B** NATALIE IMBRUGLIA **C** JASON DONOVAN

8/7 ▶ What animals are Aimless and Graceless in the novel *Cold Comfort Farm*?

> **A** COWS **B** PIGS **C** HORSES

The Barrister Quiz 8: Contestant 4

Answer at least 5 questions correctly to progress on to the Final Chase.

8/1 ▶ The sou was a low-value coin in what European country?

> **A** DENMARK **B** FRANCE **C** PORTUGAL

8/2 ▶ Who said 'I have not become the King's First Minister in order to preside over the liquidation of the British Empire'?

> **A** ANTHONY EDEN **B** WINSTON CHURCHILL **C** ALEC DOUGLAS-HOME

8/3 ▶ Which of these island groups is also the name of a shipping forecast area?

> **A** HEBRIDES **B** ORKNEY **C** SHETLAND

8/4 ▶ In a 1997 disaster film, what threatens the community of *Dante's Peak*?

> **A** TIDAL WAVE **B** EARTHQUAKE **C** VOLCANO

8/5 ▶ What word refers to a style of sandal and a small burger?

> **A** SLIDER **B** DRIFTER **C** SKIDDER

8/6 ▶ Which of these comedy stars was NOT born in Britain?

> **A** BOB HOPE **B** STAN LAUREL **C** MIKE MYERS

8/7 ▶ In 2014, India successfully put its first satellite into orbit around which planet?

> **A** MARS **B** JUPITER **C** NEPTUNE

The Barrister Quiz 8: Final Chase

⭐ Prize fund in the Final Chase was £35,000

⭐ Your target is 19 correct

Three contestants made it through to the Final Chase. After a slow start with a few wrong answers, the team recovered to notch up a strong score of 17. Ian, a 53-year-old oil rig facilities manager from Glenrothes was their top scorer. Four successful push backs secured their win against The Barrister.

8/1 ▶ Putting usually takes place on what part of a golf course?

8/2 ▶ On what continent do ospreys usually spend winter?

8/3 ▶ Nigel Hawthorne played a Hanoverian king in what film?

8/4 ▶ 'Overload' was the 2000 debut single by what girl group?

8/5 ▶ How many Hindu gods form the Trimurti?

8/6 ▶ The sea otter is mainly found in what ocean?

8/7 ▶ Short fine leg is a fielding position in what sport?

8/8 ▶ In what decade did 'Kaiser Bill' die?

8/9 ▶ What imperial measurement is equal to roughly 28 grams?

8/10 ▶ What large cut of beef shares its name with a peerage rank?

THE BARRISTER

8/11 ▶ Yemen has a border with Saudi Arabia and what other country?

8/12 ▶ HBS is the business school of what US university?

8/13 ▶ The original Roman 'Calendar of Romulus' had how many months?

8/14 ▶ In what sport did Kenny Logan play for Scotland?

8/15 ▶ Ian Holm played the android Ash in what 1970s sci-fi film?

8/16 ▶ Aligoté is a white wine variety of what fruit?

8/17 ▶ What type of creature is a tree-creeper?

8/18 ▶ In what modern-day country did Captain Cook die?

8/19 ▶ The adult human body normally has 206 what?

8/20 ▶ Who played Fontaine Khaled in the film *The Stud*?

8/21 ▶ The word 'virtuoso' comes from what language?

8/22 ▶ The Sydney Harbour Bridge is in what Australian state?

8/23 ▶ Henry the Eighth's sister Mary was queen of what country?

8/24 ▶ Which number is 'two little ducks' in bingo?

8/25 ▶ What nationality is singer-songwriter Leonard Cohen?

The Barrister Quiz 9: Contestant 1

Answer at least 5 questions correctly to progress on to the Final Chase.

9/1 ▶ The phrase expressing opposition to excessive political correctness is 'It's PC gone...' what?

A MAD B FISHIN' C WALKABOUT

9/2 ▶ The writers Laurence Marks and Maurice Gran are best known for what type of TV programme?

A DOCUMENTARIES B MURDER MYSTERIES C SITCOMS

9/3 ▶ Which of these Oscar-winning actors has also won a Broadway Tony award?

A EDDIE REDMAYNE B FOREST WHITAKER C GEORGE CLOONEY

9/4 ▶ In the 16th century, a workhouse that used hard labour as a punishment for criminals was called a 'House of...' what?

A REFORMATION B CORRECTION C IMPROVEMENT

9/5 ▶ Which of these mountains is NOT one of the so-called 'Seven Summits'?

A ELBRUS B DENALI C FUJI

9/6 ▶ In 2014, which British women's athletics record was broken twice in eleven days?

A 100M HURDLES B HIGH JUMP C 4 X 100M RELAY

9/7 ▶ What name is given to a puppet operated by rods and strings?

A MARIONETTE B MARTINET C MAJORETTE

The Barrister Quiz 9: Contestant 2

Answer at least 5 questions correctly to progress on to the Final Chase.

9/1 ▶ Which of these works of art was completed first?

> **A** *GUERNICA* **B** *THE LAUGHING CAVALIER* **C** *WHISTLER'S MOTHER*

9/2 ▶ What unit of electric potential is equivalent to one joule per coulomb?

> **A** AMP **B** VOLT **C** WATT

9/3 ▶ Which comedian has a routine in which she plays a beret-wearing girl looking for her friend Kimberley?

> **A** JO BRAND **B** LUCY PORTER **C** VICTORIA WOOD

9/4 ▶ The African capitals Brazzaville and Kinshasa are on opposite banks of what river?

> **A** CONGO **B** NILE **C** ZAMBEZI

9/5 ▶ Which of these English kings has NOT been accused of murdering one or more of his nephews?

> **A** JOHN **B** RICHARD III **C** HENRY VIII

9/6 ▶ What kind of entertainer is sometimes called a 'hoofer'?

> **A** MIME ARTIST **B** DANCER **C** PANTOMIME HORSE

9/7 ▶ How does a sufferer of 'macropsia' often perceive objects in relation to their actual appearance?

> **A** LARGER **B** BRIGHTER **C** SMALLER

The Barrister Quiz 9: Contestant 3

Answer at least 5 questions correctly to progress on to the Final Chase.

9/1 ▶ The Gatling gun was first used during which conflict?

> **A** AMERICAN CIVIL WAR **B** ZULU WAR **C** WORLD WAR

9/2 ▶ Which of these Disney characters does NOT wear shorts?

> **A** PINOCCHIO **B** MICKEY MOUSE **C** DONALD DUCK

9/3 ▶ The cathedrals of both Lichfield and Truro have how many spires?

> **A** ONE **B** TWO **C** THREE

9/4 ▶ The Irish Guards wear what colour plume in their bearskins?

> **A** RED **B** BLUE **C** PURPLE

9/5 ▶ According to the saying, 'necessity is the mother of...' what?

> **A** RATIONING **B** INVENTION **C** THEFT

9/6 ▶ Cole Porter's last Broadway musical, an adaptation of the 1939 film *Ninotchka*, was entitled *Silk... what?

> **A** *STOCKINGS* **B** *PYJAMAS* **C** *TIE*

9/7 ▶ Which bridge was made a UNESCO World Heritage site in 2015?

> **A** TOWER BRIDGE **B** FORTH BRIDGE **C** TYNE BRIDGE

The Barrister Quiz 9: Contestant 4

Answer at least 5 questions correctly to progress on to the Final Chase.

9/1 ▶ In horse racing, which group of people are known as layers?

> **A** BOOKMAKERS **B** JOCKEYS **C** STEWARDS

9/2 ▶ Which artist wrote 'I am the first to be surprised and often terrified by the images I see appear upon my canvas'?

> **A** SALVADOR DALÍ **B** FRANCISCO DE GOYA **C** PABLO PICASSO

9/3 ▶ Which of these words means 'friend' in Swahili?

> **A** SIMBA **B** PUMBAA **C** RAFIKI

9/4 ▶ What is the subject of the TV programme *Who Do You Think You Are?*?

> **A** GEOGRAPHY **B** GEOLOGY **C** GENEALOGY

9/5 ▶ Of the six species of deer in the UK, only two are classified as native – roe and which other?

> **A** SIKA **B** MUNTJAC **C** RED

9/6 ▶ Which of these authors has NOT written a Booker Prize-winning novel with the word 'Tiger' in the title?

> **A** ARAVIND ADIGA **B** PENELOPE LIVELY **C** YANN MARTEL

9/7 ▶ The conflict over what to call Czechoslovakia after the fall of Communism was given what humorous nickname?

> **A** COMMA WAR **B** HYPHEN WAR **C** FORWARD SLASH WAR

The Barrister Quiz 9: Final Chase

⭐ Prize fund in the Final Chase was £35,000

⭐ Your target is 19 correct

Three contestants in the team for the final achieved a score of 16, heralding a close finish. The team's highest scorer was Nick, a 63-year-old company director from Hampshire. The pursuit from The Barrister, was nailbiting, with 3 executed push backs enabling the team to notch up a win.

9/1 ▶ The TV show known as *BGT* is *Britain's Got...* what?

9/2 ▶ How many bails are needed in total for a game of cricket?

9/3 ▶ What's the title of Arnold Schwarzenegger's 2015 zombie film?

9/4 ▶ Which contemporary of Shakespeare wrote *The Alchemist*?

9/5 ▶ What aromatic herb flavours an American 'julep' cocktail?

9/6 ▶ The Matterhorn was first conquered in what century?

9/7 ▶ Cromarty shipping forecast area is in what sea?

9/8 ▶ Which Beatle was taught the sitar by Ravi Shankar?

9/9 ▶ 'Stroller' is the American word for what type of chair?

THE BARRISTER

9/10 ▶ Ménière's syndrome affects the inner part of what organs?

9/11 ▶ Which Nobel Prize-winner acted under the name David Baron?

9/12 ▶ Who is the youngest child of Victoria and David Beckham?

9/13 ▶ The Slaughter Stone forms part of what Wiltshire monument?

9/14 ▶ Water is the oxide of what element?

9/15 ▶ Cosimo the Elder was a member of what Florentine family?

9/16 ▶ In a personal ads column what is 'ads' short for?

9/17 ▶ How is Arthur Fonzarelli in TV's *Happy Days* better known?

9/18 ▶ What Bowie song features 'Sailors fighting in the dance hall'?

9/19 ▶ Isis was a major goddess in what mythology?

9/20 ▶ What nationality is TV chef Richard Corrigan?

9/21 ▶ What colour lends its name to a UK political party?

9/22 ▶ Litigation is the process of taking what type of action?

9/23 ▶ The Dnieper River empties into what sea?

The Barrister Quiz 10: Contestant 1

Answer at least 5 questions correctly to progress on to the Final Chase.

10/1 ▶ Which of these was NOT a chart-topping group of the 1960s?

> A THE HUNTERS B THE SEARCHERS C THE SEEKERS

10/2 ▶ Alexandra of Denmark was the mother of which king?

> A HENRY V B EDWARD V C GEORGE V

10/3 ▶ 'I'm a writer, but then nobody's perfect' is inscribed on which Hollywood director's grave?

> A BILLY WILDER B ALFRED HITCHCOCK C DAVID LEAN

10/4 ▶ In the human body, synapses can be found between two of what type of cells?

> A NERVE CELLS B RED BLOOD CELLS C EPITHELIAL CELLS

10/5 ▶ What cycling event involves teams of two trying to gain laps on other pairs?

> A CLEVELAND B POLK C MADISON

10/6 ▶ In 2015, the town of Bridlington announced plans to twin with what fictional location?

> A LILLIPUT B HOGSMEADE C WALMINGTON-ON-SEA

10/7 ▶ James Ivory directed three films based on the novels of which British author?

> A E M FORSTER B G K CHESTERTON C E L JAMES

The Barrister Quiz 10: Contestant 2

Answer at least 5 questions correctly to progress on to the Final Chase.

10/1 ▶ What does the word 'ventriloquism' literally mean?

> **A** WORD-SENDING **B** VOICE-THROWING **C** STOMACH-SPEAKING

10/2 ▶ Which of these actors was born in the USA?

> **A** DOLPH LUNDGREN **B** MICHAEL FASSBENDER **C** VIGGO MORTENSEN

10/3 ▶ Large stores where businesses can buy in bulk at lower than normal prices are called what?

> **A** PAY AND PACK **B** TENDER AND TAKE **C** CASH AND CARRY

10/4 ▶ Sir Reginald Sheffield is the father-in-law of which famous politician?

> **A** BORIS JOHNSON **B** GEORGE OSBORNE **C** DAVID CAMERON

10/5 ▶ Which of these is NOT a pilgrim in Chaucer's *Canterbury Tales*?

> **A** THE MERCER **B** THE MILLER **C** THE MONK

10/6 ▶ What connects former athletics world record-holders Seb Coe and Chris Chataway?

> **A** BECAME MPS **B** MARRIED TWO SISTERS **C** WON *CELEBRITY BIG BROTHER*

10/7 ▶ The equites formed what part of a Roman army?

> **A** ARTILLERY **B** INFANTRY **C** CAVALRY

The Barrister Quiz 10: Contestant 3

Answer at least 5 questions correctly to progress on to the Final Chase.

10/1 ▶ *Do You Want the Truth or Something Beautiful?* was the debut album of which singer?

> **A** DIDO **B** PIXIE LOTT **C** PALOMA FAITH

10/2 ▶ The ash tree has a fruit with a single wing called what?

> **A** LOCK **B** BARREL **C** KEY

10/3 ▶ Which iconic fashion designer was known for the saying 'luxury must be comfortable, otherwise it is not luxury'?

> **A** COCO CHANEL **B** YVES SAINT LAURENT **C** PACO RABANNE

10/4 ▶ Which favourite of Elizabeth I was executed in 1601 after attempting to depose her?

> **A** ROBERT DEVEREUX **B** WALTER RALEIGH **C** PHILIP SIDNEY

10/5 ▶ In art, a sculpture with a design protruding from the plane surface is called what?

> **A** CURE **B** EASE **C** RELIEF

10/6 ▶ Anthony Hopkins won his *The Silence of the Lambs* Oscar for a performance of approximately how many minutes on screen?

> **A** 8 **B** 16 **C** 64

10/7 ▶ Which company manufactures the F-35, the first 'stealth fighter' to be used by the Royal Air Force?

> **A** NORTHROP **B** BOEING **C** LOCKHEED MARTIN

THE BARRISTER QUIZ 10: Contestant 3

The Barrister Quiz 10: Contestant 4

Answer at least 5 questions correctly to progress on to the Final Chase.

10/1 ▶ In horse racing, how much will your stake be if you make a bet of £5 each-way?

A £2.50 B £5 C £10

10/2 ▶ Axilla is the anatomical name for what part of the body?

A ARMPIT B HEEL C EAR

10/3 ▶ Which of these 19th-century scientists discovered six elements of the periodic table?

A MICHAEL FARADAY B CHARLES BABBAGE C HUMPHRY DAVY

10/4 ▶ What national newspaper took the motto 'Was, is and will be'?

A *DAILY EXPRESS* B *THE DAILY TELEGRAPH* C *DAILY MAIL*

10/5 ▶ Which of these appears on the periodic table of elements?

A PEWTER B QUARTZ C RADON

10/6 ▶ What is Marge Simpson's full first name?

A MARGOT B MARJORIE C MARTHA

10/7 ▶ In 2014, George Ezra's first Top Ten hit shares its name with what capital city?

A BELGRADE B BRUSSELS C BUDAPEST

The Barrister Quiz 10: Final Chase

★ Prize fund in the Final Chase was £35,000

★ Your target is 19 correct

In this programme 3 contestants made it through to the final. All three made valuable contributions to the team's score of 16. The Barrister got off to a flying start but was eventually thwarted in his pursuit by 5 successful push backs from the team.

10/1 ▶ What human rights organisation is known by the initials AI?

10/2 ▶ How many pins are in the front row of a ten-pin bowling triangle?

10/3 ▶ Which Victorian author wrote *The Great Winglebury Duel*?

10/4 ▶ An LED is a diode that emits what?

10/5 ▶ The Dorfman Theatre is part of what London South Bank venue?

10/6 ▶ Martin Bormann was secretary to which German leader?

10/7 ▶ Which apostle was known in Aramaic as 'Cephas'?

10/8 ▶ What part of a pair of sunglasses can be mirrored or polarised?

10/9 ▶ What officer is in charge of a polling station during elections?

THE BARRISTER

10/10 ▷ Crowdie is a soft Scottish variety of what food?

10/11 ▷ In sport, a 'trampette' is a small what?

10/12 ▷ Harajuku is a district in what Asian capital city?

10/13 ▷ How many inches are there in a foot and a half?

10/14 ▷ Which Victorian Prime Minister was nicknamed Pam?

10/15 ▷ The 'Fab' in the Beatles nickname 'Fab Four' is short for what?

10/16 ▷ St Margaret's Church is in the grounds of what London abbey?

10/17 ▷ 'I Feel Good' is the subtitle of what James Brown hit?

10/18 ▷ What type of snack are 'Space Raiders'?

10/19 ▷ In what TV sci-fi show has Alex Kingston played River Song?

10/20 ▷ If you begin something, you are said to start what rolling?

The
BEAST

The Beast

The Beast. What other name could be given to Mark Labbett, *The Chase's* physical and intellectual colossus? His towering presence – he is 6 foot 6 inches tall – and unflinching determination to win make him a fearsome opponent. He has said, 'Ego and pride are the whips that drive me' and the players who encounter this Chaser need to match that commitment to win. A man of few words, he never wastes time on idle banter, preferring to embark on the Chase without delay.

His accolades include having achieved the highest score set by an individual in the Final Chase but not won (23), and jointly (with Anne) holding the record for the highest scores caught in the Final Chase (26).

But even The Beast is not invincible, and Mark has conceded the highest number of push backs by a team in the Final Chase – his opponents executed 8 out of 9 opportunities. Yet in defeat The Beast is magnanimous. He has said, 'Sometimes you've got to take your whopping like a man' – and he does.

The Beast Quiz 1: Contestant 1

Answer at least 5 questions correctly to progress on to the Final Chase.

1/1 ▶ Which comedian published the 2006 autobiography *Me: Moir – Volume One*?

> **A** EDDIE IZZARD **B** PETER KAY **C** VIC REEVES

1/2 ▶ Crocodiles are found in the wild on every continent apart from Antarctica and where else?

> **A** ASIA **B** EUROPE **C** SOUTH AMERICA

1/3 ▶ A 'Kamikaze' cocktail consists of triple sec, lime juice and which spirit?

> **A** BRANDY **B** GIN **C** VODKA

1/4 ▶ Which of these films did NOT star Bill Murray?

> **A** *GHOSTBUSTERS* **B** *GOOD WILL HUNTING* **C** *GROUNDHOG DAY*

1/5 ▶ In computing, four bits are called a what?

> **A** CRUMB **B** NIBBLE **C** TIDBIT

1/6 ▶ Which of these classic horse races is run over the longest distance?

> **A** THE DERBY **B** 1,000 GUINEAS **C** ST LEGER

1/7 ▶The Stetson company predominantly makes what style of hat?

> **A** COWBOY **B** BOWLER **C** PORK-PIE

The Beast Quiz 1: Contestant 2

Answer at least 5 questions correctly to progress on to the Final Chase.

1/1 ▶ Which of these schools is the oldest?

> A ETON B HARROW C RUGBY

1/2 ▶ In the title of the traditional song, who or what is 'The Irish Rover'?

> A A SOLDIER B A SHIP C A DOG

1/3 ▶ In 1990, which athlete set the British record for the men's 400-metre hurdles?

> A KRISS AKABUSI B LINFORD CHRISTIE C COLIN JACKSON

1/4 ▶ Who is the only Osmond to have had a solo Number One single on the US *Billboard* Hot 100 chart?

> A DONNY B JIMMY C MARIE

1/5 ▶ Which Renaissance artist designed the tapestries for the walls of the Sistine Chapel?

> A RAPHAEL B DONATELLO C TITIAN

1/6 ▶ What's the correct name for a portion of a circle's circumference?

> A ARCH B BOW C ARC

1/7 ▶ In August 2014, three of the cast members of which US sitcom secured deals for $1 million each per episode?

> A *THE BIG BANG THEORY* B *NEW GIRL* C *HOW I MET YOUR MOTHER*

The Beast Quiz 1: Contestant 3

Answer at least 5 questions correctly to progress on to the Final Chase.

1/1 ▶ What collective noun is used to describe a group of moles?

A LABOUR B SLOG C TOIL

1/2 ▶ Which of these acts did NOT win the Eurovision Song Contest?

A SANDIE SHAW B LULU C CILLA BLACK

1/3 ▶ 30 kilometres north of Paris there is a theme park dedicated to which cartoon character?

A ASTERIX B PAPA SMURF C TINTIN

1/4 ▶ Which of these British foods is the subject of a museum in Mexico?

A CORNISH PASTY B LANCASHIRE HOTPOT C YORKSHIRE PUDDING

1/5 ▶ What major league American sport is played over four scheduled periods of 12 minutes each?

A ICE HOCKEY B BASEBALL C BASKETBALL

1/6 ▶ Which of these Hollywood legends did NOT win a Best Director Oscar?

A ALFRED HITCHCOCK B FRANK CAPRA C JOHN HUSTON

1/7 ▶ Which of these weights is equal to a quintal?

A 5 POUNDS B 100 POUNDS C 500 POUNDS

The Beast Quiz 1: Contestant 4

Answer at least 5 questions correctly to progress on to the Final Chase.

1/1 ▶ Who caused controversy by calling the £250,000 he earned for writing a column in *The Daily Telegraph* 'chicken feed'?

> **A** MICHAEL GOVE **B** BORIS JOHNSON **C** WILLIAM HAGUE

1/2 ▶ The adjective 'auroral' refers to what time of day?

> **A** DAWN **B** MIDDAY **C** DUSK

1/3 ▶ Who was the only Brontë sister to marry?

> **A** ANNE **B** EMILY **C** CHARLOTTE

1/4 ▶ What is the name of the animation technique used in the *Wallace and Gromit* films?

> **A** E MOTION **B** LOCO MOTION **C** STOP MOTION

1/5 ▶ Which of these wedding anniversaries comes last?

> **A** CORAL **B** PEARL **C** CHINA

1/6 ▶ The Clarendon Way is a 24-mile walk between Winchester and what other city?

> **A** OXFORD **B** PORTSMOUTH **C** SALISBURY

1/7 ▶ Which of these writers was NOT born in Ireland?

> **A** J M BARRIE **B** G B SHAW **C** W B YEATS

The Beast Quiz 1: Final Chase

★ Prize fund in the Final Chase was £35,000

★ Your target is 19 correct

In this programme 3 contestants were in the team for the Final Chase. Adam, a 43-year-old plastic surgeon from Manchester, was the their top scorer, contributing 12 of their 17 correct answers. Their healthy score was made unassailable by a total of 8 executed push backs. Mark, The Beast, was massively outrun.

1/1 ▶ The surface AstroTurf is made to look like artificial what?

1/2 ▶ NATO was founded four years after the end of what war?

1/3 ▶ Jazz singer Elinore Harris was known by what stage name?

1/4 ▶How many times was Silvio Berlusconi Italian Prime Minister?

1/5 ▶ Kuwait is at the head of what gulf?

1/6 ▶ Jack and Billy Boswell were brothers in what TV sitcom?

1/7 ▶ What's half of 78?

1/8 ▶ The Gordon breed of what dog is named after a Scottish duke?

1/9 ▶ St Peter Port is a town in what island group?

1/10 ▶ Fans of which Hawaiian singer are known as Hooligans?

1/11 ▶ Wine-sap is a large red variety of what fruit?

THE BEAST

1/12 ▷ In the *Star Wars* films, who is Darth Vader's daughter?

1/13 ▷ What playing card is nicknamed the Death Card?

1/14 ▷ What Texas city is named after St Anthony of Padua?

1/15 ▷ Which of Henry the Eighth's wives was born last?

1/16 ▷ What line is the climax to a joke?

1/17 ▷ What insects are also known as 'white ants'?

1/18 ▷ What luxury fashion brand makes the Bayswater handbag?

1/19 ▷ The Thames Challenge Cup is awarded at what rowing regatta?

1/20 ▷ Which English crime author wrote *The Tuesday Club Murders*?

1/21 ▷ The longest wall in the world is located in what country?

1/22 ▷ What Ant & Dec TV show had a live arena tour in 2014?

1/23 ▷ Shakespeare's *King Lear* is written in how many acts?

1/24 ▷ Radix is a term for what part of a plant?

1/25 ▷ Which *Carry On* film was set in India?

1/26 ▷ What company makes the Core range of ice-cream products?

THE BEAST QUIZ 1: Final Chase

The Beast Quiz 2: Contestant 1

Answer at least 5 questions correctly to progress on to the Final Chase.

2/1 ▶ Which of these capital cities is NOT in Europe?

> A REYKJAVIK B RIGA C RIYADH

2/2 ▶ Born in 2014, what did Christina Aguilera name her first daughter?

> A SUMMER RAIN B WINTER SNOW C AUTUMN LEAVES

2/3 ▶ What type of bridge is Sydney Harbour Bridge?

> A ARCH B CANTILEVER C SUSPENSION

2/4 ▶ Which of these British middle-distance runners won Olympic gold?

> A STEVE CRAM B BRENDAN FOSTER C STEVE OVETT

2/5 ▶ What process produces the energy given off by the Sun?

> A FUSION B FISSION C FRICTION

2/6 ▶ Olly Murs was a contestant on what TV game show before he became famous?

> A *FRIENDS LIKE THESE* B *DEAL OR NO DEAL* C *TOTAL WIPEOUT*

2/7 ▶ In the standard version of Monopoly, what colour are the first properties on the board after 'Go'?

> A BROWN B DARK BLUE C RED

The Beast Quiz 2: Contestant 2

Answer at least 5 questions correctly to progress on to the Final Chase.

2/1 ▶ Which of these is a form of dance, traditionally performed in East Anglia in January?

> **A** MILLY DANCING   **B** MOLLY DANCING   **C** MANDY DANCING

2/2 ▶ What company made the space suits worn by Neil Armstrong and his crew?

> **A** FRED PERRY   **B** LEVI STRAUSS   **C** PLAYTEX

2/3 ▶ On the HB scale, which of these pencils has the blackest lead?

> **A** B   **B** 2B   **C** 4B

2/4 ▶ The comic-book hero Judge Dredd has what first name?

> **A** FRANK   **B** JOE   **C** NIGEL

2/5 ▶ To a swimming coach, dps means 'distance per...' what?

> **A** SECOND   **B** SESSION   **C** STROKE

2/6 ▶ Alastair Sawday is a famous name in what field?

> **A** GARDENING BOOKS   **B** TRAVEL BOOKS   **C** DIY BOOKS

2/7 ▶ An exclusive beauty and cosmetics line based on which of these period dramas was launched in 2013?

> **A** *DOWNTON ABBEY*   **B** *MR SELFRIDGE*   **C** *CALL THE MIDWIFE*

The Beast Quiz 2: Contestant 3

Answer at least 5 questions correctly to progress on to the Final Chase.

2/1 ▶ The noun 'cordovan' refers to something made from what material?

A GLASS B LEATHER C PAPER

2/2 ▶ After a debate in the House of Commons, MPs usually have how long to vote on a motion?

A EIGHT MINUTES B EIGHT HOURS C EIGHT DAYS

2/3 ▶ Which of these was the title of a 2005 hit single for Girls Aloud?

A 'BIOLOGY' B 'CHEMISTRY' C 'PHYSICS'

2/4 ▶ Which British sculptor was the first living artist to have a solo show at the Royal Academy of Arts?

A JACOB EPSTEIN B RACHEL WHITEREAD C ANISH KAPOOR

2/5 ▶ Which dam in the United States was constructed between 1930 and 1936?

A HOOVER DAM B ROOSEVELT DAM C TRUMAN DAM

2/6 ▶ In Roman mythology, which three sisters lived in the underworld and ascended to earth to pursue the wicked?

A THE FATES B THE GORGONS C THE FURIES

2/7 ▶ Which of these drinks was produced first?

A BLUE NUN B NEWCASTLE BROWN ALE C RED BULL

The Beast Quiz 2: Contestant 4

Answer at least 5 questions correctly to progress on to the Final Chase.

2/1 ▶ What has Katherine Heigl's character been 27 times in the film *27 Dresses*?

> **A** A GODMOTHER **B** A BRIDESMAID **C** A PROM QUEEN

2/2 ▶ The Welsh Corgi was developed to round up what animals?

> **A** CATTLE **B** CHICKENS **C** PIGS

2/3 ▶ How many grams does a 20-pence piece weigh?

> **A** 5 **B** 10 **C** 15

2/4 ▶ Ofgem is the 'Office of the Gas and Electricity...' what?

> **A** MAINTENANCE **B** MARKETS **C** MANAGEMENT

2/5 ▶ 6 and 28 are examples of what type of number?

> **A** FANTASTIC NUMBER **B** PERFECT NUMBER **C** SUPER NUMBER

2/6 ▶ What is the stage surname of the actor-director born Kevin Matthew Fowler in 1959?

> **A** SPACEY **B** BACON **C** KLINE

2/7 ▶ What does pasteurising milk improve?

> **A** TASTE **B** CALCIUM CONTENT **C** SHELF LIFE

The Beast Quiz 2: Final Chase

★ Prize fund in the Final Chase was £35,000

★ Your target is 19 correct

The full complement of 4 players made it to the Final Chase. They amassed an astonishing total of 24 for The Beast to chase. The top scorer was Kevin, a 34-year-old insurance broker from Hartlepool. Their success in the opening phase was matched by an impressive 6 executed push backs against The Beast, who was soundly beaten.

2/1 ▶ The sport of figure skating takes place on what surface?

2/2 ▶ Panadol is a trade name for what drug?

2/3 ▶ The Dog in the Pond is a pub in what TV soap?

2/4 ▶ What vegetable is also known as 'turnip-cabbage'?

2/5 ▶ What animal is T S Eliot's Old Deuteronomy?

2/6 ▶ At night, what colour light indicates 'starboard' on a ship?

2/7 ▶ Which George Cole character often said 'a nice little earner'?

2/8 ▶ Which royal is patron of The Scout Association?

2/9 ▶ What's 10 per cent of 120?

2/10 ▶ The Indian team Rajasthan Royals plays what sport?

2/11 ▶ *Sweet Baby James* and *Hourglass* are albums by which singer?

THE BEAST QUIZ 2: Final Chase

THE BEAST

2/12 ▶ Brandenburg and Lower Saxony are states in what country?

2/13 ▶ 'The infernal serpent' is a phrase in what Milton epic poem?

2/14 ▶ What Football League team is known as the Shrews?

2/15 ▶ What car company makes the B-Max and C-Max models?

2/16 ▶ Singer Ernest Evans was known as 'Chubby...' who?

2/17 ▶ What is the most westerly point of mainland England?

2/18 ▶ What radioactive noble gas is produced by the decay of radium?

2/19 ▶ The vibrations of what part of a bee make a buzzing noise?

2/20 ▶ Who illustrated Roald Dahl's poetry book *Revolting Rhymes*?

2/21 ▶ Swaziland is a country on what continent?

2/22 ▶ Cherry Blossom is a brand of what type of polish?

2/23 ▶ Who played J J McClure in the film *The Cannonball Run*?

2/24 ▶ What is the nickname of Bradford's Rugby League team?

2/25 ▶ How many milliamps are there in an amp?

2/26 ▶ What surname is shared by film directors Spike and Ang?

2/27 ▶ The River Wye flows through what two countries of the UK?

The Beast Quiz 3: Contestant 1

Answer at least 5 questions correctly to progress on to the Final Chase.

3/1 ▶ Bobby Brown reached the Top Ten in 1988 singing about 'My...' what?

> **A** PREROGATIVE **B** GENERATION **C** DING-A-LING

3/2 ▶ James Howlett is the real name of which Marvel superhero?

> **A** HAWKEYE **B** DAREDEVIL **C** WOLVERINE

3/3 ▶ According to legend, which patron saint agreed to let women propose to men on Leap Year Day?

> **A** ST ANDREW **B** ST GEORGE **C** ST PATRICK

3/4 ▶ In which sport is the wearing of one glove common?

> **A** CRICKET **B** GOLF **C** BOXING

3/5 ▶ Immortalised by Glenn Miller, what was the original telephone number of the Pennsylvania Hotel in New York?

> **A** 6-5000 **B** 5-4000 **C** 4-3000

3/6 ▶ The title of 'Mahatma' bestowed on Gandhi has what meaning in Sanskrit?

> **A** GREAT SOUL **B** PEOPLE'S SOLDIER **C** WISE TEACHER

3/7 ▶ On TV, Dirk Benedict played which member of *The A-Team*?

> **A** B A BARACUS **B** FACEMAN **C** MURDOCK

The Beast Quiz 3: Contestant 2

Answer at least 5 questions correctly to progress on to the Final Chase.

3/1 ▶ Which of these is NOT an axial bone?

> **A** SKULL **B** RIB **C** KNEECAP

3/2 ▶ Winning over two million francs in eight days, Joseph Hobson Jagger 'broke the bank' at Monte Carlo by playing what game?

> **A** BLACKJACK **B** CRAPS **C** ROULETTE

3/3 ▶ Which of these buildings was NOT destroyed in the Great Fire of London?

> **A** TOWER OF LONDON **B** ST PAUL'S CATHEDRAL **C** GUILDHALL

3/4 ▶ What combined distance is covered in the four track events of an Olympic Men's Decathlon?

> **A** 1,400 METRES **B** 1,660 METRES **C** 2,110 METRES

3/5 ▶ Which of these is one of the 'Big Five' safari animals?

> **A** BUFFALO **B** HIPPOPOTAMUS **C** GIRAFFE

3/6 ▶ Complete this closing line from a Shakespeare play 'For never was a story of more woe, than this of...' what?

> **A** ANTONY AND HIS CLEOPATRA **B** JULIET AND HER ROMEO **C** PUCK AND HIS BOTTOM

3/7 ▶ In Spain, a *bombero* would work for which of the emergency services?

> **A** FIRE **B** POLICE **C** AMBULANCE

The Beast Quiz 3: Contestant 3

Answer at least 5 questions correctly to progress on to the Final Chase.

3/1 ▶ What was Miss Piggy's surname in *The Muppet Show*?

> **A** BANKS **B** MITCHELL **C** LEE

3/2 ▶ What does it mean if two words are synonyms of each other?

> **A** THEY SOUND THE SAME **B** THEY MEAN THE SAME **C** THEY'RE SPELT THE SAME

3/3 ▶ Which of these is a popular tourist destination in Australia?

> **A** THE BUNGLE BUNGLES **B** THE GEOFFREY GEOFFREYS **C** THE ZIPPY ZIPPIES

3/4 ▶ Which board game was invented during the Depression by out-of-work American architect, Alfred Butts?

> **A** MONOPOLY **B** SCRABBLE **C** CLUEDO

3/5 ▶ Which of these darts scores is the highest?

> **A** DOUBLE THIRTEEN **B** TREBLE NINE **C** OUTER BULL

3/6 ▶ What pair of initials are shared by the authors of *The Third Man* and *The Female Eunuch*?

> **A** B B **B** F F **C** G G

3/7 ▶ What UK landmark was sold as 'Lot 15' for £6,600 in 1915?

> **A** LAND'S END **B** BLACKPOOL TOWER **C** STONEHENGE

The Beast Quiz 3: Contestant 4

Answer at least 5 questions correctly to progress on to the Final Chase.

3/1 ▶ Which of these would be most likely to have a thermal tog rating?

> **A** HANDBAG **B** SLEEPING BAG **C** AIRBAG

3/2 ▶ Which leader of the Liberal Democrats was born in India?

> **A** CHARLES KENNEDY **B** MENZIES CAMPBELL **C** PADDY ASHDOWN

3/3 ▶ Which of these songs was a UK hit first?

> **A** 'D.I.V.O.R.C.E.' **B** 'D.I.S.C.O.' **C** 'Y.M.C.A.'

3/4 ▶ What is the internal angle between the minute and hour hands of a clock when it is one o'clock?

> **A** 30 DEGREES **B** 45 DEGREES **C** 90 DEGREES

3/5 ▶ The name of which dance means 'the cracking of a whip' in Portuguese?

> **A** MACARENA **B** FANDANGO **C** LAMBADA

3/6 ▶ The A A Milne character Eeyore mainly eats what plants?

> **A** ROSES **B** ROSES **C** DANDELIONS

3/7 ▶ John 'Calico Jack' Rackham was a famous 18th-century what?

> **A** PIRATE **B** HIGHWAYMAN **C** MP

The Beast Quiz 3: Final Chase

★ Prize fund in the Final Chase was £35,000

★ Your target is 19 correct

Four contestants won a place in the Final Chase. A heroic contribution from Steve, a bar owner originating from Skegness, who provided 13 of their 19 correct answers, gave the team a challenging lead. They secured a comfortable win against the best efforts of The Beast, helped by 4 successfully executed push backs.

3/1 ▶ St Petersburg and Miami are cities in what U S state?

3/2 ▶ What relation was Elizabeth the First to Catherine Parr?

3/3 ▶ The Pathetic Sharks are characters in what adult comic?

3/4 ▶ What Tim Minchin musical features the song 'This Little Girl'?

3/5 ▶ The Lambretta scooter originated in what country?

3/6 ▶ Who replaced Alex Salmond as leader of the SNP in 2014?

3/7 ▶ Haile Selassie was the last emperor of what African country?

3/8 ▶ In the computing term HTML, what does the 'HT' stand for?

3/9 ▶ In the Max Bygraves song, what flowers came from Amsterdam?

3/10 ▶ The viceroy is a species of what winged insect?

THE BEAST

3/11 ▷ Who released the 2014 memoir *More Fool Me*?

3/12 ▷ Colorado's ski resorts are in what major mountain range?

3/13 ▷ Which Irish actor played Tony in the TV drama *The Missing*?

3/14 ▷ The video game 'Oh, Behave!' features what Mike Myers character?

3/15 ▷ Which Greek goddess is depicted on the Jules Rimet Trophy?

3/16 ▷ Weatherfield General is a hospital in what soap?

3/17 ▷ Which fictional jungle character has a son called Korak?

3/18 ▷ Who starred in *The Protectors* and *The Man from U.N.C.L.E.*?

3/19 ▷ George Washington was born in what century?

3/20 ▷ What big cat is on the British Army logo?

3/21 ▷ The Gagarin Cosmonaut Training Center is in what country?

3/22 ▷ Which TV character referred to his wife as 'er indoors'?

3/23 ▷ Which Roman emperor had his ex-wife put to death in AD 62?

3/24 ▷ What's the young of a wombat called?

The Beast Quiz 4: Contestant 1

Answer at least 5 questions correctly to progress on to the Final Chase.

4/1 ▶ What name is given to the edible ends of asparagus spears?

> **A** CRESTS **B** PEAKS **C** TIPS

4/2 ▶ In the US, the Patient Protection and Affordable Care Act is given what nickname?

> **A** CLINTONCARE **B** OBAMACARE **C** BUSHCARE

4/3 ▶ Spain's highest mountain is on which island?

> **A** LANZAROTE **B** MALLORCA **C** TENERIFE

4/4 ▶ Which of these is a species of monkey?

> **A** DRILL **B** SPANNER **C** WRENCH

4/5 ▶ In musical notation, a 'treble clef' takes the stylised form of which letter?

> **A** A **B** D **C** G

4/6 ▶ Which Brontë sister shares her name with the heroine of Jane Austen's *Persuasion*?

> **A** EMILY **B** ANNE **C** CHARLOTTE

4/7 ▶ Which of these is the name of a traditional folk song?

> **A** 'SCARBOROUGH FAIR' **B** 'SOUTHEND MARKET' **C** 'SWANAGE FÊTE'

The Beast Quiz 4: Contestant 2

Answer at least 5 questions correctly to progress on to the Final Chase.

4/1 ▶ A tetradecagon has how many sides?

> A 14 B 24 C 40

4/2 ▶ Which of these is a fear of clothing?

> A VESTIPHOBIA B SHIRTIPHOBIA C PANTIPHOBIA

4/3 ▶ The 1976 *Daily Mirror* front page headline 'The Filth and the Fury' referred to which group?

> A QUEEN B SEX PISTOLS C BAY CITY ROLLERS

4/4 ▶ Which of these actresses was made a Dame first?

> A HELEN MIRREN B DIANA RIGG C MAGGIE SMITH

4/5 ▶ Collagen and calcium phosphate are the principal components of what natural material?

> A SHELL B BONE C ENAMEL

4/6 ▶ In 2015, who said 'I can't live in a world where Ed Sheeran is headlining Wembley'?

> A ELTON JOHN B WILL.I.AM C NOEL GALLAGHER

4/7 ▶ In what sport might a 'death spiral' be performed?

> A SKATEBOARDING B FIGURE SKATING C TRAMPOLINING

The Beast Quiz 4: Contestant 3

Answer at least 5 questions correctly to progress on to the Final Chase.

4/1 ▶ Edward I was named after which other king?

> **A** EDWARD THE ELDER **B** EDWARD THE MARTYR **C** EDWARD THE CONFESSOR

4/2 ▶ Which of these terms means to withdraw a coin or note from use as legal tender?

> **A** DECAPITALISE **B** DEMONETISE **C** DETENDERISE

4/3 ▶ 'When Children Rule the World' is a song from which musical?

> **A** *WHISTLE DOWN THE WIND* **B** *BUGSY MALONE* **C** *MATILDA*

4/4 ▶ Which of these world capitals is a UNESCO World Heritage site?

> **A** BRASILIA **B** BRATISLAVA **C** BRUSSELS

4/5 ▶ An MP who does not represent a political party is known by what term?

> **A** AUTONOMOUS **B** INDEPENDENT **C** NON-ALIGNED

4/6 ▶ Which TV show centred around a GP surgery in the fictional town of Cardale?

> **A** *DOC MARTIN* **B** *PEAK PRACTICE* **C** *WHERE THE HEART IS*

4/7 ▶ Which of these was a UK Number One for Elvis Presley?

> **A** 'SURRENDER' **B** 'SUSPICIOUS MINDS' **C** 'STUCK ON YOU'

The Beast Quiz 4: Contestant 4

Answer at least 5 questions correctly to progress on to the Final Chase.

4/1 ▶ In a painting, what name is given to the point on the horizon at which parallel lines appear to meet?

> **A** DECLINING POINT **B** FADING POINT **C** VANISHING POINT

4/2 ▶ Which of these is a bottom-dwelling ray-like fish?

> **A** GUITAR FISH **B** HARP FISH **C** PIANO FISH

4/3 ▶ A cocktail of port, brandy, sugar, coffee and an egg is a 'Yankee...' what?

> **A** REJUVENATOR **B** EXHILARATOR **C** INVIGORATOR

4/4 ▶ The beginning of which science fiction film features a group of apes and no human characters?

> **A** *ALIEN* **B** *2001: A SPACE ODYSSEY* **C** *STAR WARS*

4/5 ▶ Which of these was a fragrance launched by the singer Rihanna?

> **A** 'NATURAL' **B** 'NUDE' **C** 'NAKED'

4/6 ▶ In what century did the Roman Republic become the Roman Empire?

> **A** 2ND CENTURY BC **B** 1ST CENTURY BC **C** 1ST CENTURY AD

4/7 ▶ Which of these is part of the alimentary canal?

> **A** MOUTH **B** EARS **C** NOSE

The Beast Quiz 4: Final Chase

★ Prize fund in the Final Chase was £35,000

★ Your target is 19 correct

In this programme 4 players reached the Final Chase. They hit the ground running and racked up a highly impressive score of 22. After a slow start in which he conceded several push backs, The Beast made a concerted assault on the target, but ultimately failed in his pursuit.

4/1 ▶ What's Dannii Minogue's full first name?

4/2 ▶ How many people originally formed the comedy group The Goons?

4/3 ▶ Compton is a notorious area of what American city?

4/4 ▶ 'Chandelier' was a hit for which Australian singer-songwriter?

4/5 ▶ Chris Patten served as chairman of what political party?

4/6 ▶ Bobby Zamora has represented England in what sport?

4/7 ▶ What tree-like plant is nicknamed 'the friend of China'?

4/8 ▶ Which co-rulers of Great Britain were first cousins?

4/9 ▶ What's four times seven?

4/10 ▶ What European language is the official language of Zambia?

4/11 ▶ Who composed the theme for ITV's *South Bank Show*?

THE BEAST

4/12 ▶ The duo Appleton was formed by ex-members of what girl group?

4/13 ▶ In 1960, Cameroon gained independence from which country?

4/14 ▶ In horse racing, what Grand National is run at Chepstow?

4/15 ▶ Who directed the 1942 film *Saboteur*?

4/16 ▶ 'Mossy' is a media nickname for which supermodel?

4/17 ▶ Traditional Cumberland sausages are made from what meat?

4/18 ▶ What Eleanor Catton novel won the 2013 Man Booker Prize?

4/19 ▶ Lucy is a flatmate and landlady in what Lee Mack TV comedy?

4/20 ▶ What brewery makes London Pride ale?

4/21 ▶ What's the only letter to appear twice in the word 'across'?

4/22 ▶ Who is patron saint of the Order of the Thistle?

4/23 ▶ 'Digging' is a poem by which Irish Nobel Prize-winner?

4/24 ▶ Which organisation bought George Lucas' film company in 2012?

4/25 ▶ Who hosts the UK TV version of *Deal Or No Deal*?

4/26 ▶ Espresso romano coffee is served with a twist of what fruit?

4/27 ▶ What bank uses the slogan 'Helpful Banking'?

THE BEAST QUIZ 4: Final Chase

The Beast Quiz 5: Contestant 1

Answer at least 5 questions correctly to progress on to the Final Chase.

5/1 ▶ Which fictional bear is first introduced sitting on a suitcase?

> **A** PADDINGTON BEAR **B** WINNIE-THE-POOH **C** RUPERT BEAR

5/2 ▶ What relation was 1980s Indian Premier Rajiv Gandhi to the country's first Prime Minister Pandit Nehru?

> **A** NEPHEW **B** COUSIN **C** GRANDSON

5/3 ▶ Horseradish is a member of the same family as which of these vegetables?

> **A** ONION **B** BEETROOT **C** CABBAGE

5/4 ▶ What day falls 50 days before Christmas Day?

> **A** FATHER'S DAY **B** GUY FAWKES DAY **C** ST DAVID'S DAY

5/5 ▶ How does the name of the German football team Eintracht Frankfurt translate into English?

> **A** FRANKFURT WANDERERS **B** FRANKFURT ATHLETIC **C** FRANKFURT UNITED

5/6 ▶ Who had a Number One single in 2014 with 'It's My Birthday'?

> **A** CALVIN HARRIS **B** WILL.I.AM **C** PHARRELL WILLIAMS

5/7 ▶ Focaccia bread is usually flavoured with what?

> **A** DRIED FRUIT **B** HERBS **C** NUTS

The Beast Quiz 5: Contestant 2

Answer at least 5 questions correctly to progress on to the Final Chase.

5/1 ▶ In *EastEnders*, which member of the Mitchell family killed Heather Trott?

> **A** BEN **B** PHIL **C** RONNIE

5/2 ▶ 'Manchester, England' is a song from which musical?

> **A** *HAIR* **B** *LEGALLY BLONDE* **C** *HAIRSPRAY*

5/3 ▶ What is the orbicularis oculi muscle responsible for?

> **A** CLOSING EYELIDS **B** FLARING NOSTRILS **C** PURSING LIPS

5/4 ▶ Which of these films was released most recently?

> **A** *A PLACE IN THE SUN* **B** *GORILLAS IN THE MIST* **C** *SINGIN' IN THE RAIN*

5/5 ▶ At the World Haggis Hurling Championship, contestants must stand on what?

> **A** MOUND OF THISTLES **B** TARTAN RUG **C** WHISKY BARREL

5/6 ▶ Which of these is NOT the name of a fictional detective?

> **A** SAM SPADE **B** MIKE HAMMER **C** JACK SAW

5/7 ▶ UK parliamentary constituencies are divided into what smaller areas?

> **A** DISTRICTS **B** PARISHES **C** WARDS

The Beast Quiz 5: Contestant 3

Answer at least 5 questions correctly to progress on to the Final Chase.

5/1 ▶ In 2014, who was the last member of England's 2003 Rugby World Cup-winning team to retire?

> **A** IAN BALSHAW **B** MIKE TINDALL **C** JONNY WILKINSON

5/2 ▶ In the US, the pumpkin is also known by what name?

> **A** SALSIFY **B** SQUASH **C** SUCCOTASH

5/3 ▶ Which of these holiday resorts is NOT located on an island?

> **A** AYIA NAPA **B** CANCUN **C** FALIRAKI

5/4 ▶ People who call themselves velologists collect what?

> **A** TAX DISCS **B** ENVELOPES **C** BICYCLE SEATS

5/5 ▶ Pub landlord Harry Bailly suggests a story-telling competition in which book?

> **A** *THE HOBBIT* **B** *TREASURE ISLAND* **C** *THE CANTERBURY TALES*

5/6 ▶ Which of these men never served as US President?

> **A** JOHN ADAMS **B** BENJAMIN FRANKLIN **C** JAMES MADISON

5/7 ▶ Which sitcom character revealed at school she was known as Starchy Sturgess?

> **A** HYACINTH BUCKET **B** SYBIL FAWLTY **C** MARGO LEADBETTER

The Beast Quiz 5: Contestant 4

Answer at least 5 questions correctly to progress on to the Final Chase.

5/1 ▶ The UK road sign indicating 'no motor vehicles' has a picture of a car and what else?

> **A** BICYCLE **B** LORRY **C** MOTORCYCLE

5/2 ▶ Which of these films was based on a Stephen King novella?

> **A** *SLIDING DOORS* **B** *SECRET WINDOW* **C** *PANIC ROOM*

5/3 ▶ The writer Caitlin Moran once said which politician resembled 'a slightly camp robot made of gammon'?

> **A** DAVID CAMERON **B** NICK CLEGG **C** ED MILIBAND

5/4 ▶ In 2014, 'Chapter One' was the chart topping debut album of which contestant from *The X Factor*?

> **A** JAMES ARTHUR **B** ELLA HENDERSON **C** CHER LLOYD

5/5 ▶ Which of these is NOT classed as an 'oily' fish?

> **A** ANCHOVY **B** SALMON **C** PLAICE

5/6 ▶ Which of these is a figure adopted in synchronised swimming?

> **A** EIFFEL TOWER **B** GRAND CANYON **C** SYDNEY OPERA HOUSE

5/7 ▶ What country does tennis player Victoria Azarenka represent?

> **A** AUSTRALIA **B** BELARUS **C** CROATIA

The Beast Quiz 5: Final Chase

★ Prize fund in the Final Chase was £35,000

★ Your target is 19 correct

Three contestants confronted The Beast in the final. They notched up a creditable score of 17. The Beast's pursuit was going well until the last 25 seconds, during which he stumbled on four questions, allowing the team to add a further 2 executed push backs to the 2 they had already won and thereby win the Chase.

5/1 ▶ What bones protect the human heart and lungs?

5/2 ▶ The film *12 Years A Slave* is set in what country?

5/3 ▶ Betty Jackson is a famous designer of what?

5/4 ▶ In what decade did McDonald's open in the UK?

5/5 ▶ The five rings on what flag represent five continents?

5/6 ▶ Which boy band had the 2014 hit song 'Steal My Girl'?

5/7 ▶ What type of transport is a frigate?

5/8 ▶ Gillian Gilks was a star of what sport?

5/9 ▶ A praying mantis has how many legs?

5/10 ▶ General Von Klinkerhoffen was a character in what TV sitcom?

THE BEAST

5/11 ▶ Who's the first Briton to win the Man Booker Prize twice?

5/12 ▶ The dessert zabaglione comes from what country?

5/13 ▶ Who became Russian President in 1991?

5/14 ▶ What glands secrete the hormone adrenaline?

5/15 ▶ Marcella Detroit was one half of what pop duo?

5/16 ▶ How often does a centennial event take place?

5/17 ▶ Bardarbunga volcano is in what North Atlantic country?

5/18 ▶ Which monarch made his first Christmas speech in 1932?

5/19 ▶ Farfalle is a type of what Italian food?

5/20 ▶ Who played the baddie White Goodman in the film *Dodgeball*?

5/21 ▶ In 'The Twelve Days of Christmas', what are the maids doing?

5/22 ▶ Bearded and Border are varieties of what dog breed?

5/23 ▶ What Italian river flows through Pisa to the sea?

5/24 ▶ What primary colour are Bayern Munich's home shirts?

5/25 ▶ Khmer is the official language of what Asian country?

The Beast Quiz 6: Contestant 1

Answer at least 5 questions correctly to progress on to the Final Chase.

6/1 ▶ *Atticus* was an early working title for which American novel?

> **A** *GONE WITH THE WIND* **B** *THE CATCHER IN THE RYE* **C** *TO KILL A MOCKINGBIRD*

6/2 ▶ Which of these countries joined the EU most recently?

> **A** FINLAND **B** IRELAND **C** POLAND

6/3 ▶ Who is the youngest member of The Saturdays?

> **A** FRANKIE **B** VANESSA **C** UNA

6/4 ▶ 'Golden Ball' and 'Green Globe' are varieties of what vegetable?

> **A** CARROT **B** POTATO **C** TURNIP

6/5 ▶ Which sportsman became the father of twins for the second time in 2014?

> **A** FERNANDO ALONSO **B** JONAH LOMU **C** ROGER FEDERER

6/6 ▶ In 2015, a French court prevented a couple from giving their daughter what name?

> **A** VOLVIC **B** NUTELLA **C** AIRBUS

6/7 ▶ What specific part of the ear is responsible for 'equilibrium' or a sense of balance?

> **A** OUTER EAR **B** MIDDLE EAR **C** INNER EAR

The Beast Quiz 6: Contestant 2

Answer at least 5 questions correctly to progress on to the Final Chase.

6/1 ▶ In poetry, what's another name for a couplet written in iambic pentameter?

> **A** HEROIC COUPLET **B** GALLANT COUPLET **C** NOBLE COUPLET

6/2 ▶ What hit song for Donna Summer in the 1970s also charted in the 1980s and 1990s?

> **A** *LOVE TO LOVE YOU BABY* **B** *I FEEL LOVE* **C** *LOVE'S UNKIND*

6/3 ▶ Which of these is NOT a flower?

> **A** GANSY **B** TANSY **C** PANSY

6/4 ▶ Who succeeded Tom Baker as the Doctor in *Doctor Who*?

> **A** SYLVESTER MCCOY **B** PETER DAVISON **C** COLIN BAKER

6/5 ▶ The horse-racing turf flat season officially begins at what course?

> **A** DONCASTER **B** NEWMARKET **C** GOODWOOD

6/6 ▶ What musical instrument is nicknamed a 'slush pump'?

> **A** TRUMPET **B** TROMBONE **C** SAXOPHONE

6/7 ▶ Who said at a famous event in 1985, 'Don't go to the pub tonight – please stay in and give us your money'?

> **A** BOB GELDOF **B** DAVID FROST **C** TERRY WOGAN

The Beast Quiz 6: Contestant 3

Answer at least 5 questions correctly to progress on to the Final Chase.

6/1 ▶ Approximately how many people live in the Commonwealth?

> **A** 1.1 BILLION **B** 2.2 BILLION **C** 3.3 BILLION

6/2 ▶ Which of these was NOT a category in the original Trivial Pursuit game?

> **A** GEOGRAPHY **B** HISTORY **C** MUSIC

6/3 ▶ By what name is Seventh Avenue in New York City also known?

> **A** FASHION AVENUE **B** FOOD AVENUE **C** FURNITURE AVENUE

6/4 ▶ Which Irish dramatist wrote a play called *Play* and a film called *Film*?

> **A** GEORGE BERNARD SHAW **B** OSCAR WILDE **C** SAMUEL BECKETT

6/5 ▶ A cockerel is a young male of what domestic bird?

> **A** DUCK **B** PIGEON **C** CHICKEN

6/6 ▶ How often is the magazine *Vanity Fair* published?

> **A** MONTHLY **B** FORTNIGHTLY **C** QUARTERLY

6/7 ▶ What was the first Ian Rankin novel to feature Detective Inspector Rebus?

> **A** *EXIT MUSIC* **B** *SET IN DARKNESS* **C** *KNOTS AND CROSSES*

The Beast Quiz 6: Contestant 4

Answer at least 5 questions correctly to progress on to the Final Chase.

6/1 ▶ Germany was divided into East and West countries in what decade?

A 1920S B 1930S C 1940S

6/2 ▶ In *EastEnders* who is the mother of Tanya Branning?

A CORA B DORA C NORA

6/3 ▶ In 1786, Margaret Nicholson tried to assassinate which king with a blunt ivory-handled dessert knife?

A GEORGE I B GEORGE II C GEORGE III

6/4 ▶ Which of these is a fish capable of living out of water for months?

A HEARTFISH B LUNGFISH C SPLEENFISH

6/5 ▶ The Taw, Tamar and Torridge are all rivers in what English county?

A DEVON B DORSET C DURHAM

6/6 ▶ Wilbur and Orville Wright built their pioneering aircraft using their knowledge from making and selling which vehicles?

A AUTOMOBILES B BICYCLES C SPEEDBOATS

6/7 ▶ In 1997, who dressed as King Louis XIV for his 50th birthday party at the Hammersmith Palais?

A DAVID BOWIE B ROD STEWART C ELTON JOHN

The Beast Quiz 6: Final Chase

⭐ Prize fund in the Final Chase was £35,000

⭐ Your target is 19 correct

In this programme 3 players made it to the final. They got off to a flying start, with all the team contributing, but they lost impetus towards the end of their 2 minutes. With a total of 17 to chase, The Beast conceded 7 push backs of which the players executed 5, sealing their victory.

6/1 ▶ The Taj Mahal Palace Hotel is located in what country?

6/2 ▶ Which Teletubby has a one-syllable name?

6/3 ▶ What canal was closed by the Six Day War?

6/4 ▶ Which scientist discovered the atomic nucleus in 1911?

6/5 ▶ Which children's writer created the world of Wonderland?

6/6 ▶ Yellow-necked is what type of small rodent?

6/7 ▶ What vowel appears twice in the word 'protagonist'?

6/8 ▶ Who played newlywed Maddy in the sitcom *Life of Riley*?

6/9 ▶ The Great White North is a colloquial term for what country?

THE BEAST

6/10 ▶ Which female singer had the 1980s hit 'Love Resurrection'?

6/11 ▶ Which poet was denied burial in Poets' Corner in 1824?

6/12 ▶ The *Western Mail* newspaper is based in what Welsh city?

6/13 ▶ The gladiolus is a member of what larger family of plants?

6/14 ▶ Waka is a classic form of poetry from what Asian country?

6/15 ▶ The Kickflip and Fakie Heelflip are tricks in what activity?

6/16 ▶ Who's the paternal grandfather of Princess Eugenie?

6/17 ▶ In what Elvis hit was the rhythm section called the Purple Gang?

6/18 ▶ Eastern diamondback is the deadliest species of what snake?

6/19 ▶ *Training a Tiger* was a 1997 guide-book about what sport?

6/20 ▶ Actress Mickey Sumner is the daughter of which pop star?

6/21 ▶ How many decades are there in two centuries?

6/22 ▶ The word 'scampi' comes directly from what language?

The Beast Quiz 7: Contestant 1

Answer at least 5 questions correctly to progress on to the Final Chase.

7/1 ▶ In the song about Molly Malone, how are the girls of Dublin described?

> **A** WITTY **B** PRETTY **C** GRITTY

7/2 ▶ A thrush appears on the badge of what Midlands football club?

> **A** ASTON VILLA **B** BIRMINGHAM **C** WEST BROMWICH ALBION

7/3 ▶ The Hubble sequence is used to categorise what?

> **A** CONSTELLATIONS **B** GALAXIES **C** PLANETARY RINGS

7/4 ▶ What middle names did the Duke and Duchess of Cambridge give to Princess Charlotte, born in 2015?

> **A** CAMILLA SARAH **B** ZARA BEATRICE **C** ELIZABETH DIANA

7/5 ▶ Which of these UK locations is the furthest south?

> **A** ST ANDREWS UNIVERSITY **B** ST GEORGE'S CHAPEL **C** ST DAVID'S HEAD

7/6 ▶ Fifteen fathoms is equal to what unit of length?

> **A** CUFF **B** MANACLE **C** SHACKLE

7/7 ▶ Which of these terms means the same thing as 'subcutaneous'?

> **A** SUBCOSTAL **B** SUBDERMAL **C** SUBTEXTUAL

THE BEAST

The Beast Quiz 7: Contestant 2

Answer at least 5 questions correctly to progress on to the Final Chase.

7/1 ▶ 'Cause I try and I try and I try and I try' are lyrics from which Rolling Stones song?

> **A** *HONKY TONK WOMEN* **B** *PAINT IT, BLACK* **C** *(I CAN'T GET NO) SATISFACTION*

7/2 ▶ What does the name of the Hindu god Kama mean?

> **A** FIRE **B** LOVE **C** RAIN

7/3 ▶ In 2004, how did the *EastEnders* character Barry Evans meet his end?

> **A** BITTEN BY A DOG **B** HIT BY A TRAM **C** PUSHED OFF A CLIFF

7/4 ▶ Henry III was the eldest son of which king who immediately preceded him?

> **A** GEORGE I **B** HENRY II **C** JOHN

7/5 ▶ Which of these US Presidents did NOT serve two full terms?

> **A** HARRY TRUMAN **B** DWIGHT EISENHOWER **C** RONALD REAGAN

7/6 ▶ The sugar is stored in what part of the sugar-cane?

> **A** LEAVES **B** ROOTS **C** STALK

7/7 ▶ LAND, a 2015 art commission consisting of cast-iron sculptures at five UK locations, was created by which artist?

> **A** DAMIEN HIRST **B** TRACEY EMIN **C** ANTONY GORMLEY

The Beast Quiz 7: Contestant 3

Answer at least 5 questions correctly to progress on to the Final Chase.

7/1 ▶ Which of these pets did NOT appear on *Blue Peter* in the 1960s?

A GOLDIE B JASON C PETRA

7/2 ▶ The Orkneys lie off what coast of Scotland?

A EAST B WEST C NORTH

7/3 ▶ Which Quentin Tarantino film is about what happens before and after a jewellery store robbery?

A *DJANGO UNCHAINED* B *PULP FICTION* C *RESERVOIR DOGS*

7/4 ▶ Which famous Briton was born in the same year as Beethoven?

A WILLIAM WALLACE B WILLIAM WILBERFORCE C WILLIAM WORDSWORTH

7/5 ▶ What is the national currency of the British Virgin Islands?

A EURO B DOLLAR C BRANSON

7/6 ▶ Which of these is a character in the Shakespeare play *The Merchant of Venice*?

A GOBBO B MOUTHY C CHATTY

7/7 ▶ What is 'Jerry and David's Guide to the World Wide Web' now called?

A GOOGLE B BING C YAHOO!

The Beast Quiz 7: Contestant 4

Answer at least 5 questions correctly to progress on to the Final Chase.

7/1 ▶ Which of these letters does NOT represent a regular character in the *James Bond* films?

> A F B M C Q

7/2 ▶ A 'scratch test' is a common way of checking for what?

> **A** ALLERGIES **B** BLOOD POISONING **C** REFLEXES

7/3 ▶ In 2013, Nobel Prize-winning physicist Peter Higgs said he had never done what?

> **A** READ STEPHEN HAWKING **B** SENT AN E-MAIL **C** UNDERSTOOD CALCULUS

7/4 ▶ Who created the film comedies *Dumb and Dumber* and *There's Something About Mary*?

> **A** THE FARRELLY BROTHERS **B** THE COEN BROTHERS **C** THE WAYANS BROTHERS

7/5 ▶ A winged form of what animal is used in art to represent St Mark?

> **A** LION **B** HORSE **C** PIG

7/6 ▶ What is used to make the base of a quiche?

> **A** SPONGE **B** BREAD **C** PASTRY

7/7 ▶ Which of these is a real accent in Ireland?

> **A** LEINSTER WELSH **B** MUNSTER ENGLISH **C** ULSTER SCOTS

The Beast Quiz 7: Final Chase

★ Prize fund in the Final Chase was £35,000

★ Your target is 19 correct

Just 2 contestants reached the final in this programme. London-born Sonny, a 43-year-old recruitment consultant, contributed 17 of the pair's 20 correct answers, giving The Beast a total of 22 to chase. Successful execution of only 3 out of 8 push back chances was nevertheless sufficient for the duo to outrun their pursuer.

7/1 ▷ A standard UK plug socket has how many holes?

7/2 ▷ Which member of Girls Aloud was born in Newcastle?

7/3 ▷ In what year did Austria-Hungary cease to be an Empire?

7/4 ▷ In 1902, the Henry Ford Company became what luxury carmaker?

7/5 ▷ The twelve pairs of cerebral nerves arise from what organ?

7/6 ▷ In the US government, the DOJ is the 'Department of...' what?

7/7 ▷ What name is given to a person who runs a pawnshop?

7/8 ▷ Which cartoon title character has a pet snail named Gary?

7/9 ▷ What was the first name of the US President known as 'FDR'?

7/10 ▷ What type of creature is a crimson topaz?

7/11 ▷ The Double Deuce bar features in what Patrick Swayze film?

THE BEAST

7/12 ▷ A limequat is a cross between a key lime and which other fruit?

7/13 ▷ The novel *Red Planet Blues* is set on what planet?

7/14 ▷ Who played Bob Wallace in the 1950s film *White Christmas*?

7/15 ▷ What is the highest prime number on a roulette wheel?

7/16 ▷ Brazil is the largest country on what continent?

7/17 ▷ Riff and Bernardo are rival gang leaders in what musical?

7/18 ▷ Which children's author wrote the *Mary Mouse* series?

7/19 ▷ What Devon airport has the code EXT?

7/20 ▷ 'Uptown Funk' in 2014 was which DJ's first UK Number One?

7/21 ▷ 'Sheltie' is a nickname for what small breed of pony?

7/22 ▷ 'Bring Out The Best' is a trademark of what mayonnaise brand?

7/23 ▷ How is 'Basin City' known in a series of comics by Frank Miller?

7/24 ▷ In which of the Home Counties is Amersham?

7/25 ▷ The computing abbreviation VPN stands for 'virtual private...' what?

7/26 ▷ Joey Essex won what winter sports reality show in 2015?

The Beast Quiz 8: Contestant 1

Answer at least 5 questions correctly to progress on to the Final Chase.

8/1 ▶On his official Twitter account, which actor's biography states: 'I told you I'd be back'?

> **A** BRAD PITT **B** ARNOLD SCHWARZENEGGER **C** TOM CRUISE

8/2 ▶ In 2014, which country presented a claim to the UN for ownership of the North Pole?

> **A** DENMARK **B** NORWAY **C** SWEDEN

8/3 ▶ In George Orwell's *Animal Farm*, Old Major promoted ideas based on which philosophy?

> **A** COMMUNISM **B** FASCISM **C** CAPITALISM

8/4 ▶ The name of what condiment comes from a Hindi word meaning 'to lick'?

> **A** CHUTNEY **B** MAYONNAISE **C** MUSTARD

8/5 ▶ The 1997 Royal Parks and Other Open Spaces Regulations forbids feeding or touching which bird?

> **A** PARROT **B** PELICAN **C** PENGUIN

8/6 ▶ Who is the only English monarch to have been crowned King of France in France?

> **A** JOHN **B** RICHARD II **C** HENRY VI

8/7 ▶ Which of these US sitcoms was broadcast first?

> **A** *MORK & MINDY* **B** *SEX AND THE CITY* **C** *WILL & GRACE*

The Beast Quiz 8: Contestant 2

Answer at least 5 questions correctly to progress on to the Final Chase.

8/1 ▶ The Royal Navy's Museum of Naval Firepower in Gosport is called what?

> **A** EXPLOSION! **B** IGNITION! **C** BOOM!

8/2 ▶ Which of these is the symbol of a chemical element?

> **A** AS **B** IT **C** IS

8/3 ▶ What film series featured the voices of Eddie Murphy and Antonio Banderas?

> **A** *MONSTERS INC.* **B** *TOY STORY* **C** *SHREK*

8/4 ▶ What is the only prime number between 90 and 100?

> **A** 91 **B** 93 **C** 97

8/5 ▶ Which of these was the name of a real American blues pianist?

> **A** PINETOP PERKINS **B** OAKTOP OSBORNE **C** ELMTOP EDWARDS

8/6 ▶ Which term describes evidence that is not able to be used in a court of law?

> **A** INADMISSIBLE **B** OBJECTIONABLE **C** UNDESIRABLE

8/7 ▶ *The Magic Whip* in 2015 was which band's first new studio album for 12 years?

> **A** BLUR **B** PULP **C** OASIS

The Beast Quiz 8: Contestant 3

Answer at least 5 questions correctly to progress on to the Final Chase.

8/1 ▶ Which of these authors was NOT knighted?

> A KINGSLEY AMIS B ARTHUR CONAN DOYLE C J R R TOLKIEN

8/2 ▶ The name of what sea precedes 'climate' to describe areas with hot, dry summers and mild, wet winters?

> A BALTIC B CASPIAN C MEDITERRANEAN

8/3 ▶ The song 'Maniac' appears on the soundtrack of which 1980s film?

> A *FLASHDANCE* B *FOOTLOOSE* C *DIRTY DANCING*

8/4 ▶ In 2015, a hawkweed became the first new plant species discovered in the UK to be named after which broadcaster?

> A DAVID ATTENBOROUGH B JOHN CRAVEN C CHRIS PACKHAM

8/5 ▶ Which of these is the name of two books of the Old Testament?

> A KINGS B QUEENS C PRINCES

8/6 ▶ When it first opened, Chelsea's Stamford Bridge football ground was originally offered to what team?

> A ARSENAL B FULHAM C QPR

8/7 ▶ In what film does the actress Rebel Wilson say 'I'm gonna kill him! I'm gonna finish him like a cheesecake!'?

> A *BRIDESMAIDS* B *PITCH PERFECT* C *BACHELORETTE*

THE BEAST QUIZ 8: Contestant 3

THE BEAST

The Beast Quiz 8: Contestant 4

Answer at least 5 questions correctly to progress on to the Final Chase.

8/1 ▶ The oldest axes ever discovered are made of what material?

> **A** IRON **B** BRONZE **C** STONE

8/2 ▶ Which of these occupations would be most likely to use French chalk?

> **A** TAILOR **B** TEACHER **C** TILER

8/3 ▶ An audiologist would treat which of these medical problems?

> **A** ANOSMIA **B** MYOPIA **C** TINNITUS

8/4 ▶ Formed in Victorian times, what did members of the 'Band of Hope' pledge to avoid?

> **A** ALCOHOL **B** GAMBLING **C** SMOKING

8/5 ▶ Which king was made a saint by the Church of England?

> **A** WILLIAM II **B** EDWARD V **C** CHARLES I

8/6 ▶ Which of these singers uses their real first name?

> **A** LORDE **B** BONO **C** MADONNA

8/7 ▶ The seemingly random movement of particles in a liquid or gas is commonly known as what?

> **A** ALEXANDER MOTION **B** BROWNIAN MOTION **C** PERRIN MOTION

The Beast Quiz 8: Final Chase

★ Prize fund in the Final Chase was £35,000

★ Your target is 19 correct

Three contestants earned a place in the final. With 53-year-old Southampton supply teacher Ken leading the scoring, the team achieved a total of 16. After a confident start, The Beast became impatient and his interruptions to the questions conceded 13 push back chances of which the team capitalised on 7. The result was a catastrophic failure for The Beast.

8/1 ▶ What planet lies between Venus and Mars?

8/2 ▶ 'Princess of Pop' is a nickname of which Australian singer?

8/3 ▶ Buckingham Palace is in what London borough?

8/4 ▶ How many planets are closer to the Sun than Jupiter?

8/5 ▶ The Confed Cup is a short name for what football tournament?

8/6 ▶ What company was established in 1516 as 'The King's Posts'?

8/7 ▶ In what decade was the 50-pence piece first circulated?

8/8 ▶ Cartoonist Robert Crumb created *Fritz the...* what?

8/9 ▶ 'Weetos' are made by what cereal brand?

THE BEAST

8/10 ▶ Drogon is a dragon in what American TV show?

8/11 ▶ Which English philosopher wrote the 1859 work *On Liberty*?

8/12 ▶ What is the brightest object in the night sky?

8/13 ▶ What European city-state covers 109 acres?

8/14 ▶ *The Adventures of Parsley* was a spin off from what TV series?

8/15 ▶ Who was the Greek goddess of the dawn?

8/16 ▶ How many lions appear on the England cricket team's jumper?

8/17 ▶ In what city is the National Library of Scotland?

8/18 ▶ Jeff Daniels played anchorman Will McAvoy in what TV show?

8/19 ▶ 'Tis the season to be jolly' is a line from what carol?

8/20 ▶ A lactate is a salt of what acid?

8/21 ▶ *Hoop* is an American magazine dedicated to what sport?

8/22 ▶ On pencils, the letter 'H' indicates the hardness of what?

8/23 ▶ 'I Don't Need A Man' was a hit for what American girl group?

The Beast Quiz 9: Contestant 1

Answer at least 5 questions correctly to progress on to the Final Chase.

9/1 ▶ Which of these pop hits was released first?

> A 'DREAMS' – GABRIELLE B 'SWEET DREAMS' – BEYONCÉ C 'I HAVE A DREAM' – ABBA

9/2 ▶ What is the earliest known unit of length?

> A CUBIT B MILE C YARD

9/3 ▶ In 2015, who broke the record for women's alpine skiing World Cup wins?

> A ANNA FENNINGER B TINA MAZE C LINDSEY VONN

9/4 ▶ Which of these cheese-related places is NOT in the Netherlands?

> A JARLSBERG B EDAM C GOUDA

9/5 ▶ Alec Guinness described which of his films as 'fairy-tale rubbish'?

> A *DOCTOR ZHIVAGO* B *STAR WARS* C *LAWRENCE OF ARABIA*

9/6 ▶ When he crashed his McLaren F1 in 2011, who set a record of £910,000 for a car-repair insurance claim?

> A ROWAN ATKINSON B CHRIS EVANS C URI GELLER

9/7 ▶ In literature, what fictional language is 'the only language in the world whose vocabulary gets smaller every year'?

> A ELVISH B KLINGON C NEWSPEAK

The Beast Quiz 9: Contestant 2

Answer at least 5 questions correctly to progress on to the Final Chase.

9/1 ▶ George II and George IV both had wives with what name?

> **A** CAROLINE **B** CATHERINE **C** CHARLOTTE

9/2 ▶ Which actress stars as Fish Mooney in the TV series *Gotham*?

> **A** JADA PINKETT SMITH **B** HALLE BERRY **C** SALMA HAYEK

9/3 ▶ What is the only rock that floats on water?

> **A** FLINT **B** MARBLE **C** PUMICE

9/4 ▶ Who was the first Spice Girl to have a Number One single away from the group?

> **A** EMMA BUNTON **B** MELANIE BROWN **C** GERI HALLIWELL

9/5 ▶ Something that is 'anguine' resembles what animal?

> **A** OX **B** ROOSTER **C** SNAKE

9/6 ▶ Which of these days is NOT named after a Norse deity?

> **A** THURSDAY **B** FRIDAY **C** SATURDAY

9/7 ▶ What is a philocubist?

> **A** A LOVER OF DICE GAMES **B** A PHASE OF CUBIST PAINTING **C** A MAKER OF BOXES

The Beast Quiz 9: Contestant 3

Answer at least 5 questions correctly to progress on to the Final Chase.

9/1 ▶ The philosopher Albert Camus said 'Everything I know about morality and the obligations of men, I owe to...' what?

> **A** FOOTBALL **B** BEING FRENCH **C** TINTIN

9/2 ▶ Which chef developed 'cherry bakewell vodka'?

> **A** HESTON BLUMENTHAL **B** JAMIE OLIVER **C** KEITH FLOYD

9/3 ▶ In April 2015, the Americas were declared the first region to be free from what disease?

> **A** CHICKENPOX **B** RUBELLA **C** ATHLETE'S FOOT

9/4 ▶ Who sang on the 2010 Swedish House Mafia hit 'One (Your Name)'?

> **A** ANDRÉ 3000 **B** FLO RIDA **C** PHARRELL WILLIAMS

9/5 ▶ Between 1973 and 2006, which tennis star played in 325 matches at Wimbledon?

> **A** BILLIE JEAN KING **B** STEFFI GRAF **C** MARTINA NAVRATILOVA

9/6 ▶ Which of these films did NOT star Grace Kelly?

> **A** *HIGH ANXIETY* **B** *HIGH NOON* **C** *HIGH SOCIETY*

9/7 ▶ The Battle of Actium features in which Shakespeare play?

> **A** *ANTONY AND CLEOPATRA* **B** *TIMON OF ATHENS* **C** *TROILUS AND CRESSIDA*

The Beast Quiz 9: Contestant 4

Answer at least 5 questions correctly to progress on to the Final Chase.

9/1 ▶ The term 'relevé' refers to the heels rising off the ground in which form of dance?

> **A** BALLET **B** FLAMENCO **C** TANGO

9/2 ▶ To date, who is the longest-serving Leader of the Opposition in the House of Commons?

> **A** WINSTON CHURCHILL **B** NEIL KINNOCK **C** MARGARET THATCHER

9/3 ▶ Which coastal town is home to the Royal Navy Submarine Museum?

> **A** CHATHAM **B** SALCOMBE **C** GOSPORT

9/4 ▶ Which of these US sitcoms was NOT named after the actress who starred in it?

> **A** *ELLEN* **B** *ROSEANNE* **C** *RHODA*

9/5 ▶ What is the usual job of someone with the letters MICE after their name?

> **A** CIVIL ENGINEER **B** CHIEF EXECUTIVE **C** CAT EXTERMINATOR

9/6 ▶ Which saint has his feast day on New Year's Eve?

> **A** ST ARNOLD **B** ST VINCENT **C** ST SYLVESTER

9/7 ▶ The Benjamin Britten opera *The Turn of the Screw* is based on a story by which author?

> **A** HENRY FIELDING **B** HENRY MILLER **C** HENRY JAMES

The Beast Quiz 9: Final Chase

⭐ Prize fund in the Final Chase was £35,000

⭐ Your target is 19 correct

In this programme 3 players made it to the final. They amassed an astonishing total of 25 for The Beast to chase, with contributions from all three. The Beast motored through his questions, but the team were able to execute only 1 out of 5 push back opportunities. With his target within reach, The Beast suffered 'brain freeze' and failed to outrun the contestants.

9/1 ▷ In what sport are dogs raced from traps?

9/2 ▷ What area of Moscow do the French call La Place Rouge?

9/3 ▷ Megan Mullally played Karen Walker in what US sitcom?

9/4 ▷ Carthaginian is another name for what series of wars?

9/5 ▷ In the game 'Rock Paper Scissors' what beats 'Rock'?

9/6 ▷ What Verdi opera was commissioned by the Khedive of Egypt?

9/7 ▷ 'Stena Line' specialises in what sort of shipping?

9/8 ▷ *Allan Quatermain* is the sequel to what H Rider Haggard novel?

9/9 ▷ W is the symbol for what unit of power?

9/10 ▷ Na'vi is a fictional language in what James Cameron film?

THE BEAST

9/11 ▷ Which Austrian was UN Secretary-General in the 1970s?

9/12 ▷ A transdermal patch delivers medicine through what organ?

9/13 ▷ Who sang lead vocals on the 1980 Number One 'Brass in Pocket'?

9/14 ▷ 'Aardvark' and 'meerkat' are words from what African language?

9/15 ▷ Which Rugby League Super League team is based in France?

9/16 ▷ What's the legal process by which a marriage is ended?

9/17 ▷ What surname links pop singer David and *TOWIE* star Joey?

9/18 ▷ The Kuiper Belt extends beyond the orbit of what planet?

9/19 ▷ What company makes the chocolate bar TimeOut?

9/20 ▷ The Munch Museum is in what European capital?

9/21 ▷ What's three-quarters of forty?

9/22 ▷ The myxoma virus causes what disease in rabbits?

9/23 ▷ Thomas Jefferson was what US President's Secretary of State?

9/24 ▷ Which TV chef owns a restaurant called 'Fifteen'?

9/25 ▷ What film industry's name is a blend of Bombay and Hollywood?

THE BEAST QUIZ 9: Final Chase

The Beast Quiz 10: Contestant 1

Answer at least 5 questions correctly to progress on to the Final Chase.

10/1 ▶ Somebody who does something too soon is said to have done what?

A DRIVEN THE RIFLE B THROWN THE PISTOL C JUMPED THE GUN

10/2 ▶ A 'Brucie Bonus' was a regular feature of which TV game show?

A *PLAY YOUR CARDS RIGHT* B *THE GENERATION GAME* C *THE PRICE IS RIGHT*

10/3 ▶ Which of these is the name of a mountain range on New Zealand's South Island?

A THE BRILLIANTS B THE PHENOMENALS C THE REMARKABLES

10/4 ▶ On what mode of transport would you find a bowsprit?

A CAR B AEROPLANE C BOAT

10/5 ▶ Which future Labour leader stood unsuccessfully at a by-election in Beaconsfield in 1982?

A ED MILIBAND B GORDON BROWN C TONY BLAIR

10/6 ▶ In gambling, what odds are also known as 'scotch'?

A EVENS B THREE TO ONE C TEN TO ONE

10/7 ▶ Which of these structures was NOT built by the ancient Romans?

A PANTHEON B COLOSSEUM C PARTHENON

The Beast Quiz 10: Contestant 2

Answer at least 5 questions correctly to progress on to the Final Chase.

10/1 ▶ The drink known as a B&B consists of Bénédictine and what?

> **A** BEER **B** BRANDY **C** BURGUNDY

10/2 ▶ Which of these is NOT a play by Oscar Wilde?

> **A** *A FLORENTINE TRAGEDY* **B** *THE DUCHESS OF PADUA* **C** *DEATH IN VENICE*

10/3 ▶ What is the most numerous instrument in a standard symphony orchestra?

> **A** TRUMPET **B** FLUTE **C** VIOLIN

10/4 ▶ In 1986, which future James Bond had to turn down an initial offer of the role because of contractual obligations on TV?

> **A** TIMOTHY DALTON **B** PIERCE BROSNAN **C** DANIEL CRAIG

10/5 ▶ What nickname was given to Lord Chancellor Derry Irvine because of his controversial spending of public money?

> **A** LORD WALLPAPER **B** LORD IPAD **C** LORD DUCK POND

10/6 ▶ What name is given to the colonies in which true oysters are found?

> **A** BEDS **B** CHAIRS **C** TABLES

10/7 ▶ Bertie Carvel and Eddie Marsan played the title characters in the fantasy TV series *Jonathan Strange &...* who?

> **A** *MR NORRELL* **B** *MR JOLLY* **C** *MR HYDE*

The Beast Quiz 10: Contestant 3

Answer at least 5 questions correctly to progress on to the Final Chase.

10/1 ▶ Which of these major corporations does **NOT** have its headquarters in Seattle?

> **A** STARBUCKS **B** AMAZON **C** EBAY

10/2 ▶ In sumo wrestling, what does the referee wear?

> **A** KIMONO **B** PONCHO **C** TUXEDO

10/3 ▶ What name was given to Ancient Greek philosophers who didn't attach themselves to a particular school?

> **A** EPICURES **B** CYNICS **C** ECLECTICS

10/4 ▶ Which of these authors was born first?

> **A** J G BALLARD **B** J D SALINGER **C** J K ROWLING

10/5 ▶ Which Oscar-winning actress was a star of the British gangster film *The Long Good Friday*?

> **A** GLENDA JACKSON **B** HELEN MIRREN **C** EMMA THOMPSON

10/6 ▶ What is the meaning of the word 'veracity'?

> **A** WEALTH **B** LOVE **C** TRUTH

10/7 ▶ Jessica Drew is the alias of which superheroine?

> **A** SUPERWOMAN **B** BATWOMAN **C** SPIDER-WOMAN

The Beast Quiz 10: Contestant 4

Answer at least 5 questions correctly to progress on to the Final Chase.

10/1 ▶ In 2014, what was the second most commonly held reserve currency after the US dollar?

> **A** EURO **B** JAPANESE YEN **C** POUND STERLING

10/2 ▶ In what sitcom are the main characters Max and Caroline trying to set up their own business?

> **A** *2 BROKE GIRLS* **B** *NEW GIRL* **C** *THE GOLDEN GIRLS*

10/3 ▶ Which *Harry Potter* star was named 2015 male 'Rear of the Year'?

> **A** DANIEL RADCLIFFE **B** ALAN RICKMAN **C** ROBBIE COLTRANE

10/4 ▶ 20 kilograms is approximately how many pounds?

> **A** 22 **B** 33 **C** 44

10/5 ▶ What is the only British bird that can climb down trees as well as up them?

> **A** NIGHTINGALE **B** NIGHTJAR **C** NUTHATCH

10/6 ▶ Which of these singing voices is the highest?

> **A** ALTO **B** BARITONE **C** TENOR

10/7 ▶ With earnings of $300 million, which sportsman topped the *Forbes* 2015 list of the world's highest-paid athletes?

> **A** NOVAK DJOKOVIC **B** FLOYD MAYWEATHER **C** TIGER WOODS

The Beast Quiz 10: Final Chase

★ Prize fund in the Final Chase was £35,000

★ Your target is 19 correct

Two contestants reached the final in this programme. Helen, a 46-year-old science and maths tutor from Melton Mowbray, provided all 15 of the pair's correct answers, producing a total of 17 for The Beast to chase. In a nail-biting finish, The Beast stumbled on the final question to allow the pair to outrun him, having executed 4 out of 7 push back chances.

10/1 ▶ Alongside chips, what's the main ingredient in a chip butty?

10/2 ▶ Ophthalmia affects which parts of the body?

10/3 ▶ The River Tweed rises in the Borders and flows into what sea?

10/4 ▶ The Levellers were a democratic party during what war?

10/5 ▶ What term for a Formula One race means 'big prize' in French?

10/6 ▶ In the game 'Hearts', what playing card is 'The Black Lady'?

10/7 ▶ What confectionery company owns Milky Way?

10/8 ▶ Nicodemus Boffin features in what Charles Dickens novel?

10/9 ▶ *Backwoods Barbie* was an album by which country singer?

THE BEAST

10/10 ▶ The name of what royal house is the Welsh form of Theodore?

10/11 ▶ Named after a Turkish town, what fruit is a casaba?

10/12 ▶ The *Mona Lisa* was stolen from what museum in 1911?

10/13 ▶ Bristol Zoo featured in what Johnny Morris TV wildlife show?

10/14 ▶ What name is given to a viaduct that carries a canal?

10/15 ▶ London's first public playhouses were built in what century?

10/16 ▶ Members of which of the armed forces 'go ashore'?

10/17 ▶ 'Let Me Entertain You' was a 1990s hit for which singer?

10/18 ▶ What mode of transport is a Super Voyager?

10/19 ▶ Cover and point are fielding positions in what sport?

10/20 ▶ Anna Chancellor played Juliet Shaw in what BBC spy drama?

10/21 ▶ What element is added to table salt to make iodised salt?

10/22 ▶ In what hobby are loppers used as a pruning tool?

ANSWERS

The Governess Quiz 1

Contestant 1

1/1 ▶ C	1/3 ▶ B	1/5 ▶ C	1/7 ▶ B
1/2 ▶ A	1/4 ▶ C	1/6 ▶ A	

Contestant 2

1/1 ▶ C	1/3 ▶ A	1/5 ▶ A	1/7 ▶ B
1/2 ▶ C	1/4 ▶ C	1/6 ▶ A	

Contestant 3

1/1 ▶ C	1/3 ▶ C	1/5 ▶ A	1/7 ▶ B
1/2 ▶ A	1/4 ▶ A	1/6 ▶ A	

Contestant 4

1/1 ▶ A	1/3 ▶ B	1/5 ▶ C	1/7 ▶ C
1/2 ▶ A	1/4 ▶ B	1/6 ▶ C	

Final Chase

1/1 ▶ Euro	1/14 ▶ Francis of Assisi
1/2 ▶ *The Voice*	1/15 ▶ Toni Collette
1/3 ▶ The Queen	1/16 ▶ Mumbai
1/4 ▶ Norway	1/17 ▶ Rodents
1/5 ▶ 90	1/18 ▶ Andy Carroll
1/6 ▶ Lee Ryan	1/19 ▶ The Terrible
1/7 ▶ March	1/20 ▶ Britney Spears
1/8 ▶ Quito	1/21 ▶ Their onions
1/9 ▶ Tennis	1/22 ▶ Gino D'Acampo
1/10 ▶ Nadine Coyle	1/23 ▶ *Cuban Fury*
1/11 ▶ George Washington	1/24 ▶ Glucose
1/12 ▶ Johnson's	1/25 ▶ Hawaii
1/13 ▶ Tennyson	

The Governess Quiz 2

Contestant 1

2/1 ▶ C	2/3 ▶ C	2/5 ▶ A	2/7 ▶ B
2/2 ▶ C	2/4 ▶ A	2/6 ▶ C	

Contestant 2

2/1 ▶ C	2/3 ▶ C	2/5 ▶ A	2/7 ▶ A
2/2 ▶ B	2/4 ▶ B	2/6 ▶ B	

Contestant 3

2/1 ▶ C	2/3 ▶ A	2/5 ▶ C	2/7 ▶ A
2/2 ▶ C	2/4 ▶ A	2/6 ▶ A	

Contestant 4

2/1 ▶ A	2/3 ▶ B	2/5 ▶ A	2/7 ▶ B
2/2 ▶ C	2/4 ▶ C	2/6 ▶ B	

Final Chase

2/1 ▶ Blackcurrant	2/14 ▶ Brain
2/2 ▶ Willow	2/15 ▶ Three
2/3 ▶ Timothy West	2/16 ▶ Son
2/4 ▶ Cullen	2/17 ▶ 1940s
2/5 ▶ Windows	2/18 ▶ Malcolm McDowell
2/6 ▶ Ten	2/19 ▶ French
2/7 ▶ USA	2/20 ▶ Lungs
2/8 ▶ Lime	2/21 ▶ Swansea City
2/9 ▶ Sean Connery	2/22 ▶ One Hundred
2/10 ▶ White	2/23 ▶ Spring tide
2/11 ▶ Dutch	2/24 ▶ Hazelnut
2/12 ▶ Canterbury	2/25 ▶ New Jersey
2/13 ▶ Mediterranean	2/26 ▶ Abyssinian
	2/27 ▶ Four

The Governess Quiz 3

Contestant 1

3/1 ▶ A	3/3 ▶ C	3/5 ▶ C	3/7 ▶ C
3/2 ▶ C	3/4 ▶ C	3/6 ▶ B	

Contestant 2

3/1 ▶ C	3/3 ▶ A	3/5 ▶ A	3/7 ▶ C
3/2 ▶ B	3/4 ▶ A	3/6 ▶ A	

Contestant 3

3/1 ▶ A	3/3 ▶ C	3/5 ▶ B	3/7 ▶ A
3/2 ▶ B	3/4 ▶ C	3/6 ▶ A	

Contestant 4

3/1 ▶ C	3/3 ▶ A	3/5 ▶ C	3/7 ▶ A
3/2 ▶ A	3/4 ▶ A	3/6 ▶ A	

Final Chase

3/1 ▶ Dressing	3/14 ▶ World War Two
3/2 ▶ Atlantic	3/15 ▶ Bedfordshire
3/3 ▶ Rob Roy	3/16 ▶ Bread
3/4 ▶ Stieg Larsson	3/17 ▶ *Mamma Mia!*
3/5 ▶ Foghorn Leghorn	3/18 ▶ Jack Straw
3/6 ▶ Monocle	3/19 ▶ Dick Whittington
3/7 ▶ *Discworld*	3/20 ▶ Robert the Bruce
3/8 ▶ Austria	3/21 ▶ Hawaii
3/9 ▶ Christopher Columbus	3/22 ▶ Dublin
3/10 ▶ *The Good, The Bad and The Ugly*	3/23 ▶ *Adam Bede*
3/11 ▶ The America's Cup	3/24 ▶ Vendetta
3/12 ▶ Brain	3/25 ▶ 'We'll Meet Again'
3/13 ▶ Alan Bennett	

The Governess Quiz 4

Contestant 1

| 4/1 ▶ A | 4/3 ▶ C | 4/5 ▶ C | 4/7 ▶ A |
| 4/2 ▶ B | 4/4 ▶ A | 4/6 ▶ A | |

Contestant 2

| 4/1 ▶ A | 4/3 ▶ B | 4/5 ▶ C | 4/7 ▶ A |
| 4/2 ▶ C | 4/4 ▶ B | 4/6 ▶ C | |

Contestant 3

| 4/1 ▶ A | 4/3 ▶ A | 4/5 ▶ C | 4/7 ▶ C |
| 4/2 ▶ A | 4/4 ▶ A | 4/6 ▶ B | |

Contestant 4

| 4/1 ▶ A | 4/3 ▶ C | 4/5 ▶ C | 4/7 ▶ A |
| 4/2 ▶ B | 4/4 ▶ B | 4/6 ▶ A | |

Final Chase

4/1 ▶ will.i.am	4/14 ▶ Blue
4/2 ▶ Thirty-six	4/15 ▶ Julie Andrews
4/3 ▶ *Hot Fuzz*	4/16 ▶ Teeth
4/4 ▶ William Wordsworth	4/17 ▶ World War Two
4/5 ▶ The Stature of Liberty	4/18 ▶ South Carolina
4/6 ▶ Paul Weller	4/19 ▶ Venus
4/7 ▶ White	4/20 ▶ Bear Grylls
4/8 ▶ Herbert Asquith	4/21 ▶ Helium
4/9 ▶ Porky Pig	4/22 ▶ San Francisco Bay
4/10 ▶ Richard II	4/23 ▶ *The Man with the Golden Gun*
4/11 ▶ Men At Work	4/24 ▶ Magaluf
4/12 ▶ Golf	4/25 ▶ Tee
4/13 ▶ 1940s	4/26 ▶ Mason-Dixon

The Governess Quiz 5

Contestant 1

5/1 ▶ C	5/3 ▶ B	5/5 ▶ A	5/7 ▶ C
5/2 ▶ C	5/4 ▶ C	5/6 ▶ A	

Contestant 2

5/1 ▶ A	5/3 ▶ C	5/5 ▶ C	5/7 ▶ C
5/2 ▶ A	5/4 ▶ B	5/6 ▶ B	

Contestant 3

5/1 ▶ B	5/3 ▶ C	5/5 ▶ B	5/7 ▶ C
5/2 ▶ C	5/4 ▶ C	5/6 ▶ C	

Contestant 4

5/1 ▶ A	5/3 ▶ B	5/5 ▶ C	5/7 ▶ B
5/2 ▶ C	5/4 ▶ B	5/6 ▶ B	

Final Chase

5/1 ▶ Teeth	5/14 ▶ National
5/2 ▶ Australia	5/15 ▶ Kaufman
5/3 ▶ Butterfly	5/16 ▶ London
5/4 ▶ Judges	5/17 ▶ Boiling
5/5 ▶ Swansea	5/18 ▶ Lea Michele
5/6 ▶ Disney	5/19 ▶ Winston Churchill
5/7 ▶ Matches	5/20 ▶ Hydrogen
5/8 ▶ Germany	5/21 ▶ The Beatles
5/9 ▶ 180	5/22 ▶ P G Wodehouse
5/10 ▶ Post Office	5/23 ▶ 540
5/11 ▶ Elmore Leonard	5/24 ▶ Belfast
5/12 ▶ Kingston	5/25 ▶ Jones
5/13 ▶ Tinky Winky	

THE GOVERNESS

The Governess Quiz 6

Contestant 1

6/1 ▶ A	6/3 ▶ C	6/5 ▶ A	6/7 ▶ A
6/2 ▶ A	6/4 ▶ A	6/6 ▶ A	

Contestant 2

6/1 ▶ C	6/3 ▶ A	6/5 ▶ A	6/7 ▶ A
6/2 ▶ C	6/4 ▶ C	6/6 ▶ B	

Contestant 3

6/1 ▶ C	6/3 ▶ B	6/5 ▶ C	6/7 ▶ B
6/2 ▶ C	6/4 ▶ A	6/6 ▶ B	

Contestant 4

6/1 ▶ A	6/3 ▶ C	6/5 ▶ A	6/7 ▶ A
6/2 ▶ C	6/4 ▶ C	6/6 ▶ C	

Final Chase

6/1 ▶ April and August	6/13 ▶ Thrush
6/2 ▶ Wolverine	6/14 ▶ Tank
6/3 ▶ 1960s	6/15 ▶ Katy Perry
6/4 ▶ Buddhism	6/16 ▶ Six
6/5 ▶ Cheese	6/17 ▶ Oxford
6/6 ▶ 'Don't Cry for Me Argentina'	6/18 ▶ Poker
6/7 ▶ Isle of Wight	6/19 ▶ Medusa
6/8 ▶ Elizabeth the First	6/20 ▶ *Peter Pan*
6/9 ▶ S Club 7	6/21 ▶ Russian
6/10 ▶ Cricket	6/22 ▶ Grave
6/11 ▶ Mazda	6/23 ▶ Dominic
6/12 ▶ Morocco	6/24 ▶ Nineteenth

The Governess Quiz 7

Contestant 1

7/1 ▶ B	7/3 ▶ A	7/5 ▶ C	7/7 ▶ C
7/2 ▶ A	7/4 ▶ A	7/6 ▶ A	

Contestant 2

7/1 ▶ A	7/3 ▶ A	7/5 ▶ A	7/7 ▶ C
7/2 ▶ A	7/4 ▶ C	7/6 ▶ C	

Contestant 3

7/1 ▶ A	7/3 ▶ C	7/5 ▶ A	7/7 ▶ C
7/2 ▶ C	7/4 ▶ B	7/6 ▶ C	

Contestant 4

7/1 ▶ A	7/3 ▶ B	7/5 ▶ A	7/7 ▶ C
7/2 ▶ C	7/4 ▶ A	7/6 ▶ B	

Final Chase

7/1 ▶ Mediterranean	7/14 ▶ Connecticut
7/2 ▶ Message	7/15 ▶ Red
7/3 ▶ George the Fifth	7/16 ▶ Marian
7/4 ▶ Fifty	7/17 ▶ Christopher Columbus
7/5 ▶ Gustav	7/18 ▶ *Kim*
7/6 ▶ (The) Montague(s)	7/19 ▶ October
7/7 ▶ J R R Tolkien	7/20 ▶ John Brown
7/8 ▶ Salisbury	7/21 ▶ Liverpool
7/9 ▶ Cow	7/22 ▶ Park
7/10 ▶ Scotland	7/23 ▶ Buck Rarebit
7/11 ▶ *Madam Butterfly*	7/24 ▶ Obituaries
7/12 ▶ Leeward	7/25 ▶ *The Archers*
7/13 ▶ Fish	

The Governess Quiz 8

Contestant 1

8/1 ▶ C	8/3 ▶ A	8/5 ▶ C	8/7 ▶ A
8/2 ▶ C	8/4 ▶ A	8/6 ▶ A	

Contestant 2

8/1 ▶ B	8/3 ▶ C	8/5 ▶ B	8/7 ▶ B
8/2 ▶ C	8/4 ▶ A	8/6 ▶ A	

Contestant 3

8/1 ▶ B	8/3 ▶ A	8/5 ▶ B	8/7 ▶ C
8/2 ▶ A	8/4 ▶ B	8/6 ▶ C	

Contestant 4

8/1 ▶ B	8/3 ▶ C	8/5 ▶ C	8/7 ▶ A
8/2 ▶ A	8/4 ▶ A	8/6 ▶ A	

Final Chase

8/1 ▶ Philadelphia	8/13 ▶ Betty Rubble
8/2 ▶ *Supermarket Sweep*	8/14 ▶ Stumped
8/3 ▶ Barack Obama	8/15 ▶ *London Fields*
8/4 ▶ 12th	8/16 ▶ Anne
8/5 ▶ Rafael Nadal	8/17 ▶ France
8/6 ▶ Andromeda	8/18 ▶ John Legend
8/7 ▶ Hotel California	8/19 ▶ Heel
8/8 ▶ Victor Hugo	8/20 ▶ Bluebell
8/9 ▶ One-fifth	8/21 ▶ Flour
8/10 ▶ Emmanuel	8/22 ▶ One
8/11 ▶ Peru	8/23 ▶ Muffler
8/12 ▶ 1950s	

The Governess Quiz 9

Contestant 1

9/1 ▶ B   9/3 ▶ B   9/5 ▶ A   9/7 ▶ C
9/2 ▶ A   9/4 ▶ A   9/6 ▶ C

Contestant 2

9/1 ▶ B   9/3 ▶ B   9/5 ▶ C   9/7 ▶ A
9/2 ▶ C   9/4 ▶ A   9/6 ▶ B

Contestant 3

9/1 ▶ B   9/3 ▶ B   9/5 ▶ A   9/7 ▶ A
9/2 ▶ C   9/4 ▶ B   9/6 ▶ B

Contestant 4

9/1 ▶ B   9/3 ▶ C   9/5 ▶ A   9/7 ▶ C
9/2 ▶ A   9/4 ▶ B   9/6 ▶ B

Final Chase

9/1 ▶ Yolk
9/2 ▶ *Coronation Street*
9/3 ▶ Saturn
9/4 ▶ Literature
9/5 ▶ Patrick Swayze
9/6 ▶ Newmarket
9/7 ▶ The Queen
9/8 ▶ *Girls*
9/9 ▶ Nelson Mandela
9/10 ▶ Domestic
9/11 ▶ M62
9/12 ▶ Dog

9/13 ▶ Jerusalem
9/14 ▶ 1960s
9/15 ▶ *La Bohème*
9/16 ▶ 17
9/17 ▶ Greek
9/18 ▶ Cumbria
9/19 ▶ Andrew Lloyd Webber
9/20 ▶ Salt Lake City
9/21 ▶ 31
9/22 ▶ North Sea
9/23 ▶ Alana Hamilton

The Governess Quiz 10

Contestant 1

10/1 ▶ C	10/3 ▶ B	10/5 ▶ A	10/7 ▶ A
10/2 ▶ C	10/4 ▶ A	10/6 ▶ A	

Contestant 2

10/1 ▶ C	10/3 ▶ A	10/5 ▶ A	10/7 ▶ B
10/2 ▶ C	10/4 ▶ A	10/6 ▶ B	

Contestant 3

10/1 ▶ C	10/3 ▶ A	10/5 ▶ C	10/7 ▶ A
10/2 ▶ C	10/4 ▶ C	10/6 ▶ C	

Contestant 4

10/1 ▶ C	10/3 ▶ B	10/5 ▶ A	10/7 ▶ A
10/2 ▶ B	10/4 ▶ C	10/6 ▶ C	

Final Chase

10/1 ▶ Head	10/14 ▶ Hand-cuffs
10/2 ▶ Jazz	10/15 ▶ Panthéon
10/3 ▶ Six	10/16 ▶ 41
10/4 ▶ 1920s	10/17 ▶ The Navy
10/5 ▶ *EastEnders*	10/18 ▶ Rugby
10/6 ▶ Trident	10/19 ▶ Two
10/7 ▶ Chariot race	10/20 ▶ Cranberry
10/8 ▶ Cold blooded	10/21 ▶ Bird
10/9 ▶ Frankie Howerd	10/22 ▶ Billie Piper
10/10 ▶ US dollar	10/23 ▶ 19th
10/11 ▶ Dr. Dre	10/24 ▶ Hinduism
10/12 ▶ Arsenal	10/25 ▶ Chancellor of the Exchequer
10/13 ▶ Gus	

The Sinnerman Quiz 1

Contestant 1

1/1 ▶ C	1/3 ▶ C	1/5 ▶ A	1/7 ▶ C
1/2 ▶ C	1/4 ▶ C	1/6 ▶ C	

Contestant 2

1/1 ▶ C	1/3 ▶ C	1/5 ▶ C	1/7 ▶ C
1/2 ▶ B	1/4 ▶ C	1/6 ▶ B	

Contestant 3

1/1 ▶ C	1/3 ▶ A	1/5 ▶ C	1/7 ▶ C
1/2 ▶ C	1/4 ▶ C	1/6 ▶ C	

Contestant 4

1/1 ▶ A	1/3 ▶ A	1/5 ▶ A	1/7 ▶ C
1/2 ▶ B	1/4 ▶ A	1/6 ▶ C	

Final Chase

1/1 ▶ Conservative	1/13 ▶ Spain
1/2 ▶ *Brookside*	1/14 ▶ Golf
1/3 ▶ Gold	1/15 ▶ *Goodnight Mister Tom*
1/4 ▶ Cumbria	1/16 ▶ Green
1/5 ▶ Three	1/17 ▶ Hyde Park
1/6 ▶ David Guetta	1/18 ▶ Kanye West
1/7 ▶ Surfing	1/19 ▶ Treasure map
1/8 ▶ Straw	1/20 ▶ Two
1/9 ▶ Four	1/21 ▶ Cows
1/10 ▶ Mary Jane	1/22 ▶ Football
1/11 ▶ 'The Iliad'	1/23 ▶ *The Big Bang Theory*
1/12 ▶ Bette	1/24 ▶ Certificate of Secondary Education

The Sinnerman Quiz 2

Contestant 1

2/1 ▶ C	2/3 ▶ A	2/5 ▶ C	2/7 ▶ C
2/2 ▶ A	2/4 ▶ C	2/6 ▶ B	

Contestant 2

2/1 ▶ B	2/3 ▶ C	2/5 ▶ A	2/7 ▶ C
2/2 ▶ A	2/4 ▶ C	2/6 ▶ A	

Contestant 3

2/1 ▶ C	2/3 ▶ C	2/5 ▶ C	2/7 ▶ C
2/2 ▶ B	2/4 ▶ A	2/6 ▶ C	

Contestant 4

2/1 ▶ B	2/3 ▶ C	2/5 ▶ A	2/7 ▶ C
2/2 ▶ A	2/4 ▶ C	2/6 ▶ B	

Final Chase

2/1 ▶ Wednesday	2/13 ▶ Austria
2/2 ▶ Knee	2/14 ▶ World War Two
2/3 ▶ *Fight Club*	2/15 ▶ All Saints' Day
2/4 ▶ Tony Blair	2/16 ▶ *Superman*
2/5 ▶ Ten	2/17 ▶ Fidel Castro
2/6 ▶ Australia	2/18 ▶ Puccini
2/7 ▶ Wilde	2/19 ▶ Rhode Island
2/8 ▶ Jamaica Inn	2/20 ▶ Kanye West
2/9 ▶ Uncle	2/21 ▶ Shoes
2/10 ▶ A	2/22 ▶ Jet
2/11 ▶ Vitali Klitschko	2/23 ▶ LX
2/12 ▶ Guinevere	

The Sinnerman Quiz 3

Contestant 1

3/1 ▶ C   3/3 ▶ C   3/5 ▶ A   3/7 ▶ A
3/2 ▶ C   3/4 ▶ A   3/6 ▶ C

Contestant 2

3/1 ▶ B   3/3 ▶ C   3/5 ▶ C   3/7 ▶ B
3/2 ▶ A   3/4 ▶ A   3/6 ▶ A

Contestant 3

3/1 ▶ C   3/3 ▶ B   3/5 ▶ C   3/7 ▶ A
3/2 ▶ B   3/4 ▶ C   3/6 ▶ C

Contestant 4

3/1 ▶ A   3/3 ▶ A   3/5 ▶ C   3/7 ▶ B
3/2 ▶ C   3/4 ▶ A   3/6 ▶ C

Final Chase

3/1 ▶ Paris
3/2 ▶ Tomato
3/3 ▶ Carol Ann Duffy
3/4 ▶ Gladstone
3/5 ▶ Barcelona
3/6 ▶ Four
3/7 ▶ Missy Elliott
3/8 ▶ *Funny Girl*
3/9 ▶ Oxford
3/10 ▶ Fletcher Christian
3/11 ▶ *The O.C.*

3/12 ▶ Switzerland
3/13 ▶ Frida Kahlo
3/14 ▶ Liverpool
3/15 ▶ *Chess*
3/16 ▶ 1970s
3/17 ▶ A pub
3/18 ▶ United States
3/19 ▶ Rubber
3/20 ▶ Romeo
3/21 ▶ RAF
3/22 ▶ Chocolate Orange

The Sinnerman Quiz 4

Contestant 1

4/1 ▶ C	4/3 ▶ B	4/5 ▶ B	4/7 ▶ C
4/2 ▶ B	4/4 ▶ A	4/6 ▶ C	

Contestant 2

4/1 ▶ C	4/3 ▶ B	4/5 ▶ A	4/7 ▶ A
4/2 ▶ A	4/4 ▶ A	4/6 ▶ A	

Contestant 3

4/1 ▶ A	4/3 ▶ A	4/5 ▶ A	4/7 ▶ A
4/2 ▶ B	4/4 ▶ A	4/6 ▶ C	

Contestant 4

4/1 ▶ B	4/3 ▶ C	4/5 ▶ A	4/7 ▶ A
4/2 ▶ C	4/4 ▶ B	4/6 ▶ C	

Final Chase

4/1 ▶ Biscuit	4/14 ▶ Indira Gandhi
4/2 ▶ *Tootsie*	4/15 ▶ Yugoslav
4/3 ▶ North America	4/16 ▶ Hot water
4/4 ▶ Methuselah	4/17 ▶ Three
4/5 ▶ Ice hockey	4/18 ▶ Georges Seurat
4/6 ▶ easyJet	4/19 ▶ Eddie Redmayne
4/7 ▶ *The Lord of the Rings*	4/20 ▶ Humerus
4/8 ▶ JLS	4/21 ▶ Train
4/9 ▶ 19th	4/22 ▶ Henry the Eighth
4/10 ▶ Chile	4/23 ▶ *Cold Comfort Farm*
4/11 ▶ Monkey	4/24 ▶ Wyclef Jean
4/12 ▶ Forsythia	4/25 ▶ Atlantic
4/13 ▶ *Emmerdale*	4/26 ▶ Omar Sharif

The Sinnerman Quiz 5

Contestant 1

5/1 ▶ A	5/3 ▶ C	5/5 ▶ C	5/7 ▶ A
5/2 ▶ A	5/4 ▶ C	5/6 ▶ A	

Contestant 2

5/1 ▶ A	5/3 ▶ B	5/5 ▶ C	5/7 ▶ A
5/2 ▶ C	5/4 ▶ B	5/6 ▶ A	

Contestant 3

5/1 ▶ C	5/3 ▶ A	5/5 ▶ A	5/7 ▶ A
5/2 ▶ C	5/4 ▶ B	5/6 ▶ A	

Contestant 4

5/1 ▶ B	5/3 ▶ C	5/5 ▶ A	5/7 ▶ C
5/2 ▶ B	5/4 ▶ B	5/6 ▶ C	

Final Chase

5/1 ▶ Head	5/12 ▶ Medieval
5/2 ▶ Australia	5/13 ▶ Gin
5/3 ▶ *Casualty*	5/14 ▶ Daffy Duck
5/4 ▶ *The Night Watch*	5/15 ▶ King Arthur
5/5 ▶ 89	5/16 ▶ Children
5/6 ▶ 'Making Your Mind Up'	5/17 ▶ North America
5/7 ▶ Sugar	5/18 ▶ Carlos Acosta
5/8 ▶ Durban	5/19 ▶ Two
5/9 ▶ Water	5/20 ▶ Inspector Wexford
5/10 ▶ *The Iron Lady*	5/21 ▶ Cadbury's
5/11 ▶ *Carmina Burana*	5/22 ▶ Earth

THE SINNERMAN

The Sinnerman Quiz 6

Contestant 1

6/1 ▶ B	6/3 ▶ C	6/5 ▶ C	6/7 ▶ B
6/2 ▶ C	6/4 ▶ A	6/6 ▶ B	

Contestant 2

6/1 ▶ A	6/3 ▶ B	6/5 ▶ B	6/7 ▶ A
6/2 ▶ A	6/4 ▶ A	6/6 ▶ A	

Contestant 3

6/1 ▶ C	6/3 ▶ A	6/5 ▶ C	6/7 ▶ A
6/2 ▶ A	6/4 ▶ C	6/6 ▶ A	

Contestant 4

6/1 ▶ C	6/3 ▶ B	6/5 ▶ C	6/7 ▶ C
6/2 ▶ C	6/4 ▶ A	6/6 ▶ B	

Final Chase

6/1 ▶ Beehive	6/14 ▶ Seal
6/2 ▶ Barbie	6/15 ▶ The KLF
6/3 ▶ Two	6/16 ▶ Blue
6/4 ▶ Modern pentathlon	6/17 ▶ Spain
6/5 ▶ Feast	6/18 ▶ Evangeline Lilly
6/6 ▶ Teri Hatcher	6/19 ▶ Lamb
6/7 ▶ Beef	6/20 ▶ Wine
6/8 ▶ Netherlands	6/21 ▶ Soap opera
6/9 ▶ Science	6/22 ▶ Glasgow
6/10 ▶ Monster	6/23 ▶ Italian
6/11 ▶ Leo Tolstoy	6/24 ▶ Quadriceps
6/12 ▶ Cowboy boot	6/25 ▶ Romans
6/13 ▶ 17th	

The Sinnerman Quiz 7

Contestant 1

7/1 ▶ C   7/3 ▶ C   7/5 ▶ B   7/7 ▶ C
7/2 ▶ B   7/4 ▶ B   7/6 ▶ B

Contestant 2

7/1 ▶ C   7/3 ▶ C   7/5 ▶ A   7/7 ▶ A
7/2 ▶ A   7/4 ▶ B   7/6 ▶ A

Contestant 3

7/1 ▶ C   7/3 ▶ C   7/5 ▶ C   7/7 ▶ C
7/2 ▶ C   7/4 ▶ A   7/6 ▶ A

Contestant 4

7/1 ▶ A   7/3 ▶ A   7/5 ▶ C   7/7 ▶ A
7/2 ▶ A   7/4 ▶ C   7/6 ▶ A

Final Chase

7/1 ▶ Mountain
7/2 ▶ German
7/3 ▶ *Blazing Saddles*
7/4 ▶ *Porgy and Bess*
7/5 ▶ Theresa May
7/6 ▶ Bird
7/7 ▶ Wimpy
7/8 ▶ The Saturdays
7/9 ▶ Israel
7/10 ▶ *The Matrix*
7/11 ▶ Prospero
7/12 ▶ Rome

7/13 ▶ HMS *Victory*
7/14 ▶ Ice hockey
7/15 ▶ Methane
7/16 ▶ Lungs
7/17 ▶ Toys 'R' Us
7/18 ▶ Louis the 16th
7/19 ▶ Whisky
7/20 ▶ Sandra Bullock
7/21 ▶ Football
7/22 ▶ Russia
7/23 ▶ 5 Seconds of Summer

The Sinnerman Quiz 8

Contestant 1

8/1 ▶ B	8/3 ▶ C	8/5 ▶ A	8/7 ▶ A
8/2 ▶ B	8/4 ▶ C	8/6 ▶ C	

Contestant 2

8/1 ▶ A	8/3 ▶ B	8/5 ▶ B	8/7 ▶ C
8/2 ▶ C	8/4 ▶ A	8/6 ▶ A	

Contestant 3

8/1 ▶ C	8/3 ▶ C	8/5 ▶ A	8/7 ▶ A
8/2 ▶ B	8/4 ▶ A	8/6 ▶ B	

Contestant 4

8/1 ▶ A	8/3 ▶ A	8/5 ▶ B	8/7 ▶ A
8/2 ▶ B	8/4 ▶ A	8/6 ▶ A	

Final Chase

8/1 ▶ Guitar	8/14 ▶ B
8/2 ▶ Henry the Eighth	8/15 ▶ Judi Dench
8/3 ▶ 1930s	8/16 ▶ Wales
8/4 ▶ Trixie	8/17 ▶ New York Yankees
8/5 ▶ *Macbeth*	8/18 ▶ Numbers
8/6 ▶ Coca-Cola	8/19 ▶ The Smiths
8/7 ▶ Flattery	8/20 ▶ 63
8/8 ▶ Dennis Potter	8/21 ▶ White
8/9 ▶ Engine	8/22 ▶ James
8/10 ▶ Annie Mac	8/23 ▶ Shetland
8/11 ▶ Southern Rhodesia	8/24 ▶ Home Secretary
8/12 ▶ Diana Ross	8/25 ▶ Red and white
8/13 ▶ Beetle	

The Sinnerman Quiz 9

Contestant 1

9/1 ▶ B		9/3 ▶ A		9/5 ▶ C		9/7 ▶ C
9/2 ▶ A		9/4 ▶ C		9/6 ▶ A		

Contestant 2

9/1 ▶ A		9/3 ▶ A		9/5 ▶ C		9/7 ▶ C
9/2 ▶ C		9/4 ▶ A		9/6 ▶ C		

Contestant 3

9/1 ▶ A		9/3 ▶ B		9/5 ▶ A		9/7 ▶ A
9/2 ▶ A		9/4 ▶ B		9/6 ▶ B		

Contestant 4

9/1 ▶ B		9/3 ▶ A		9/5 ▶ C		9/7 ▶ A
9/2 ▶ A		9/4 ▶ B		9/6 ▶ A		

Final Chase

9/1 ▶ Dog	9/13 ▶ 4 x 400 metres
9/2 ▶ Air Force	9/14 ▶ Latin
9/3 ▶ *Escape to the Country*	9/15 ▶ Brahmaputra
9/4 ▶ Venus de Milo	9/16 ▶ 125
9/5 ▶ Delia Smith	9/17 ▶ Ben Stiller
9/6 ▶ *12 Years a Slave*	9/18 ▶ Ursula Le Guin
9/7 ▶ Spencer	9/19 ▶ Napoleon
9/8 ▶ The Alamo	9/20 ▶ Toyota
9/9 ▶ Karate	9/21 ▶ Genesis
9/10 ▶ 'The Living Daylights'	9/22 ▶ Central Park
9/11 ▶ Thailand	9/23 ▶ Jan Kodes
9/12 ▶ *The Hobbit*	9/24 ▶ The knee

The Sinnerman Quiz 10

Contestant 1

10/1 ▶ C   10/3 ▶ A   10/5 ▶ A   10/7 ▶ C
10/2 ▶ A   10/4 ▶ C   10/6 ▶ A

Contestant 2

10/1 ▶ A   10/3 ▶ A   10/5 ▶ C   10/7 ▶ A
10/2 ▶ C   10/4 ▶ C   10/6 ▶ A

Contestant 3

10/1 ▶ A   10/3 ▶ B   10/5 ▶ C   10/7 ▶ A
10/2 ▶ C   10/4 ▶ C   10/6 ▶ A

Contestant 4

10/1 ▶ C   10/3 ▶ A   10/5 ▶ A   10/7 ▶ B
10/2 ▶ C   10/4 ▶ A   10/6 ▶ C

Final Chase

10/1 ▶ White
10/2 ▶ San
10/3 ▶ Pathology
10/4 ▶ 18th
10/5 ▶ *Under Milk Wood*
10/6 ▶ Gary Numan
10/7 ▶ Jeremy Corbyn
10/8 ▶ pH scale
10/9 ▶ Princess
10/10 ▶ Bill Bryson
10/11 ▶ *Gone Girl*
10/12 ▶ Catwoman
10/13 ▶ The Oval
10/14 ▶ *The Godfather*
10/15 ▶ Thomas Gainsborough
10/16 ▶ Amanda
10/17 ▶ Williams sisters
10/18 ▶ *The Tudors*
10/19 ▶ Atlantic
10/20 ▶ Black mamba
10/21 ▶ *Peter Pan*
10/22 ▶ King Arthur
10/23 ▶ *CSI*

The Vixen Quiz 1

Contestant 1

1/1 ▶ B	1/3 ▶ C	1/5 ▶ A	1/7 ▶ C
1/2 ▶ B	1/4 ▶ C	1/6 ▶ B	

Contestant 2

1/1 ▶ A	1/3 ▶ B	1/5 ▶ C	1/7 ▶ C
1/2 ▶ C	1/4 ▶ B	1/6 ▶ A	

Contestant 3

1/1 ▶ C	1/3 ▶ C	1/5 ▶ B	1/7 ▶ A
1/2 ▶ C	1/4 ▶ A	1/6 ▶ A	

Contestant 4

1/1 ▶ A	1/3 ▶ C	1/5 ▶ A	1/7 ▶ C
1/2 ▶ B	1/4 ▶ B	1/6 ▶ A	

Final Chase

1/1 ▶ April		1/11 ▶ Armani
1/2 ▶ India		1/12 ▶ Architecture
1/3 ▶ Arsenal		1/13 ▶ The Saturdays
1/4 ▶ Dwight Eisenhower		1/14 ▶ West Berlin
1/5 ▶ North		1/15 ▶ Dorian Gray
1/6 ▶ *Beverly Hills Cop*		1/16 ▶ Boiling
1/7 ▶ Tennis		1/17 ▶ Sole
1/8 ▶ Paraguay		1/18 ▶ Katherine Jenkins
1/9 ▶ *Coronation Street*		1/19 ▶ Three
1/10 ▶ *Aïda*		

THE VIXEN

The Vixen Quiz 2

Contestant 1

2/1 ▶ B	2/3 ▶ A	2/5 ▶ A	2/7 ▶ B
2/2 ▶ C	2/4 ▶ C	2/6 ▶ B	

Contestant 2

2/1 ▶ C	2/3 ▶ C	2/5 ▶ C	2/7 ▶ A
2/2 ▶ A	2/4 ▶ A	2/6 ▶ A	

Contestant 3

2/1 ▶ C	2/3 ▶ A	2/5 ▶ B	2/7 ▶ C
2/2 ▶ A	2/4 ▶ C	2/6 ▶ A	

Contestant 4

2/1 ▶ A	2/3 ▶ A	2/5 ▶ A	2/7 ▶ C
2/2 ▶ A	2/4 ▶ A	2/6 ▶ C	

Final Chase

2/1 ▶ Abel	2/12 ▶ Royal Air Force
2/2 ▶ Cassidy	2/13 ▶ Charlton Heston
2/3 ▶ Westminster Abbey	2/14 ▶ Hawaii
2/4 ▶ Michelle Pfeiffer	2/15 ▶ *Keeping Up Appearances*
2/5 ▶ Dog	2/16 ▶ John
2/6 ▶ French	2/17 ▶ Duchess of Cornwall
2/7 ▶ Vodka	2/18 ▶ Prometheus
2/8 ▶ Sikhism	2/19 ▶ One
2/9 ▶ Costa del Sol	2/20 ▶ Isle of Wight
2/10 ▶ Heimlich manoevre	2/21 ▶ Communist
2/11 ▶ The Joker	

The Vixen Quiz 3

Contestant 1

3/1 ► C	3/3 ► B	3/5 ► C	3/7 ► A
3/2 ► A	3/4 ► B	3/6 ► A	

Contestant 2

3/1 ► C	3/3 ► C	3/5 ► A	3/7 ► A
3/2 ► A	3/4 ► C	3/6 ► C	

Contestant 3

3/1 ► B	3/3 ► C	3/5 ► B	3/7 ► B
3/2 ► C	3/4 ► A	3/6 ► A	

Contestant 4

3/1 ► A	3/3 ► C	3/5 ► B	3/7 ► A
3/2 ► A	3/4 ► B	3/6 ► C	

Final Chase

3/1 ► Kylie		3/13 ► The Stort	
3/2 ► *Elle*		3/14 ► O	
3/3 ► NATO		3/15 ► Emilio Estevez	
3/4 ► Crystal Palace		3/16 ► Drum	
3/5 ► Two		3/17 ► Lemon	
3/6 ► M1		3/18 ► Chrysler Building	
3/7 ► Adidas		3/19 ► *Star Wars*	
3/8 ► *Charlotte's Web*		3/20 ► 1950s	
3/9 ► Disrespect		3/21 ► Pancreas	
3/10 ► 800		3/22 ► Shoes	
3/11 ► Namibian dollar		3/23 ► Bristol	
3/12 ► *The Sound of Music*			

The Vixen Quiz 4

Contestant 1
4/1 ▶ C	4/3 ▶ B	4/5 ▶ B	4/7 ▶ A
4/2 ▶ C	4/4 ▶ C	4/6 ▶ A	

Contestant 2
4/1 ▶ C	4/3 ▶ A	4/5 ▶ B	4/7 ▶ C
4/2 ▶ C	4/4 ▶ A	4/6 ▶ B	

Contestant 3
4/1 ▶ A	4/3 ▶ A	4/5 ▶ A	4/7 ▶ C
4/2 ▶ A	4/4 ▶ C	4/6 ▶ B	

Contestant 4
4/1 ▶ B	4/3 ▶ C	4/5 ▶ C	4/7 ▶ A
4/2 ▶ C	4/4 ▶ B	4/6 ▶ A	

Final Chase

4/1 ▶ Pasta	4/12 ▶ Henry the Eighth
4/2 ▶ World War Two	4/13 ▶ Women
4/3 ▶ Gwyneth Paltrow	4/14 ▶ Atlantic
4/4 ▶ Dolce & Gabbana	4/15 ▶ *Finding Neverland*
4/5 ▶ North America	4/16 ▶ Eating
4/6 ▶ Wet Wet Wet	4/17 ▶ Latin
4/7 ▶ Princess Anne	4/18 ▶ Paloma Faith
4/8 ▶ *The Joy Luck Club*	4/19 ▶ Twenty
4/9 ▶ Canberra	4/20 ▶ Sulphuric acid
4/10 ▶ Jim Henson	4/21 ▶ B
4/11 ▶ Pastoral Symphony	4/22 ▶ Manchester Victoria

The Vixen Quiz 5

Contestant 1

5/1 ▶ B   5/3 ▶ B   5/5 ▶ C   5/7 ▶ B
5/2 ▶ C   5/4 ▶ C   5/6 ▶ B

Contestant 2

5/1 ▶ C   5/3 ▶ A   5/5 ▶ A   5/7 ▶ A
5/2 ▶ C   5/4 ▶ C   5/6 ▶ C

Contestant 3

5/1 ▶ A   5/3 ▶ B   5/5 ▶ A   5/7 ▶ A
5/2 ▶ B   5/4 ▶ C   5/6 ▶ B

Contestant 4

5/1 ▶ A   5/3 ▶ A   5/5 ▶ A   5/7 ▶ A
5/2 ▶ C   5/4 ▶ B   5/6 ▶ B

Final Chase

5/1 ▶ Cricket

5/2 ▶ Led Zeppelin

5/3 ▶ Pacific

5/4 ▶ Sharp

5/5 ▶ Capricorn

5/6 ▶ Cardiff

5/7 ▶ Headlights

5/8 ▶ Kidney

5/9 ▶ *Cats*

5/10 ▶ The Body Shop

5/11 ▶ Kristin Scott Thomas

5/12 ▶ Large Goods Vehicle

5/13 ▶ Blue and white

5/14 ▶ Elizabeth the First

5/15 ▶ Delaware

5/16 ▶ Saturated fat

5/17 ▶ Hugh Fearnley-Whittingstall

5/18 ▶ 1970s

5/19 ▶ Wembley Stadium

5/20 ▶ Investment

5/21 ▶ 40

5/22 ▶ Shiraz

THE VIXEN

The Vixen Quiz 6

Contestant 1

6/1 ▶ A	6/3 ▶ C	6/5 ▶ C	6/7 ▶ A
6/2 ▶ A	6/4 ▶ A	6/6 ▶ C	

Contestant 2

6/1 ▶ C	6/3 ▶ A	6/5 ▶ A	6/7 ▶ B
6/2 ▶ B	6/4 ▶ A	6/6 ▶ B	

Contestant 3

6/1 ▶ A	6/3 ▶ A	6/5 ▶ C	6/7 ▶ C
6/2 ▶ B	6/4 ▶ C	6/6 ▶ A	

Contestant 4

6/1 ▶ A	6/3 ▶ B	6/5 ▶ A	6/7 ▶ A
6/2 ▶ C	6/4 ▶ C	6/6 ▶ A	

Final Chase

6/1 ▶ *Harry Potter*	6/12 ▶ Vladimir Putin
6/2 ▶ French	6/13 ▶ Lord Greystoke
6/3 ▶ *Footballers' Wives*	6/14 ▶ Umpires
6/4 ▶ Habsburg	6/15 ▶ Norway
6/5 ▶ Three	6/16 ▶ Red
6/6 ▶ Kristen Stewart	6/17 ▶ Roman
6/7 ▶ Germany	6/18 ▶ *How I Met Your Mother*
6/8 ▶ Verdi	6/19 ▶ Asia
6/9 ▶ Book	6/20 ▶ Olivia Newton-John
6/10 ▶ Skin	6/21 ▶ Bread
6/11 ▶ Rizzle Kicks	6/22 ▶ Edward the Eighth

The Vixen Quiz 7

Contestant 1

7/1 ▶ A	7/3 ▶ C	7/5 ▶ B	7/7 ▶ A
7/2 ▶ A	7/4 ▶ C	7/6 ▶ B	

Contestant 2

7/1 ▶ A	7/3 ▶ A	7/5 ▶ C	7/7 ▶ B
7/2 ▶ B	7/4 ▶ C	7/6 ▶ B	

Contestant 3

7/1 ▶ C	7/3 ▶ A	7/5 ▶ A	7/7 ▶ C
7/2 ▶ C	7/4 ▶ C	7/6 ▶ B	

Contestant 4

7/1 ▶ C	7/3 ▶ A	7/5 ▶ C	7/7 ▶ B
7/2 ▶ C	7/4 ▶ C	7/6 ▶ A	

Final Chase

7/1 ▶ North Korea	7/13 ▶ Queen
7/2 ▶ Anne	7/14 ▶ Horseracing
7/3 ▶ *Grease*	7/15 ▶ Jimmy Choo
7/4 ▶ Actinium	7/16 ▶ Pride
7/5 ▶ Asia	7/17 ▶ 1970s
7/6 ▶ Charlie Higson	7/18 ▶ Van Gogh
7/7 ▶ Lactic acid	7/19 ▶ Cow
7/8 ▶ Basketball	7/20 ▶ *We Will Rock You*
7/9 ▶ November	7/21 ▶ Eyes
7/10 ▶ MC Hammer	7/22 ▶ Japan
7/11 ▶ Mario Testino	7/23 ▶ Adam Richman
7/12 ▶ Mercury	

THE VIXEN

The Vixen Quiz 8

Contestant 1

8/1 ▶ A	8/3 ▶ A	8/5 ▶ C	8/7 ▶ A
8/2 ▶ A	8/4 ▶ C	8/6 ▶ C	

Contestant 2

8/1 ▶ A	8/3 ▶ B	8/5 ▶ A	8/7 ▶ A
8/2 ▶ C	8/4 ▶ C	8/6 ▶ B	

Contestant 3

8/1 ▶ A	8/3 ▶ C	8/5 ▶ A	8/7 ▶ C
8/2 ▶ B	8/4 ▶ C	8/6 ▶ C	

Contestant 4

8/1 ▶ B	8/3 ▶ A	8/5 ▶ B	8/7 ▶ C
8/2 ▶ C	8/4 ▶ A	8/6 ▶ B	

Final Chase

8/1 ▶ Stone	8/12 ▶ 180 degrees
8/2 ▶ Cycling	8/13 ▶ All Saints
8/3 ▶ Scandium	8/14 ▶ Elizabeth the First
8/4 ▶ Robert Webb	8/15 ▶ Francis Beaufort
8/5 ▶ Three	8/16 ▶ US
8/6 ▶ *Chicago*	8/17 ▶ *Frozen*
8/7 ▶ Davis	8/18 ▶ Ice Cube
8/8 ▶ Athens	8/19 ▶ Femur
8/9 ▶ *Neighbours*	8/20 ▶ *Leaving Las Vegas*
8/10 ▶ Dog	8/21 ▶ Ten
8/11 ▶ Paris	8/22 ▶ Florence Nightingale

The Vixen Quiz 9

Contestant 1

9/1 ▶ C	9/3 ▶ C	9/5 ▶ C	9/7 ▶ A
9/2 ▶ C	9/4 ▶ A	9/6 ▶ A	

Contestant 2

9/1 ▶ B	9/3 ▶ C	9/5 ▶ B	9/7 ▶ A
9/2 ▶ A	9/4 ▶ C	9/6 ▶ B	

Contestant 3

9/1 ▶ A	9/3 ▶ A	9/5 ▶ C	9/7 ▶ A
9/2 ▶ B	9/4 ▶ B	9/6 ▶ C	

Contestant 4

9/1 ▶ B	9/3 ▶ B	9/5 ▶ A	9/7 ▶ C
9/2 ▶ C	9/4 ▶ A	9/6 ▶ C	

Final Chase

9/1 ▶ Diana Spencer	9/12 ▶ Kylie Minogue
9/2 ▶ Army	9/13 ▶ Chlorophyll
9/3 ▶ Roald Dahl	9/14 ▶ Music
9/4 ▶ Al Pacino	9/15 ▶ Greece
9/5 ▶ Seven	9/16 ▶ Ralph Lauren
9/6 ▶ Andrew Jackson	9/17 ▶ Ian Fleming
9/7 ▶ Fish	9/18 ▶ American football
9/8 ▶ *Interstellar*	9/19 ▶ English Channel
9/9 ▶ Yeoman warders	9/20 ▶ 1960s
9/10 ▶ *The Color of Money*	9/21 ▶ Bird
9/11 ▶ France	9/22 ▶ Brazil

THE VIXEN

The Vixen Quiz 10

Contestant 1

| 10/1 ▶ C | 10/3 ▶ C | 10/5 ▶ A | 10/7 ▶ A |
| 10/2 ▶ A | 10/4 ▶ C | 10/6 ▶ C | |

Contestant 2

| 10/1 ▶ C | 10/3 ▶ B | 10/5 ▶ A | 10/7 ▶ B |
| 10/2 ▶ A | 10/4 ▶ B | 10/6 ▶ B | |

Contestant 3

| 10/1 ▶ B | 10/3 ▶ A | 10/5 ▶ A | 10/7 ▶ C |
| 10/2 ▶ C | 10/4 ▶ B | 10/6 ▶ A | |

Contestant 4

| 10/1 ▶ C | 10/3 ▶ B | 10/5 ▶ C | 10/7 ▶ A |
| 10/2 ▶ C | 10/4 ▶ A | 10/6 ▶ B | |

Final Chase

10/1 ▶ Journalist	10/13 ▶ Green and white
10/2 ▶ *Rainbow*	10/14 ▶ Bill Bailey
10/3 ▶ Amsterdam	10/15 ▶ Kaiser
10/4 ▶ Edward the First	10/16 ▶ Monmouthshire
10/5 ▶ Ten	10/17 ▶ June
10/6 ▶ Kinetic	10/18 ▶ Pig
10/7 ▶ *Despicable Me*	10/19 ▶ Margaret Thatcher
10/8 ▶ Athletics	10/20 ▶ *David Copperfield*
10/9 ▶ *Coronation Street*	10/21 ▶ Star
10/10 ▶ *Apollo 11*	10/22 ▶ Buckingham Palace
10/11 ▶ Mimi Rogers	10/23 ▶ Pink
10/12 ▶ South Africa	

The Barrister Quiz 1

Contestant 1

1/1 ▶ C	1/3 ▶ C	1/5 ▶ C	1/7 ▶ B
1/2 ▶ A	1/4 ▶ C	1/6 ▶ C	

Contestant 2

1/1 ▶ B	1/3 ▶ C	1/5 ▶ C	1/7 ▶ A
1/2 ▶ A	1/4 ▶ B	1/6 ▶ A	

Contestant 3

1/1 ▶ A	1/3 ▶ B	1/5 ▶ C	1/7 ▶ C
1/2 ▶ A	1/4 ▶ A	1/6 ▶ A	

Contestant 4

1/1 ▶ B	1/3 ▶ A	1/5 ▶ B	1/7 ▶ C
1/2 ▶ A	1/4 ▶ C	1/6 ▶ C	

Final Chase

1/1 ▶ The Simpsons	1/14 ▶ Katie Price
1/2 ▶ Lions	1/15 ▶ Gabrielle Aplin
1/3 ▶ The Milkybar Kid	1/16 ▶ December
1/4 ▶ 1896	1/17 ▶ Conservative
1/5 ▶ Cher	1/18 ▶ Valerie Mendes
1/6 ▶ Fish	1/19 ▶ 'Save Your Love'
1/7 ▶ American	1/20 ▶ Frog
1/8 ▶ Stafford	1/21 ▶ Black Jack
1/9 ▶ White	1/22 ▶ Paris
1/10 ▶ 19th	1/23 ▶ Pollux
1/11 ▶ Stravinsky	1/24 ▶ Chlorine
1/12 ▶ Prince Charles	1/25 ▶ Bollywood
1/13 ▶ Mohammed Al Fayed	

The Barrister Quiz 2

Contestant 1

2/1 ▶ A	2/3 ▶ C	2/5 ▶ A	2/7 ▶ A
2/2 ▶ A	2/4 ▶ A	2/6 ▶ C	

Contestant 2

2/1 ▶ C	2/3 ▶ A	2/5 ▶ B	2/7 ▶ B
2/2 ▶ C	2/4 ▶ A	2/6 ▶ A	

Contestant 3

2/1 ▶ C	2/3 ▶ A	2/5 ▶ C	2/7 ▶ C
2/2 ▶ C	2/4 ▶ C	2/6 ▶ C	

Contestant 4

2/1 ▶ B	2/3 ▶ C	2/5 ▶ C	2/7 ▶ C
2/2 ▶ C	2/4 ▶ B	2/6 ▶ C	

Final Chase

2/1 ▶ Hairstyles	2/14 ▶ Beef
2/2 ▶ Waltz	2/15 ▶ Liam Hemsworth
2/3 ▶ *Downton Abbey*	2/16 ▶ Camel
2/4 ▶ Red Sea	2/17 ▶ *Dynasty*
2/5 ▶ Book club	2/18 ▶ Edward Elgar
2/6 ▶ Gin	2/19 ▶ Alpha
2/7 ▶ Brass	2/20 ▶ Dr Seuss
2/8 ▶ Philippa Gregory	2/21 ▶ Red
2/9 ▶ Michael Jackson	2/22 ▶ *Jesus Christ Superstar*
2/10 ▶ Portuguese	2/23 ▶ Mary Robinson
2/11 ▶ Gainsborough	2/24 ▶ Mario Puzo
2/12 ▶ *The X Factor*	2/25 ▶ Tears
2/13 ▶ José María Olazábal	

The Barrister Quiz 3

Contestant 1

3/1 ▶ A	3/3 ▶ A	3/5 ▶ A	3/7 ▶ A
3/2 ▶ C	3/4 ▶ B	3/6 ▶ C	

Contestant 2

3/1 ▶ A	3/3 ▶ A	3/5 ▶ C	3/7 ▶ B
3/2 ▶ B	3/4 ▶ C	3/6 ▶ C	

Contestant 3

3/1 ▶ B	3/3 ▶ B	3/5 ▶ B	3/7 ▶ C
3/2 ▶ A	3/4 ▶ C	3/6 ▶ B	

Contestant 4

3/1 ▶ C	3/3 ▶ A	3/5 ▶ A	3/7 ▶ C
3/2 ▶ C	3/4 ▶ C	3/6 ▶ C	

Final Chase

3/1 ▶ Los Angeles		3/14 ▶ Shakespeare
3/2 ▶ Melanie Brown		3/15 ▶ Joel Grey
3/3 ▶ Salsa		3/16 ▶ Horses
3/4 ▶ 1960s		3/17 ▶ Windsor
3/5 ▶ Kent		3/18 ▶ Amazon
3/6 ▶ Percussion		3/19 ▶ Paris
3/7 ▶ Frankie Dettori		3/20 ▶ Angel Falls
3/8 ▶ Richard Hannay		3/21 ▶ Red
3/9 ▶ *Jesus Christ Superstar*		3/22 ▶ Mussolini
3/10 ▶ *Frasier*		3/23 ▶ Goat
3/11 ▶ Casablanca		3/24 ▶ Gareth Bale
3/12 ▶ 35		3/25 ▶ Grange Hill
3/13 ▶ James Garfield		3/26 ▶ 13

The Barrister Quiz 4

Contestant 1

4/1 ▶ A	4/3 ▶ C	4/5 ▶ A	4/7 ▶ A
4/2 ▶ C	4/4 ▶ C	4/6 ▶ C	

Contestant 2

4/1 ▶ A	4/3 ▶ A	4/5 ▶ B	4/7 ▶ C
4/2 ▶ C	4/4 ▶ C	4/6 ▶ A	

Contestant 3

4/1 ▶ A	4/3 ▶ A	4/5 ▶ C	4/7 ▶ C
4/2 ▶ B	4/4 ▶ C	4/6 ▶ C	

Contestant 4

4/1 ▶ C	4/3 ▶ C	4/5 ▶ C	4/7 ▶ A
4/2 ▶ B	4/4 ▶ A	4/6 ▶ C	

Final Chase

4/1 ▶ Teeth	4/13 ▶ Portugal
4/2 ▶ Judi Dench	4/14 ▶ Jay Z
4/3 ▶ Twice	4/15 ▶ Juliana
4/4 ▶ Open University	4/16 ▶ Mane
4/5 ▶ Blood	4/17 ▶ John Paul the Second
4/6 ▶ Mark Owen	4/18 ▶ Krypton
4/7 ▶ Terrier	4/19 ▶ Charles de Gaulle
4/8 ▶ Percy Shelley	4/20 ▶ Davy Jones
4/9 ▶ Russia	4/21 ▶ Feet
4/10 ▶ Captain Scarlet	4/22 ▶ Carnivore
4/11 ▶ 17th	4/23 ▶ Oslo
4/12 ▶ Green	4/24 ▶ Sergio Leone

The Barrister Quiz 5

Contestant 1

5/1 ▶ B	5/3 ▶ C	5/5 ▶ B	5/7 ▶ A
5/2 ▶ C	5/4 ▶ B	5/6 ▶ A	

Contestant 2

5/1 ▶ A	5/3 ▶ A	5/5 ▶ C	5/7 ▶ C
5/2 ▶ C	5/4 ▶ C	5/6 ▶ B	

Contestant 3

5/1 ▶ B	5/3 ▶ B	5/5 ▶ C	5/7 ▶ B
5/2 ▶ C	5/4 ▶ A	5/6 ▶ A	

Contestant 4

5/1 ▶ A	5/3 ▶ B	5/5 ▶ C	5/7 ▶ B
5/2 ▶ A	5/4 ▶ B	5/6 ▶ B	

Final Chase

5/1 ▶ Sun	5/14 ▶ Prince Charles
5/2 ▶ North America	5/15 ▶ Joe McElderry
5/3 ▶ Four	5/16 ▶ London
5/4 ▶ Egyptian	5/17 ▶ MasterCard
5/5 ▶ Chicken	5/18 ▶ Munster
5/6 ▶ Laura Branigan	5/19 ▶ *Mrs Brown's Boys*
5/7 ▶ Wales	5/20 ▶ Four
5/8 ▶ *Much Ado About Nothing*	5/21 ▶ Pineapple
5/9 ▶ *Return of the Jedi*	5/22 ▶ Australia
5/10 ▶ Atlantic	5/23 ▶ Siegfried Sassoon
5/11 ▶ Zinc	5/24 ▶ Calvin Harris
5/12 ▶ Vauxhall	5/25 ▶ *Pride and Prejudice*
5/13 ▶ Beetle	

The Barrister Quiz 6

Contestant 1

6/1 ▶ A	6/3 ▶ A	6/5 ▶ C	6/7 ▶ A
6/2 ▶ C	6/4 ▶ B	6/6 ▶ C	

Contestant 2

6/1 ▶ C	6/3 ▶ A	6/5 ▶ C	6/7 ▶ A
6/2 ▶ C	6/4 ▶ A	6/6 ▶ C	

Contestant 3

6/1 ▶ A	6/3 ▶ A	6/5 ▶ C	6/7 ▶ A
6/2 ▶ A	6/4 ▶ B	6/6 ▶ B	

Contestant 4

6/1 ▶ A	6/3 ▶ A	6/5 ▶ A	6/7 ▶ A
6/2 ▶ C	6/4 ▶ C	6/6 ▶ C	

Final Chase

6/1 ▶ Cheese	6/13 ▶ Two
6/2 ▶ Real Madrid	6/14 ▶ Red
6/3 ▶ 'Guitar Hero'	6/15 ▶ Andrew
6/4 ▶ Buddha	6/16 ▶ Hugo Boss
6/5 ▶ Malta	6/17 ▶ First World War
6/6 ▶ Christian Louboutin	6/18 ▶ Uranus
6/7 ▶ Debbie Harry	6/19 ▶ *Vanity Fair*
6/8 ▶ Iraq	6/20 ▶ Jaguar
6/9 ▶ French	6/21 ▶ 31 December
6/10 ▶ Arm	6/22 ▶ *Jesus Christ Superstar*
6/11 ▶ *Sophie's Choice*	6/23 ▶ Victoria
6/12 ▶ *EastEnders*	6/24 ▶ Prince Edward

The Barrister Quiz 7

Contestant 1

7/1 ▶ B	7/3 ▶ B	7/5 ▶ A	7/7 ▶ A
7/2 ▶ A	7/4 ▶ A	7/6 ▶ C	

Contestant 2

7/1 ▶ A	7/3 ▶ A	7/5 ▶ A	7/7 ▶ A
7/2 ▶ B	7/4 ▶ C	7/6 ▶ C	

Contestant 3

7/1 ▶ A	7/3 ▶ A	7/5 ▶ C	7/7 ▶ C
7/2 ▶ C	7/4 ▶ C	7/6 ▶ B	

Contestant 4

7/1 ▶ A	7/3 ▶ C	7/5 ▶ C	7/7 ▶ A
7/2 ▶ A	7/4 ▶ C	7/6 ▶ A	

Final Chase

7/1 ▶ The Bible	7/12 ▶ Poseidon
7/2 ▶ Tom Cruise	7/13 ▶ The Monkees
7/3 ▶ Bird	7/14 ▶ Brain
7/4 ▶ Sweden	7/15 ▶ *The Mill On The Floss*
7/5 ▶ Square	7/16 ▶ Christmas
7/6 ▶ McVitie's	7/17 ▶ James Bond
7/7 ▶ *Prisoner: Cell Block H*	7/18 ▶ Anderlecht
7/8 ▶ Nefertiti	7/19 ▶ Five o'clock
7/9 ▶ Budapest	7/20 ▶ *On the Buses*
7/10 ▶ 1980s	7/21 ▶ NYPD
7/11 ▶ Veterinary surgeon	7/22 ▶ Tiger

The Barrister Quiz 8

Contestant 1

8/1 ▶ A	8/3 ▶ C	8/5 ▶ A	8/7 ▶ C
8/2 ▶ B	8/4 ▶ B	8/6 ▶ C	

Contestant 2

8/1 ▶ C	8/3 ▶ A	8/5 ▶ B	8/7 ▶ B
8/2 ▶ B	8/4 ▶ C	8/6 ▶ A	

Contestant 3

8/1 ▶ A	8/3 ▶ C	8/5 ▶ C	8/7 ▶ A
8/2 ▶ B	8/4 ▶ C	8/6 ▶ C	

Contestant 4

8/1 ▶ B	8/3 ▶ A	8/5 ▶ A	8/7 ▶ A
8/2 ▶ B	8/4 ▶ C	8/6 ▶ C	

Final Chase

8/1 ▶ The green	8/14 ▶ Rugby union
8/2 ▶ Africa	8/15 ▶ *Alien*
8/3 ▶ *The Madness of King George*	8/16 ▶ Grape
8/4 ▶ Sugababes	8/17 ▶ Bird
8/5 ▶ Three	8/18 ▶ USA
8/6 ▶ Pacific	8/19 ▶ Bones
8/7 ▶ Cricket	8/20 ▶ Joan Collins
8/8 ▶ 1940s	8/21 ▶ Italian
8/9 ▶ One ounce	8/22 ▶ New South Wales
8/10 ▶ Baron	8/23 ▶ France
8/11 ▶ Oman	8/24 ▶ Twenty-two
8/12 ▶ Harvard	8/25 ▶ Canadian
8/13 ▶ Ten	

The Barrister Quiz 9

Contestant 1

9/1 ▶ A 9/3 ▶ A 9/5 ▶ C 9/7 ▶ A
9/2 ▶ C 9/4 ▶ B 9/6 ▶ C

Contestant 2

9/1 ▶ B 9/3 ▶ C 9/5 ▶ B 9/7 ▶ A
9/2 ▶ B 9/4 ▶ A 9/6 ▶ A

Contestant 3

9/1 ▶ A 9/3 ▶ C 9/5 ▶ C 9/7 ▶ B
9/2 ▶ C 9/4 ▶ B 9/6 ▶ B

Contestant 4

9/1 ▶ A 9/3 ▶ C 9/5 ▶ C 9/7 ▶ B
9/2 ▶ A 9/4 ▶ C 9/6 ▶ C

Final Chase

9/1 ▶ *Talent*
9/2 ▶ Four
9/3 ▶ *Maggie*
9/4 ▶ Ben Jonson
9/5 ▶ Mint
9/6 ▶ 19th
9/7 ▶ North Sea
9/8 ▶ George Harrison
9/9 ▶ Pushchair
9/10 ▶ Ears
9/11 ▶ Harold Pinter
9/12 ▶ Harper

9/13 ▶ Stonehenge
9/14 ▶ Hydrogen
9/15 ▶ Medici
9/16 ▶ Advertisements
9/17 ▶ The Fonz
9/18 ▶ 'Life on Mars'
9/19 ▶ Egyptian
9/20 ▶ Irish
9/21 ▶ Green
9/22 ▶ Legal action
9/23 ▶ Black Sea

The Barrister Quiz 10

Contestant 1

10/1 ▶ A	10/3 ▶ A	10/5 ▶ C	10/7 ▶ A
10/2 ▶ C	10/4 ▶ A	10/6 ▶ C	

Contestant 2

10/1 ▶ C	10/3 ▶ C	10/5 ▶ A	10/7 ▶ C
10/2 ▶ C	10/4 ▶ C	10/6 ▶ A	

Contestant 3

10/1 ▶ C	10/3 ▶ A	10/5 ▶ B	10/7 ▶ C
10/2 ▶ C	10/4 ▶ A	10/6 ▶ B	

Contestant 4

10/1 ▶ C	10/3 ▶ C	10/5 ▶ C	10/7 ▶ C
10/2 ▶ A	10/4 ▶ B	10/6 ▶ B	

Final Chase

10/1 ▶ Amnesty International		10/11 ▶ Trampoline	
10/2 ▶ One		10/12 ▶ Tokyo	
10/3 ▶ Charles Dickens		10/13 ▶ Eighteen	
10/4 ▶ Light		10/14 ▶ Lord Palmerston	
10/5 ▶ National Theatre		10/15 ▶ Fabulous	
10/6 ▶ Adolf Hitler		10/16 ▶ Westminster Abbey	
10/7 ▶ Peter		10/17 ▶ 'I Got You'	
10/8 ▶ Lens		10/18 ▶ Crisps	
10/9 ▶ Presiding officer		10/19 ▶ Doctor Who	
10/10 ▶ Cheese		10/20 ▶ The ball	

The Beast Quiz 1

Contestant 1

1/1 ▶ C   1/3 ▶ C   1/5 ▶ B   1/7 ▶ A
1/2 ▶ B   1/4 ▶ B   1/6 ▶ C

Contestant 2

1/1 ▶ A   1/3 ▶ A   1/5 ▶ A   1/7 ▶ A
1/2 ▶ B   1/4 ▶ A   1/6 ▶ C

Contestant 3

1/1 ▶ A   1/3 ▶ A   1/5 ▶ C   1/7 ▶ B
1/2 ▶ C   1/4 ▶ A   1/6 ▶ A

Contestant 4

1/1 ▶ B   1/3 ▶ C   1/5 ▶ A   1/7 ▶ A
1/2 ▶ A   1/4 ▶ C   1/6 ▶ C

Final Chase

1/1 ▶ Grass
1/2 ▶ Second World War
1/3 ▶ Billie Holiday
1/4 ▶ Three
1/5 ▶ Persian Gulf
1/6 ▶ *Bread*
1/7 ▶ 39
1/8 ▶ Setter
1/9 ▶ Channel Islands
1/10 ▶ Bruno Mars
1/11 ▶ Apple
1/12 ▶ Princess Leia
1/13 ▶ Ace of Spades
1/14 ▶ San Antonio
1/15 ▶ Catherine Howard
1/16 ▶ Punchline
1/17 ▶ Termites
1/18 ▶ Mulberry
1/19 ▶ Henley
1/20 ▶ Agatha Christie
1/21 ▶ China
1/22 ▶ *Saturday Night Takeaway*
1/23 ▶ Five
1/24 ▶ Root
1/25 ▶ *Carry on Up the Khyber*
1/26 ▶ Ben & Jerry's

THE BEAST

The Beast Quiz 2

Contestant 1

2/1 ▶ C	2/3 ▶ A	2/5 ▶ A	2/7 ▶ A
2/2 ▶ A	2/4 ▶ C	2/6 ▶ B	

Contestant 2

2/1 ▶ B	2/3 ▶ C	2/5 ▶ C	2/7 ▶ A
2/2 ▶ C	2/4 ▶ B	2/6 ▶ B	

Contestant 3

2/1 ▶ B	2/3 ▶ A	2/5 ▶ A	2/7 ▶ A
2/2 ▶ A	2/4 ▶ C	2/6 ▶ C	

Contestant 4

2/1 ▶ B	2/3 ▶ A	2/5 ▶ B	2/7 ▶ C
2/2 ▶ A	2/4 ▶ B	2/6 ▶ A	

Final Chase

2/1 ▶ Ice	2/15 ▶ Ford
2/2 ▶ Paracetamol	2/16 ▶ Checker
2/3 ▶ *Hollyoaks*	2/17 ▶ Land's End
2/4 ▶ Kohlrabi	2/18 ▶ Radon
2/5 ▶ Cat	2/19 ▶ Wings
2/6 ▶ Green	2/20 ▶ Quentin Blake
2/7 ▶ Arthur Daley	2/21 ▶ Africa
2/8 ▶ The Queen	2/22 ▶ Shoe polish
2/9 ▶ 12	2/23 ▶ Burt Reynolds
2/10 ▶ Cricket	2/24 ▶ Bulls
2/11 ▶ James Taylor	2/25 ▶ A thousand
2/12 ▶ Germany	2/26 ▶ Lee
2/13 ▶ *Paradise Lost*	2/27 ▶ England and Wales
2/14 ▶ Shrewsbury Town	

The Beast Quiz 3

Contestant 1

3/1 ▶ A   3/3 ▶ C   3/5 ▶ A   3/7 ▶ B
3/2 ▶ C   3/4 ▶ B   3/6 ▶ A

Contestant 2

3/1 ▶ C   3/3 ▶ A   3/5 ▶ A   3/7 ▶ A
3/2 ▶ C   3/4 ▶ A   3/6 ▶ B

Contestant 3

3/1 ▶ C   3/3 ▶ A   3/5 ▶ B   3/7 ▶ C
3/2 ▶ B   3/4 ▶ B   3/6 ▶ C

Contestant 4

3/1 ▶ B   3/3 ▶ A   3/5 ▶ C   3/7 ▶ A
3/2 ▶ C   3/4 ▶ A   3/6 ▶ B

Final Chase

3/1 ▶ Florida
3/2 ▶ Step-daughter
3/3 ▶ Viz
3/4 ▶ Matilda
3/5 ▶ Italy
3/6 ▶ Nicola Sturgeon
3/7 ▶ Ethiopia
3/8 ▶ Hypertext
3/9 ▶ Tulips
3/10 ▶ Butterfly
3/11 ▶ Stephen Fry
3/12 ▶ Rockies
3/13 ▶ James Nesbitt
3/14 ▶ Austin Powers
3/15 ▶ Nike
3/16 ▶ Coronation Street
3/17 ▶ Tarzan
3/18 ▶ Robert Vaughn
3/19 ▶ 18th century
3/20 ▶ Lion
3/21 ▶ Russia
3/22 ▶ Arthur Daley
3/23 ▶ Nero
3/24 ▶ Joey

The Beast Quiz 4

Contestant 1

4/1 ▶ C	4/3 ▶ C	4/5 ▶ C	4/7 ▶ A
4/2 ▶ B	4/4 ▶ A	4/6 ▶ B	

Contestant 2

4/1 ▶ A	4/3 ▶ B	4/5 ▶ B	4/7 ▶ B
4/2 ▶ A	4/4 ▶ C	4/6 ▶ C	

Contestant 3

4/1 ▶ C	4/3 ▶ A	4/5 ▶ B	4/7 ▶ A
4/2 ▶ B	4/4 ▶ A	4/6 ▶ B	

Contestant 4

4/1 ▶ C	4/3 ▶ C	4/5 ▶ B	4/7 ▶ A
4/2 ▶ A	4/4 ▶ B	4/6 ▶ B	

Final Chase

4/1 ▶ Danielle	4/14 ▶ Welsh Grand National
4/2 ▶ Four	4/15 ▶ Alfred Hitchcock
4/3 ▶ Los Angeles	4/16 ▶ Kate Moss
4/4 ▶ Sia	4/17 ▶ Pork
4/5 ▶ Conservative	4/18 ▶ *The Luminaries*
4/6 ▶ Football	4/19 ▶ *Not Going Out*
4/7 ▶ Bamboo	4/20 ▶ Fuller's
4/8 ▶ William and Mary	4/21 ▶ S
4/9 ▶ Twenty-eight	4/22 ▶ St Andrew
4/10 ▶ English	4/23 ▶ Seamus Heaney
4/11 ▶ Andrew Lloyd Webber	4/24 ▶ Disney
4/12 ▶ All Saints	4/25 ▶ Noel Edmonds
4/13 ▶ France	4/26 ▶ Lemon
	4/27 ▶ NatWest

The Beast Quiz 5

Contestant 1

| 5/1 ▶ A | 5/3 ▶ C | 5/5 ▶ C | 5/7 ▶ B |
| 5/2 ▶ C | 5/4 ▶ B | 5/6 ▶ B | |

Contestant 2

| 5/1 ▶ A | 5/3 ▶ A | 5/5 ▶ C | 5/7 ▶ C |
| 5/2 ▶ A | 5/4 ▶ B | 5/6 ▶ C | |

Contestant 3

| 5/1 ▶ B | 5/3 ▶ B | 5/5 ▶ C | 5/7 ▶ C |
| 5/2 ▶ B | 5/4 ▶ A | 5/6 ▶ B | |

Contestant 4

| 5/1 ▶ C | 5/3 ▶ A | 5/5 ▶ B | 5/7 ▶ B |
| 5/2 ▶ B | 5/4 ▶ B | 5/6 ▶ C | |

Final Chase

5/1 ▶ Ribs	5/14 ▶ Adrenal glands
5/2 ▶ USA	5/15 ▶ Shakespears Sister
5/3 ▶ Clothes	5/16 ▶ Every 100 years
5/4 ▶ 1970s	5/17 ▶ Iceland
5/5 ▶ Olympic flag	5/18 ▶ George the Fifth
5/6 ▶ One Direction	5/19 ▶ Pasta
5/7 ▶ Ship	5/20 ▶ Ben Stiller
5/8 ▶ Badminton	5/21 ▶ Milking
5/9 ▶ Six	5/22 ▶ Collie
5/10 ▶ 'Allo 'Allo	5/23 ▶ Arno
5/11 ▶ Hilary Mantel	5/24 ▶ Red
5/12 ▶ Italy	5/25 ▶ Cambodia
5/13 ▶ Boris Yeltsin	

The Beast Quiz 6

Contestant 1

6/1 ▶ C	6/3 ▶ B	6/5 ▶ C	6/7 ▶ C
6/2 ▶ C	6/4 ▶ C	6/6 ▶ B	

Contestant 2

6/1 ▶ B	6/3 ▶ A	6/5 ▶ C	6/7 ▶ C
6/2 ▶ C	6/4 ▶ C	6/6 ▶ A	

Contestant 3

6/1 ▶ A	6/3 ▶ B	6/5 ▶ C	6/7 ▶ C
6/2 ▶ A	6/4 ▶ A	6/6 ▶ A	

Contestant 4

6/1 ▶ C	6/3 ▶ C	6/5 ▶ A	6/7 ▶ C
6/2 ▶ A	6/4 ▶ B	6/6 ▶ B	

Final Chase

6/1 ▶ India		6/12 ▶ Cardiff
6/2 ▶ Po		6/13 ▶ Irises
6/3 ▶ Suez Canal		6/14 ▶ Japan
6/4 ▶ Ernest Rutherford		6/15 ▶ Skateboarding
6/5 ▶ Lewis Carroll		6/16 ▶ Prince Philip
6/6 ▶ Mouse		6/17 ▶ 'Jailhouse Rock'
6/7 ▶ O		6/18 ▶ Rattlesnake
6/8 ▶ Caroline Quentin		6/19 ▶ Golf
6/9 ▶ Canada		6/20 ▶ Sting
6/10 ▶ Alison Moyet		6/21 ▶ Twenty
6/11 ▶ Byron		6/22 ▶ Italian

The Beast Quiz 7

Contestant 1

7/1 ▶ B	7/3 ▶ B	7/5 ▶ B	7/7 ▶ B
7/2 ▶ C	7/4 ▶ C	7/6 ▶ C	

Contestant 2

7/1 ▶ C	7/3 ▶ C	7/5 ▶ C	7/7 ▶ C
7/2 ▶ C	7/4 ▶ C	7/6 ▶ C	

Contestant 3

7/1 ▶ A	7/3 ▶ C	7/5 ▶ B	7/7 ▶ C
7/2 ▶ C	7/4 ▶ C	7/6 ▶ A	

Contestant 4

7/1 ▶ A	7/3 ▶ B	7/5 ▶ A	7/7 ▶ C
7/2 ▶ A	7/4 ▶ A	7/6 ▶ C	

Final Chase

7/1 ▶ Three		7/14 ▶ Bing Crosby
7/2 ▶ Cheryl		7/15 ▶ Thirty-one
7/3 ▶ 1918		7/16 ▶ South America
7/4 ▶ Cadillac		7/17 ▶ *West Side Story*
7/5 ▶ Brain		7/18 ▶ Enid Blyton
7/6 ▶ Justice		7/19 ▶ Exeter
7/7 ▶ Pawnbroker		7/20 ▶ Mark Ronson
7/8 ▶ SpongeBob SquarePants		7/21 ▶ Shetland
7/9 ▶ Franklin		7/22 ▶ Hellman's
7/10 ▶ Bird		7/23 ▶ Sin City
7/11 ▶ *Road House*		7/24 ▶ Buckinghamshire
7/12 ▶ Kumquat		7/25 ▶ Network
7/13 ▶ Mars		7/26 ▶ *The Jump*

The Beast Quiz 8

Contestant 1

8/1 ▶ B	8/3 ▶ A	8/5 ▶ B	8/7 ▶ A
8/2 ▶ A	8/4 ▶ A	8/6 ▶ C	

Contestant 2

8/1 ▶ A	8/3 ▶ C	8/5 ▶ A	8/7 ▶ A
8/2 ▶ A	8/4 ▶ C	8/6 ▶ A	

Contestant 3

8/1 ▶ C	8/3 ▶ A	8/5 ▶ A	8/7 ▶ B
8/2 ▶ C	8/4 ▶ A	8/6 ▶ B	

Contestant 4

8/1 ▶ C	8/3 ▶ C	8/5 ▶ C	8/7 ▶ B
8/2 ▶ A	8/4 ▶ A	8/6 ▶ C	

Final Chase

8/1 ▶ Earth		8/13 ▶ The Vatican
8/2 ▶ Kylie Minogue		8/14 ▶ *The Herbs*
8/3 ▶ Westminster		8/15 ▶ Eos
8/4 ▶ Four		8/16 ▶ Three
8/5 ▶ Confederations Cup		8/17 ▶ Edinburgh
8/6 ▶ Royal Mail		8/18 ▶ *The Newsroom*
8/7 ▶ 1960s		8/19 ▶ 'Deck The Hall'
8/8 ▶ Cat		8/20 ▶ Lactic acid
8/9 ▶ Weetabix		8/21 ▶ Basketball
8/10 ▶ *Game of Thrones*		8/22 ▶ Lead
8/11 ▶ John Stuart Mill		8/23 ▶ Pussycat Dolls
8/12 ▶ The Moon		

The Beast Quiz 9

Contestant 1

9/1 ▶ C	9/3 ▶ C	9/5 ▶ B	9/7 ▶ C
9/2 ▶ A	9/4 ▶ A	9/6 ▶ A	

Contestant 2

9/1 ▶ A	9/3 ▶ C	9/5 ▶ C	9/7 ▶ A
9/2 ▶ A	9/4 ▶ B	9/6 ▶ C	

Contestant 3

9/1 ▶ A	9/3 ▶ B	9/5 ▶ C	9/7 ▶ A
9/2 ▶ A	9/4 ▶ C	9/6 ▶ A	

Contestant 4

9/1 ▶ A	9/3 ▶ C	9/5 ▶ A	9/7 ▶ C
9/2 ▶ B	9/4 ▶ C	9/6 ▶ C	

Final Chase

9/1 ▶ Greyhound racing	9/14 ▶ Afrikaans
9/2 ▶ Red Square	9/15 ▶ Catalan Dragons
9/3 ▶ *Will & Grace*	9/16 ▶ Divorce
9/4 ▶ Punic Wars	9/17 ▶ Essex
9/5 ▶ Paper	9/18 ▶ Neptune
9/6 ▶ *Aida*	9/19 ▶ Cadbury
9/7 ▶ Ferries	9/20 ▶ Oslo
9/8 ▶ *King Solomon's Mines*	9/21 ▶ Thirty
9/9 ▶ Watt	9/22 ▶ Myxomatosis
9/10 ▶ *Avatar*	9/23 ▶ George Washington
9/11 ▶ Kurt Waldheim	9/24 ▶ Jamie Oliver
9/12 ▶ The skin	9/25 ▶ Bollywood
9/13 ▶ Chrissie Hynde	

The Beast Quiz 10

Contestant 1

10/1 ▶ C	10/3 ▶ C	10/5 ▶ C	10/7 ▶ C
10/2 ▶ A	10/4 ▶ C	10/6 ▶ A	

Contestant 2

10/1 ▶ B	10/3 ▶ C	10/5 ▶ A	10/7 ▶ A
10/2 ▶ C	10/4 ▶ B	10/6 ▶ A	

Contestant 3

10/1 ▶ C	10/3 ▶ C	10/5 ▶ B	10/7 ▶ C
10/2 ▶ A	10/4 ▶ B	10/6 ▶ C	

Contestant 4

10/1 ▶ A	10/3 ▶ A	10/5 ▶ C	10/7 ▶ B
10/2 ▶ A	10/4 ▶ C	10/6 ▶ A	

Final Chase

10/1 ▶ Bread	10/12 ▶ Louvre
10/2 ▶ Eyes	10/13 ▶ *Animal Magic*
10/3 ▶ North Sea	10/14 ▶ Aqueduct
10/4 ▶ English Civil War	10/15 ▶ 16th century
10/5 ▶ Grand prix	10/16 ▶ Royal Navy
10/6 ▶ Queen of Spades	10/17 ▶ Robbie Williams
10/7 ▶ Mars	10/18 ▶ Train
10/8 ▶ *Our Mutual Friend*	10/19 ▶ Cricket
10/9 ▶ Dolly Parton	10/20 ▶ *Spooks*
10/10 ▶ Tudor	10/21 ▶ Iodine
10/11 ▶ Melon	10/22 ▶ Gardening

ACKNOWLEDGEMENTS

Octopus Publishing Group would like to thank *The Chase* production team and all at Potato: Bradley Walsh, Michael Kelpie, Martin Scott, Helen Tumbridge, Caroline Sale, Christina Clayton, the Chasers – Mark Labbett, Anne Hegerty, Shaun Wallace, Paul Sinha and Jenny Ryan – and especially the question team – James Bovington, Luke Kelly, Mary Doyle, Rachel Armitage, Thomas Eaton, Liz Gore, Sean Carey, Stewart McCartney, Angus McDonald, Abby Brakewell and Olav Bjortomt.

PICTURE CREDITS

Photos courtesy ITV Studios Ltd. Additional image credits: 13 Andrei Simonenko/Shutterstock; 77 vectorOK/Shutterstock; 141 Irina Matyash/dreamstime.com; 205 Glam/Shutterstock; 269 AldanNi/Shutterstock.

Additional Text: Cathy Meeus

Editorial Director: Trevor Davies

Senior Editor: Leanne Bryan

Junior Designer: Jack Storey

Layout Design: Penny Stock

Picture Researcher: Jennifer Veall

Production Controller: Sarah Kulasek-Boyd